# JONATHAN, JACK, AND GBS

John O'Donovan

# JONATHAN, JACK, AND GBS

Four Plays about
Irish History and Literature
by John O'Donovan

Edited by Robert Hogan
With a Reminiscence by James Plunkett

*Published in association with the Society of Irish Playwrights*

Newark: University of Delaware Press
London and Toronto: Associated University Presses

Associated University Presses
440 Forsgate Drive
Cranbury, NJ 08512

Associated University Presses
25 Sicilian Avenue
London WC1A 2QH, England

Associated University Presses
P.O. Box 338, Port Credit
Mississauga, Ontario
Canada L5G 4L8

The paper used in this publication meets the requirements
of the American National Standard for Permanence of Paper
for Printed Library Materials Z39.48-1984.

**Library of Congress Cataloging-in-Publication Data**

O'Donovan, John, 1921—
    Jonathan, Jack, and GBS : four plays about Irish history and
literature / by John O'Donovan : edited by Robert Hogan : with a
reminiscence by James Plunkett.
        p.  cm.
    "Published in association with the Society of Irish Playwrights."
    Contents: Copperfaced Jack—The fiddler and the dean—The
Shaws of Synge Street—Carlotta.
    ISBN 0-87413-452-8 (alk. paper)
    1. Ireland—History—Drama.  2. Scott, John, Earl of Clonmell,
1739–1798—Drama.  3. Handel, George Frideric, 1685–1759—Drama.
4. Swift, Jonathan, 1667–1745—Drama.  5. Shaw, Bernard. 1856–1950–
–Drama.  6. Shaw family—Drama.  I. Hogan, Robert Goode, 1930–
II. Title.
PR6065.D63J64 1993
822'.914—dc20                                                              91-51141
                                                                                  CIP

PRINTED IN THE UNITED STATES OF AMERICA

# CONTENTS

# JOHN O'DONOVAN—A REMINISCENCE

**James Plunkett**

John O'Donovan, born in Dublin in January 1921, was a man of many parts: a musicologist, a radio personality, a Shavian scholar, a historian, but principally a man of letters and a dramatist who had five full-length plays performed at the Abbey Theatre, Dublin:

*The Half Millionaire,* 1954
*The Less We Are Together,* 1957.
*A Change of Mind,* 1958
*The Shaws of Synge Street,* 1960
*Copperfaced Jack,* 1963

In addition he wrote over forty plays for Radio Éireann and the BBC.

He and I first met in 1928 when we were delivered up—simultaneously—to the good Christian Brothers of Synge Street to see what fist they might make of educating the pair of us. So they did their honest best, finding the going soft enough with myself, because I was a malleable, even gullible kind of a child, inclined to accept authority at its word.

With John, I think, they found the going tougher. He had a mind well stocked even at that age and a vocabulary far in advance of his tender years. When he deemed it necessary to answer back, as he sometimes did, he was dangerously equipped to do so.

Much of this precocity flowed from the lifestyle he encountered from an early age in the home of his Uncle Larry and Aunt Lil. His uncle, L. P. Byrne, was literary and drama critic under his pen name Andrew E. Malone for *The Irish Times* and a man of gregarious and intellectual tastes. Authors, poets, dramatists, actors, actresses from the Abbey and other Dublin theatres were constant visitors to Aunt Lil and Uncle Larry in Ranelagh, and the talk the young John heard there was of plays and poetry and publishing and related matters.

It suited his natural gifts and bent, and he listened avidly. In addition, the books on the shelves about him ranged from the classics to the latest novels. Music was also part of the daily or weekly fare. He absorbed it all naturally and grew up thinking it was ordinary and everyday.

We became close friends, he and I, and constant companions from early on. I was expected to be able to discuss plays and dramatists and composers I had hardly heard of and to do so on an equal footing. The match was uneven, and I lost my bearings at times.

I remember, for instance, searching the library indexes fruitlessly for mention of the works of Henry Gibson before discovering that the dramatist so frequently quoted and referred to in John's conversation was, in fact, called Henrik Ibsen.

Drama occupied much of the time. I remember one of his school-day productions, Lady Gregory's *The White Cockade,* in which he himself played James II and I was entrusted with the part of Sarsfield. It received a number of public performances. Another, an impossible ambitious assault on Shakespeare's *King Richard III,* did not. John, needless to say, was Gloucester, and I can still picture him making the most agitated contortions of face and frame to recite:

> I that am rudely stamped and want love's majesty
> To strut before a wantom ambling nymph;
> I, that am curtailed of this fair proportion,
> Cheated of feature by dissembling Nature,
> Deformed, unfinished, sent before my time
> Into this breathing world, scarce half made up,
> And that so lamely and unfashionable
> That dogs bark at me as I halt by them—

As he entered his late teens, his tastes in literature and drama became firmly rooted in the classics: Shakespeare, Dickens, Voltaire, Molière, Samuel Butler, Anatole France, Ibsen, Shaw. In composers, too, he stuck with the "Greats," though he tended to advance further along the road to musical modernity than I cared to explore. (Once I remember him saying, "James, why do you always look slightly surprised when I tell you Brahms is dead?"). However, I was studying music, and on that subject we were on level terms.

All these were matters discussed and reiterated while we followed the peripatetic instincts of generations of earnest and penniless forerunners and traipsed the streets talking thirteen to the dozen.

But it was not exclusively a hell-bent pursuit of culture. I remember afternoon rambles by roads around Dundrum and Stillorgan that were still hedge-lined byways in an as yet undisturbed countryside. Longer hikes took us to Bohernabreena and longer still deep into the mountains for Sally Gap or by Wicklow Gap into the lost and secret fastness of west Wicklow. Swimming in the rivers and the sea were other delights that cost nothing and were enjoyed by both of us.

One retreat we prized above all was a hut we were allowed to use for long stretches of summer and autumn. It stood on the cliffs of Shankill looking out to Killiney and the sea and Dalkey Island, and it served our romantic tastes for moonlight walks and midnight swims.

There were occcasional more proletarian descents on the slot machines and the dodgems of Bray. We traveled in and out to work on the old Shankill to Harcourt Street line or, when a spirit altered, by bicycle. I remember flashing spokes and youthful zest and a Bray road that had hardly any traffic at all, which led us by tranquil fields where trees and grass and white palings still dreamed in the early morning peace.

I went down to that hut field only the other day in memory of John and other onetime comrades with whom I'll go no more a-roving by the light of the moon. The vista was there still, of course—Killiney and Dalkey Island and the surge of the waves below the cliffs and the mild wind with its salt and seaweed smell. But the hut was no more. And where were the buzz of the primus and the smell of paraffin and the bicycles leaning against the wall and the drying togs and all the unregainable sweetness of youth? All gone into the dark, the interstellar spaces.

Still, it occurred to me that the preoccupation and enthusiasms of his earliest days were faithful and kept their covenant with him to the end. The record of his work bears witness. As a dramatist, his five full-length plays were produced at the Abbey Theatre and over forty radio plays were presented on Radio Éireann and the BBC.

His Shavian scholarship found general recognition and was expressed in several lectures and essays, plus two published books—*Shaw and the Charlatan Genius* and *G. B. Shaw* in Gill and Macmilllan's "Irish Lives" series.

In the field of music, he acted as music critic for a number of papers and magazines, and as a musicologist he contributed regularly to Radio Éireann. In addition he was for many years a governor of the Royal Irish Academy of Music, a founder member and chairman of the Society of Irish Playwrights, and president of the Irish Anti-Vivisection Society. Perhaps for the general public, his best regarded role was that of presenter of his own "Dear Sir or Madam" series for radio which ran for twenty years right up until his death.

My abiding memory of him is of a lifelong friend, bulky in person and bulkier still in personality, but largest of all in heart and compassion. He filled a lot of space.

# JOHN O'DONOVAN—AN
# INTRODUCTION

## Robert Hogan

The excellent Irish playwright Seamus Byrne titled a play of his about Dublin *Little City,* and that mild denigration was nothing compared to how a score or so of brilliant Irishmen, from Jonathan Swift to James Joyce, have excoriated the capital of Ireland. Nevertheless, the City of the Ford of the Hurdles remained endlessly fascinating to most of those commentators, and "dear dirty Dublin" is a phrase that still encapsulates both its beguiling attractiveness and its perennial ability to exacerbate and enrage.

Perhaps one telling symptom of Dublin-ness is the extraordinary number of richly eccentric individuals that the city has, in decade after decade, created and nourished and cherished. Three of the most notable—Jonathan Swift, Lord Clonmell, and Bernard Shaw—are the principal subjects of the plays in this book; but the author of the plays was himself as individual and as memorable a Dubliner as perhaps our times have seen.

John Purcell (a second name he never used) O'Donovan should doubtless be best remembered as a playwright, but he was much else—perhaps too much else—besides. He was born in Dublin on 29 January 1921, and he attended the Synge Street Christian Brothers school until he was about seventeen. A boyhood and a lifelong friend was James Plunkett, the novelist and short-story writer who, like O'Donovan, was to spend much of his life working for Irish radio and television. One mutual interest was their devotion to music, and O'Donovan was to do some composing and to become a prolific and vastly knowledgeable music critic. This immersion in music was to serve him well when he came to write of the musical Shaws and their friends.

O'Donovan's education transcended what Synge Street had to offer. James Plunkett has pointed out the influence of his uncle, "Andrew E. Malone," who wrote that indispensable volume *The Modern Irish Drama;* but O'Donovan himself has added that much of his real education was gained in the domed reading room of the National Library of Ireland. The age for access to the National Library was seventeen; and so O'Donovan, who always looked older than his years, wrote seventeen on his application form. He was, however, only twelve, but the National Library has rarely made a more fruitful error.

Leaving school when he was about seventeen, he had a series of clerking jobs, including one in the offices of a motor company. However, petrol rationing during the Second World War caused great unemployment in Dublin, and O'Donovan was one of many to be made "redundant." Consequently, he spent most of what the neutral Southern Irish called "The Emergency" working in Belfast. From 1941 to the spring of 1944, he worked in the Royal Victoria Hospital and was obliged to become a part-time fireman. He hated Belfast, and these were the unhappiest years of his life.

Managing to return to Dublin, he began submitting articles to papers and gradually drifted into full-time journalism, working on the *Radio Review,* the *Irish Press,* and then as able Sub-Editor of the *Evening Press.* Hugh Oram in his history of Irish journalism, *The Newspaper Book,* describes O'Donovan as "one of the fittest people" ever to work on the paper; and Douglas Gageby, his managing editor, called him "precise, voluble, scathing, and a kindly uncle by turns." His formidable side as well as his erudition are apparent in an incident related by Gageby, who introduced to O'Donovan a friend who was interested in applying for the position of second-string drama critic. "Well, Mr. So and So," said O'Donovan, "you are interested in drama, I hear. Suppose we take *Coriolanus,* Act II, and you will remember where in the second scene . . . perhaps you will give me your opinion on that and on another passage with which you are no doubt familiar."

After about five years, O'Donovan gave up this solid sinecure to go into full-time free-lancing at which he was eminently successful and very busy. He wrote many scripts for Irish radio, and for many years had his own popular program, "Dear Sir or Madam," for which people around the country wrote in their opinions upon contemporary affairs, and he wisely and jovially and sometimes cuttingly commented upon them. With the coming of television in the early 1960s, he found a new outlet both as writer and presenter; and at the same time, under the pseudonym of "Andrew Marsh," he wrote a droll and discursive weekly column about Ireland's past for the *Evening Press.* Indeed, his encyclopedic knowledge of that past was the basis of his companionable posthumous book, *Life by the Liffey,* a chattily anecdotal social history of his city over the centuries.

He was a man of abounding energy, and at least two activities to which he devoted thousands of hours should also be cited. One was the Royal Irish Academy of Music, with which the great Pecksniffian character of *The Shaws of Synge Street,* Joseph Robinson, had been attached. O'Donovan became a governor of the Academy in 1950, and was elected its Vice President in 1965. He was also a founder member and the first Chairman of the Society of Irish Playwrights, which has done much to improve the miserable lot of dramatic authors in the country.

In the summer of 1985, busy as ever, he had a serious stroke. But even in the hospital, he continued to work, and even seemed to be recovering. So it was a jolting shock when, on August 26, someone so bustling and vital died.

This sketch does no justice to the rich, companionable ebullience of the man. He was something of a puritanic Falstaff or a Rabelaisian Shaw. Indeed, as a non-smoker, a teetotaler, and a vegetarian with a playful mind and a sharp tongue for folly, he seemed a burly version of Shaw, about whom he wrote two books and also the two plays which are included in this volume. Unlike Shaw, as I once remarked elsewhere, "O'Donovan could never be accused of writing sexless plays about unemotional characters. If anything, his plays tend to be—in a fashion not hitherto notably connected with the Irish drama—a bit on the ribald side." In proof, I then quoted the opening lines of one hilarious and still-unpublished play:

*Spratt.* Morning, Mr. Kilgarriff. What's the Prime Minister doing?
*Kilgarriff.* Masturbating.

Hardly a conventional opening for an Irish play even in the late 1960s. And, indeed, it was O'Donovan's misfortune that his best work was too racy in subject and too complex in characterization for the Irish theatre of his day.

The first five of O'Donovan's six Abbey pieces (and perhaps the last should not really be called a play) were produced when the company was in its fifteen-year exile in the old Queen's Theatre in Pearse Street, where they had found a home after the fire in their own theatre in 1951. These fifteen years were probably one of the artistic low points in the theatre's long and distinguished history. The management of the Abbey was then firmly in the control of Ernest Blythe, who had been Minister of Finance in the original

Free State government. Although much credit must certainly be given to Blythe for keeping the theatre's doors open through trying and difficult times, he remained more an intractable nationalist than the director of an art theatre. One of his policies was that no actor be hired without a good grasp of the Irish language, and one result was the production of the broad Christmas pantomimes in the Irish language, in which an actor might sing a song in Irish to the tune of "I'd like to get you on a slow boat to China."

Some of the actors were themselves talented, but in general the discipline of the theatre deteriorated, and many of the plays came to have a certain broad kitchen-comedy sameness about them. Another problem was that the Queen's was an old barn of a theatre which had been mainly used for low comedy and broad melodrama, and it was much too large for most of the plays that the Abbey had put on in its prime. Consequently, some new plays seem to have been chosen for their popular appeal, and the distinctive Abbey style, if any of it indeed remained at all, coagulated into a broad, stock-company playing which could elicit a superficial reaction from an audience, a reaction which one critic described as principally "a brainless, bovine laughter."

Another effect on the deterioration of the acting was the economic necessity of the long run. In the Abbey's early productive years, the program had been changed once and sometimes twice a week. However, the production of George Sheils' *The Rugged Path* in 1940 had proved so popular that the theatre was able to run it for an unprecedented twelve weeks; and now that the theatre was forced to play in a much larger house, the longer the run, the better for the balance sheet. The problem, however, with the long run was that even in a good, solid play like *The Rugged Path,* the acting got broader and broader.

The producer of many of the plays in Pearse Street was Ria Mooney, an able actress of much experience who had brilliantly created Rosie Redmond in the original *Plough and the Stars* and who had worked in America with Le Gallienne and Nazimova. However, she was overworked, unable to enforce a thorough discipline, and depressed by the quality of the plays being accepted. As she once remarked to the present writer, "No, there's nothing to do with those plays. One's just like another. You rack your mind trying to think of something new, but it boils down to last week you put the door over here, so now you'll put it over there."

In other words, during the 1950s the Abbey had become a predictable, unimaginative, and artistically slovenly theatre, its plays not demanding, its productions self-imitating, its actors not stretched. Some of O'Donovan's plays, such as *The Less We Are Together,* which ran for four months in 1957, or *A Change of Mind,* which ran for five weeks in 1958, were broad enough and funny enough to be staged with some effect. His best work, however—*The Shaws of Synge Street* and *Copperfaced Jack*—was much too subtle and demanding for the Abbey Theatre of the 1950s and early '60s; and both predictably failed.

The production of *Copperfaced Jack* on 25 February 1963 was a shambles that convinced even perceptive people in its audience that the play itself was at fault. Rehearsals were most casual, and were even underway before O'Donovan himself learned that the play was scheduled for production. Blythe, as was his frequent custom, made unauthorized changes in the text; and, as O'Donovan later wrote to me, "when I discovered at rehearsal that several lines had been cut by his order without reference to me, and indeed in spite of his verbal undertaking not to change the text, I sprang up from my seat in the theatre and emphasized an apostrophe to the heavens with a blow of my fist on the back of an iron seat that broke it (the iron seat, not my fist)." Another symptom of the casualness with which the theatre took the play was that on the Friday before the Monday opening, the play had still not been advertised; and on this occasion the beleagured playwright dashed up to the formidable managing director's office, reached over the desk, grabbed him by the lapels and—in O'Donovan's words—"I shook him, and I shook him, and I SHOOK him!" After a week's dismal run to small houses, the play closed and O'Donovan went into the hospital.

The script of the play itself is probably the best condemnation of the Abbey's quality in these years, for the play is a richly, densely comic one and its title character as complex and memorable a creation as the Abbey had seen for a long time. The play is set in 1798, and depicts the trial of a fictional patriot named Peter Shanks by the real Lord Chief Justice, John Scott, first Earl of Clonmell. As O'Donovan describes them:

> My rebel is . . . a fictional variation of Emmet, of whom I am not at all an admirer. Adventurers who proclaim a rebellion and sign themselves president of the new republic command neither my respect nor my admiration, especially when they scuttle off up a back street when the going gets hot and then whinge to their serving-maid, "It wasn't *my* fault, it wasn't." (Emmet did this.) Jack himself is a notional recreation of John Scott, first Earl of Clonmell, Lord Chief Justice of the King's Bench, who died of gluttony and drunkenness on the very day that the Rebellion of 1798 (Wolfe Tone's) broke out. On the face of it, his career

was that of an unmitigated scoundrel, but I happened to read extracts from his diary and found that he had a clear-sighted view of his own character and behaviour which kept him making attempts to reform himself until almost the day of his death. His great ability (he pulled himself up by his own bootstraps) and his ironic self-portraiture attracted me to him; and although I cannot document every trait I gave him I believe I have re-created him quite faithfully.

O'Donovan's Jack is for the stage a rarely complex character who is painted warts and all. Never before had the Abbey stage seen a description of the perverse sadism that impels Jack to whip Mary Neale. Indeed, given the simplicity of most stage characterization, that action would in most plays be enough to consign Jack to the company of such monsters of dramatic literature as Sir Giles Overreach or Richard III, if not to that of the irremediably black Rawdon Scudamores and Gideon Bloodgoods of melodrama.

It was quite a *tour de force,* then, to compel us to view Jack at other times with tolerance for his weaknesses, sympathy for his anguish, and admiration for his wit and courage. It was a *tour de force* that the Abbey company of 1963 could not pull off, and probably that the Irish audience of 1963 could not have taken in. Nevertheless, the play still awaits its sympathetic production, and that I should say would be a necessarily triumphant one.

O'Donovan's imaginary conversation between Swift and Handel, *The Fiddler and the Dean,* was written for Radio Éireann in the summer of 1961. Handel had spent some time in Dublin, and indeed on 13 April 1742, had given the first production of *The Messiah* in Fishamble Street. A few blocks away, in Patrick Street, the Dean did initially forbid his choristers to take part in Handel's concerts. Swift, of course, was like Yeats notoriously unmusical, and the juxtaposition of these two figures—probably the pre-eminent English composer and the preeminent writer in English of the day—was well-nigh irrestistible. In the playlet, O'Donovan is more successful in conjuring up the fascinating and perturbed personality of Swift than he is in creating Handel. Nevertheless, the clash of issues in the playlet, although perhaps rather more than listeners to Radio Éireann were accustomed, proved deservedly popular; and there is little reason that, with a simple open staging, the playlet should not be just as effective on the stage.

Incidentally, O'Donovan's last Abbey piece was about Swift. It was commissioned to be played in the Abbey's new theatre which had been erected on the old premises on the corner of Marlborough and Abbey streets. Originally conceived as a Swift's evening's entertainment, the piece was entitled *Dearly Beloved Roger* (after Swift's opening remarks in a sermon he once preached in a small rural church when the only member of the congregation present was his verger). Produced on 26 April 1967, *Dearly Beloved Roger,* after a nicely dramatic start, turns into a sort of documentary cum poetry recital; and this was a real pity, for Swift, like Shaw, was a figure with whom O'Donovan had much empathy and about whom he should have written brilliantly.

About Bernard Shaw, he did write brilliantly. His two books, *Shaw and the Charlatan Genius* and his short life *G. B. Shaw,* both rest solidly on new research, particularly into Shaw's family and their background. That material has not only benefited subsequent biographers up to Michael Holroyd, but it also formed the rich background for O'Donovan's fourth Abbey play, *The Shaws of Synge Street.* That play was produced by Ria Mooney at the Queen's on 23 April 1960. The cast included the usual Abbey stalwarts of the day, among whom were such solid players as Philip Flynn, Angela Newman, Edward Golden, Ray MacAnally, and Kathleen Barrington. Given the restrictions of the company, there was some inevitable miscasting, such as the theatre's broad comic Harry Brogan as the ripely selfish sexual buccaneer, Joseph Robinson. Nevertheless, the play itself was really a bit beyond the capabilities of the company, for at least nine of the roles are full, major, and demanding ones. O'Donovan was not writing here such a play as *Copperfaced Jack* which, if it has a superb leading actor, can get by with only passable performances from the rest of the cast. In *The Shaws* he was writing a play such as Chekhov or Granville-Barker might have written, full of meaty parts and demanding a subtlety and a close-knit ensemble playing which the Abbey company of the day was really not equipped to give it. Predictably, after a week of playing to small houses, the play was closed, and has not to my knowledge been revived.

It was, however, published in 1966 by my Proscenium Press in a small, error-riddled paperback edition of 400 copies. On that occasion, O'Donovan wrote this about it:

*The Shaws of Synge Street* is a chronicle play which is as faithful to the facts, in so far as they are known to the author, as the Shakespeare histories, although some events are telescoped to bring the story within the possibility of stage representation.

A play about Bernard Shaw's family was first suggested to me by Mr. B. C. Rosset, a member of the Shaw Society of America, but the idea didn't fire my imagination. I felt Shaw himself had already milked the subject dry, and I hadn't the least inclination merely to dramatize his autobiographical prefaces. But one afternoon while chatting to Lady Hanson, in company with the late Richard Irvine Best, onetime director of the National Library of Ireland, the conversation turned to the misdemeanours of Mrs. Shaw. I pricked up my ears, but it transpired that this Mrs. Shaw was not George Bernard's mother but a neighbour and friend of the family, though no relation.

Both Mrs. Shaws, it appeared, were interested in the mysterious George Vandeleur Lee, the Dublin singing teacher, impresario, and conductor who so greatly influenced the young Shaw. I was told that when the dramatist's mother managed to commandeer Lee for herself, her rival turned to Joseph Robinson, another musician, famed in his native Dublin for his passion for Handel and for women. Robinson's wife later committed suicide by taking off for heaven from the roof of her home, attired in a white nightdress and a pair of cloth wings. Knowing Dubliners hinted that her insanity was caused by her husband's infidelities, which in turn may have been caused by her inability to have children.

This, and other information, when added to Shaw's narrative, made me realize that here was the making of a play; but a play old-fashioned enough to cause me reluctance to embark on writing it. However, the unborn play continued to persecute me until I consented to bring it into the world.

It was produced at the Abbey Theatre in 1960 to the enthusiastic applause of the handful of people who came to see it. For this production I had supplied, at the insistence of Mr. Ernest Blythe, managing director of the Abbey, a short prologue in which Shaw's identity and literary rank were stressed, Mr. Blythe fearing that although the name George Bernard Shaw might have a familiar ring to Abbey audiences, they might not remember in just what connection. Since Robert Hogan assures me that no such tutelage is needed for an American audience, I am glad to ditch the prologue as a superfluity I disliked.

Mr. Blythe had also suggested an epilogue to balance the prologue, in which I could outline Bernard Shaw's subsequent career. I didn't want such an epilogue; but as I had fiercely resisted his other suggestion that I "fatten up" Shaw's part by making him the central character, I felt it would be graceful to comply in the matter of the epilogue. As things turned out, the epilogue wasn't used in this production, nor indeed in any other. But it had got into Robert Hogan's hands and he said he rather liked it, so I have fallen back upon the characteristic Irish evasion of "I leave it to yourself" as to whether he should have included it in this edition or not.

The prologue which O'Donovan refers to above I have not discovered among his papers, but the epilogue, which was not originally published for lack of funds, appears here for the first time.

Despite O'Donovan's ambivalence about the epilogue, I think it is a useful and even necessary part of the play. In one sense, it is like the concluding chapter in one of those long Victorian novels where the author not only wraps all of the ends neatly up, but also tells us the satisfying information about how the characters lived happily or unhappily ever after. Such information seems particularly necessary for this play, which properly ends with the breakup of the Shaw household, because certain of the characters like Walter Gurly are so attractive and certain others like Joseph Robinson so deliciously contemptible that we yearn to know what happened to them. But also, the audience needs to know what happened to poor George Carr Shaw afterwards, and even more important what happened to the elusive Sonny when he became a man. Also there is the utter necessity of finishing the story of that compelling and mesmerizing figure of the first two acts, George John Vandeleur Lee, the Svengali-like singing teacher who both held the Shaw family together and drove them apart. O'Donovan's *Shaw and the Charlatan Genius* is the standard study of Lee, and so he was well prepared to bring that enigmatic character to the stage.

In purely dramatic terms, the epilogue seems necessary also. The third act had ended with the breakup of the home and the poignant moment of George Carr Shaw alone on the stage. It seems really a vital counterbalance, then, to have an epilogue which shows the final sad reaction of his cold and granite-faced wife when she, too, is left alone.

O'Donovan remarked that he was not initially attracted to the story because it demanded a quite conventional form. Within the confines of that realistic form, however, he has contrived some fascinatingly human character studies. By "human" I mean that they evoke from an audience a more complicated reaction than the simple sympathy or antipathy that most theatrical characters elicit. As with his Copperfaced Jack, he has drawn a gallery of characters who often act from the most ignominious and selfish motives, and who yet nevertheless compel our attention and intermittently at least surprisingly compel even our sympathy. He is, in other words, demanding a more complex and a more realistic response than the great majority of plays ever attempt.

One of O'Donovan's last plays, which is as yet unperformed, is *Carlotta*, the final play in this book and a play which in content, if not in form, is a satisfying sequel to *The Shaws*. *Carlotta* is a four-hander in which the characters are Shaw himself, his sister Lucy whom we have already met in *The Shaws*, his wife Charlotte, and his quasi-mistress and quondam leading lady, the brilliant Mrs.

Patrick Campbell. Each of the women is a solidly drawn and rewarding part, and each in her different way is a formidable sparring partner for GBS. But it is the character of GBS that is O'Donovan's most superb creation. There have been several attempts to put the highly theatrical Shaw on the stage. Shaw himself jokingly tried it in his skit *Shakes versus Shav,* and perhaps it may be said that he was always on stage in real life. In more recent years, there have been a one-man show or two such as the Irish actor Donal Donnelly's, or a two-hander called *Dear Liar* drawn from the letters of Shaw and Mrs. Campbell. But in O'Donovan's GBS we get the authentic Shaw, the distillation of years of study of the man, and perhaps as much of that contradictory, gentle, kind, shy, witty, playful, fantastic realist as can be squeezed into two hours' playing time. It is a portrait fit to be placed next to Copperfaced Jack.

O'Donovan was a superb, satiric, jovial raconteur specializing in the manifold faults and multitudinous foibles of his countrymen, but on one occasion he told a story against himself. And, as it was a Shaw story, it seems appropriate here.

When he was a young man, John wrote an enthusiastic letter to Shaw in which he asked permission to visit the great man at his country house in Ayot St. Lawrence. Shaw shortly replied, "Absolutely not!"

John then wrote again, pointing out that he was an avid disciple who was thoroughly immersed in all of the Master's works, and that Shaw consequently owed it to such devotion to see him.

Shaw wrote back tersely, "Well, come and be damned!"

John journeyed over by the mailboat, made his way to London, then to Ayot St. Lawrence, and walked out of the village till he came to Shaw's Corner. He knocked at the front door and was greeted by a housekeeper who said that Mr. Shaw was out by the side of the house in the garden.

John retraced his steps and came to a small gate. Beyond it was the familiar, tweed-clad, white-bearded figure who looked at him from under shaggy white brows, and presently came over.

"Ah," he said, "you must be the young man from Dublin."

John, in the throes of hero-worship, could only gulp and nod in awe.

"Hmm," said Shaw, "you must have had a long and tiring journey from Dublin."

Again John could only dumbly nod.

"Well then," said Shaw, "you must be anxious to get back. Good day." And turned on his heels and walked away.

That must have been the only time that my friend was ever at a loss for words.

But, of course, some of his written words have not been lost.

In preparing these plays for the press, I have silently corrected a few obvious errors in the manuscripts and the plethora of errors that the editor and the original printer allowed to creep into *The Shaws of Synge Street*. I have also somewhat regularized the punctuation throughout and have very slightly expanded some stage directions. That is, when the author originally wrote [*Goes to door*], I have expanded the stage direction to read [*He goes to the door*]. It was the practice of Shaw himself to provide full and fluent stage directions for his readers, rather than the terse shorthand playwrights have traditionally employed for their actors, and this was also the practice that O'Donovan himself followed in the original printing of *Copperfaced Jack*. That play was originally printed in a volume entitled *7 Irish Plays,* edited by the present author, published by the University of Minnesota Press, and years out of print. *The Shaws of Synge Street* was originally published in 1966 by Proscenium Press without the epilogue and has also been many years out of print.

Finally, I must acknowledge, and not for the first time, the perceptive and helpful remarks of Professor William J. Feeney; the aid of Professor Jay L. Halio of the University of Delaware Press; the encouragement of the Society of Irish Playwrights; and most particularly, of course, the aid and encouragement of Vera O'Donovan.

# JONATHAN,
# JACK,
# AND GBS

# COPPERFACED JACK

Thus I stand, a public character alone.
—Diary of Lord Clonmell

## Characters

*John Scott,* first Earl of Clonmell, Lord Chief Justice of the
King's Bench in Ireland
*Arthur Wolfe,* attorney-general
*Francis Higgins,* an informer
*Peter Shanks, Jack Kehoe, Michael Mahon, Tom Doyle,* rebels
*Elizabeth Shanks,* a widow
*Mary Neale,* engaged to Peter Shanks
*Master Palmer,* a physician
*Jack Fennessy,* carpenter
*Brian Borroo,* a convict
*Viola, Rosalind, Bessie,* whores
*Galvin,* a hangman
*Governor* of Newgate Jail
*Milligan,* Clonmell's attendant
Turnkeys, a chaplain, prisoners, soldiers

## Act I

### SCENE I

*A shabby room in a Dublin back street in May 1798. By the light
of a candle stuck in a bottle, two men are sitting at a rickety
table. They are Jack Kehoe, middle-aged and shabby, and Michael
Mahon, ten years younger, but with scantier hair. Both are poorly
dressed and look as if they haven't had a bath since birth. Tom
Doyle, a palefaced lad of eighteen, bursts in.*

*Kehoe [Whipping his feet off the table in alarm, then relaxing]*.
My God, I thought it was somebody. *[Puts up his feet again.]*

*Doyle*. Where's the General?

*Mahon*. Gone out to the jakes.

*Doyle*. Have I missed anything?

*Kehoe*. Naw.

*Mahon*. He has formed his government. You're in it.

*Doyle [Almost awed]*. Me?! Then he really does like me. And trusts
me.

*Mahon*. You're the secretary of state for—wait now till I think.

*Kehoe [Picking his teeth]*. Jasus, don't ask me. I'm chancellor of
the exchequer, that's all I know.

*Mahon*. Secretary of State for Home Affairs—I'm nearly sure
that's what it is.

*Doyle [Disappointed]*. Oh . . . I was hoping I'd be—no matter.

*Kehoe*. D'ye think ye'll be able for the work, son?

*Doyle [In a gust of fury]*. By God, if you don't leave me alone I'll
kill you.
*[Doyle has come near to Kehoe's feet, which are still propped up
on the table. Kehoe nonchalantly raises a foot, props it against
Doyle's chest, and pushes him. He staggers back and falls over
a chair.]*

*Mahon*. Will youse pair stop—

*Doyle [Scrambling up]*. I'll kill him for that. I'll kill him.
*[Doyle rushes at Kehoe again, and again Kehoe nonchalantly
foots him backward. This time Doyle staggers into the arms of
Peter Shanks who has just entered. Shanks is young, slender,
good-looking, grave, humorless. His movements are quick and
nervous—indeed almost everything about him is quick. But although quick to lose his temper (and indeed to lose his head) he
appears calm, because anger in him takes the form of pale,
cold resentment. He has to be goaded for a long time before he
displays the more usual signs of anger. He tends to adopt ora-
torical poses; a favorite is the putting of one hand on his breast,
the other behind his back, à la Napoleon.]*

*Mahon [Jerking his thumb toward the unperturbed Kehoe]*. He
begun it, General.

*Shanks [Raising his hand]*. Desist! I command you—desist!

*Mahon*. It was him begun it.

*Shanks*. I want no recriminations. Sit down.
*[Mahon and Doyle sit. Kehoe doesn't remove his feet from the
table. Shanks remains standing in his Napoleonic pose.]*

*Shanks*. I will say no more about this unseemly episode. H'm. You
were late for the meeting, Captain Doyle.

*Doyle.* I'm sorry, General. I had to put heels on three pairs of shoes before the master would let me go.

*Kehoe.* I told Tom—Captain Doyle—about his new job.

*Doyle.* I'm very grateful to you, General, for giving me the chance to show what I can do. It's the first chance I've ever got, General. And I won't ever let you down—never!

*Shanks.* I hope that my trust in you will not prove to be misplaced.

*Kehoe.* So do we all, so do we all.

*Doyle [Springing up].* There, he's at me again. I'll choke him.

*[Mahon tries to pull Doyle down.]*

*Shanks [Looking at the floor].* Desist. I said desist.

*[A doorbell rings in the distance.]*

*Shanks.* See who it is, Colonel Kehoe.

*Kehoe.* Send the Secretary of State for Home Affairs as he's on his feet.

*Shanks.* I've given an order.

*Kehoe.* Well, give it to Tom Doyle.

*Shanks [Sharply].* Major Mahon.

*[Mahon rises.]*

*Shanks.* The door.

*Mahon.* Well now after all, General, you did tell Jack Kehoe to—

*Shanks.* Major Mahon, the door.

*[The doorbell rings again.]*

*Doyle.* It's all right, General, I'll go.

*Shanks.* Resume your seat, Captain. I've given Major Mahon an order.

*Mahon.* But surely it's the junior officer's job to—

*Shanks.* My orders are not matters for discussion.

*Kehoe.* If one of youse fellows doesn't move a leg, he'll have to go and answer it himself.

*[No one makes a move.]*

*Doyle.* Let *me* go, General.

*Shanks.* No, Captain. *[With much dignity.]* I shall go myself. *[Goes.]*

*Doyle [To Mahon].* Why didn't you go when he told you?

*Mahon.* He told him first, didn't he?

*Kehoe [Spitting on the floor].* Here's one Chancellor of the Exchequer who's not going to run messages like a whore's footman.

*Doyle.* He thinks he's going to rise me again, but he won't.

*Kehoe.* Secretary of State for Home Affairs and he wouldn't know whether you'd eat a home affair or wear it going to Mass of a Sunday.

*Doyle [Rushing at Kehoe].* Declare to God, I'll crucify him.

*[Kehoe pushes him back with his foot. When Doyle falls this time he lies still and moans.]*

*Doyle.* Me back—oh my God, me back.

*Mahon [Kneeling beside Doyle and glaring at Kehoe].* Now look
what you've done. *[He helps Doyle up.]*

*Doyle.* Me back—me back—me back.

*Mahon.* Are you hurted, lad?

*Doyle [Alarmed].* I've cut meself. I'm bleeding. I can feel the blood
running down me leg.

*Kehoe.* Are ye sure it's blood is running down your leg?

*Mahon.* It's the mercy of God you didn't kill yourself.

*Kehoe.* Well, he always wanted to die for Ireland, didn't he?

*Doyle [Feebly].* I'll rub the sneer off that fellow's face.

*Mahon.* Here—let's have a look at you.

*[Mahon begins to unfasten Doyle's belt. He lowers his trousers.]*

*Doyle [Wincing].* Oooh—go aisy, go aisy.

*Mahon.* Lean forward a bit. *[He takes a candle and lifts the tail
of Doyle's shirt.]*

*Kehoe.* Don't set fire to him now whatever you do.

*Mahon.* You've cut yourself all right.

*[Shanks and Francis Higgins appear at the door.]*

*Shanks.* What in heaven's name—! *[He turns away in disgust.]*

*Kehoe.* Good day to you, Mr. Higgins.

*Shanks.* Captain Doyle, be so kind as to cover yourself.

*Kehoe.* Yes, the view from over there must be fierce.

*Shanks [Still turned away].* Major Mahon, Captain Doyle: I require
your explanation.

*Doyle [Straightening painfully].* I fell and hurt myself.

*Shanks [Immediately all sympathy].* Hurt yourself? Oh—he's
bleeding.

*Mahon.* Just lean over the table, Tom, and I'll bathe it with a sup
of water.

*[Mahon goes to one side, pours water from a jug into a dish,
and splashes it on Doyle's wound. Meanwhile Higgins and
Shanks have come forward. Higgins is a dark, blue-chinned,
stocky man. One would imagine that no sensible man would
trust him an inch.]*

*Higgins.* I'm afraid I can only remain for a few moments. But I
had to come to find out if we are any nearer the day of liberty,
when our country shall be free and prosperous under your wise
and enlightened leadership?

*Shanks.* Very near it now.

*Higgins.* And how is the glorious army of the revolution?

*Kehoe.* Couldn't be worse. All officers and no soldiers.

*Shanks.* When the hour strikes, the soldiers will be there. My country will not fail me.

*Higgins.* And how about the list of public enemies who are to be executed, General? How's that coming on?

*Doyle [Raising his head].* Joseph Byrne. He's on *my* list.

*Higgins.* Who is this enemy of our beloved country?

*Doyle.* The bootmaker in Thomas Street. The man I work for.

*Higgins.* Joseph Byrne . . . Thomas Street. Good. I'll make a note of him. How about Mr. Wolfe?

*Kehoe.* Who's he when he's at home?

*Higgins.* Mr. Wolfe is the attorney-general.

*Kehoe.* Stick him on the list if you want him. *My* man is Copperfaced Jack.

*Higgins.* Splendid.

*Kehoe.* He had me uncle and me two cousins strung up for stealing one mangy sheep.

*Shanks.* It's not because of your uncle and your cousins that the lord chief justice is on the list, Colonel Kehoe, but because he has betrayed his great office. He has swindled widows and orphans, accepted bribes, perverted the cause of justice, disgraced the bench *[Darkly]* and defiled unprotected women.

*Higgins.* Hanging would be too good for him, gentlemen.

*Kehoe.* Wait'll I get me hands around his fat throat. . . .

*Higgins.* That's my brave comrade . . . good! *[Writing.]* For assassination . . . execution I should say . . . the lord chief justice. And let's put down Mr. Wolfe, the attorney-general as well, shall we?

*Kehoe.* You can put down anyone you like.

*Shanks [Drawing Higgins aside].* These, Mr. Higgins, are the instruments I must use to tear the tyrant's hand from my country's throat. But believe me *[Places his hand on Higgins' arm]* they shall be replaced with worthier instruments at the first opportunity.

*Higgins.* When you call on me to serve you, General, you shall not call in vain.

*[Impulsively Shanks grasps Higgins' hand. There is a loud hammering on the outer door, and a voice cries, "Open in the name of the King!"]*

*Kehoe [Jumping up].* Jasus, we're caught.

*[Kehoe snatches the candle from the table and extinguishes it. The door is battered in, and in the darkness a gleam of light shows the figures of armed soldiers rushing in. Shouts and confusion.]*


SCENE 2


*The lord chief justice's room at the Four Courts, Dublin. A huge crimson velvet curtain with a gold fringe hangs in folds at the back; at right is a window curtained in a darker hue; at left a glowing fireplace, the light from which flickers on the huddled figure of the lord chief justice in his chair. He is in a dressing gown, and without his full-bottomed wig. His face, a mass of reddish purple flesh, shows the man who had been dangerously overfeeding and overdrinking all his life. Although enormously fat, he doesn't look in the least comical. Years of deference from subordinates and toadies have turned him into a bigger bully than he is by nature. But he is saved from complete insufferabilitity by humor and by a genuine capacity for self-criticism. His wig, robe, and chain of office are draped on a lay figure, right. There is a table on which are quill pens and an ink bottle, papers, books, a decanter of brandy, and glasses. A cupboard at the far left, a door right. Milligan enters with a lighted candelabrum, which he places on the table.*

*Justice.* Have I slept long, Milligan?
*Milligan.* Only half an hour, m'lud.
*Justice.* It's dark.
*Milligan.* I drew the curtains, m'lud, so as not to have the sunlight disturb you.
*Justice.* The looking glass.
   *[Milligan gives him a hand mirror.]*
*Justice [With a grimace].* God! Milligan, have you ever been able to look at yourself without hatred, loathing?
*Milligan.* I wouldn't say I had any feelings in the matter, m'lud.
*Justice.* Then you admire yourself—?
   *[He rises. Milligan helps him to dress.]*
*Justice.* Did I ever tell you how I tried to sell my soul to the Devil?
*Milligan.* It is one of your favorite stories, m'lud.
*Justice.* I was only twelve or thirteen at the time. I wanted to go to London to see all the sights. The desire was purely instinctive. Nobody had talked to me about London. I cannot have read about it, for there were no books in my father's house . . . that I can remember. But this longing for London . . . it was extraordinary. It obsessed me. Now you or any ordinary person would have got there by simply running away from home.
*Milligan.* Will you have the under-waistcoat?
*Justice.* No. Oh very well. Yes, you would have simply run away from home. But I didn't. It never occurred to me. I have always done things the hard way. I remember a schoolmaster saying to me, "Name three flowers." Now you, like any normal human being, would have said wallflowers, buttercups, and daisies. But

I had to think hard. "Antirrhinums." "Go on," said the schoolmaster. "Ah . . . chrysanthemums." "Go on," said the schoolmaster. But I couldn't remember a third flower.

*Milligan.* The other arm, m'lud.

*Justice.* So in order to get to London I decided that the first step
was to sell my soul to the Devil. My soul for the fare to London
and a little spending money . . . ten guineas. Ten guineas, Milligan. *[Turns and stares at Milligan.]* My God, how I have always
undervalued myself. Not for a kingdom. Not for perpetual youth.
Or good looks. Or women. Just the fare to London and a little
pocket money. That's the sort of humility life in a poor country
plants in you. The Devil didn't buy, of course. I sat on the edge
of my bed waiting for him. I opened the windows for him. I
lighted a huge fire in the grate to encourage him. I thought he
might have left the money in the old jug on the dresser where
my mother kept the family fortune of three and sixpence—but
no. Have you ever offered your soul to the Devil, Milligan?

*Milligan.* I am perfectly satisfied with my situation in life, m'lud.

*Justice.* Oh Thou who wert crucified to win eternal bliss for Milligan, the just man made perfect, look on Thy handiwork and be
glad.

*[Milligan puts the wig on him.]*

*Justice.* Four treason cases today, I think.

*Milligan.* Yes, m'lud.

*Justice.* Convey to the prisoners that Copperfaced Jack is in a
merciful mood this morning. If they expedite matters by pleading
guilty without more ado, the sentences will be light.

*[The lord chief justice swings around, his crimson robe spread-
ing out behind him. He paces slowly toward the curtains, which
are drawn up on either side as he approaches. The judicial seat,
canopied in red and emblazoned with the royal arms of England,
is revealed bathed in light while everything else grows dark. He
climbs into his seat. There is a hushed murmur. At the right, a
thin, wan beam picks out the dock; Doyle climbs into it.]*

*Doyle [Hoarsely].* Guilty, my lord.

*[Doyle stands back and is replaced by Kehoe.]*

*Kehoe.* Guilty, my lord.

*[Kehoe is replaced by Mahon.]*

*Mahon.* Guilty, my lord.

*[Mahon is replaced by Peter Shanks.]*

*Shanks.* Not guilty.

*Justice.* Speak up, man, speak up. Don't mumble.

*Shanks [Involuntarily straightening himself]*. Not guilty.

*Justice [Threatening]*. What did you say?

*Shanks*. Not guilty. And I do not recognize the competence of this court to try me.

*Justice*. Nevertheless it will try you.

*Shanks*. I do not expect justice from Copperfaced Jack.

*Justice*. Who's he?

*Shanks*. A swindler. A thief. A lickspittle. A murderer. A fornicator in a fancy dress.

*Justice*. "A fornicator in a fancy dress." I like the rhythm of that. Say it again for me.

*Shanks [Angry]*. A man who filched the property of defenseless and innocent widows and orphans—

*Justice*. "Defenseless and innocent!" Why do platitudes and patriotism always go together? So you plead not guilty?

*Shanks*. I plead nothing.

*[A dark figure emerges from the shadows behind the dock and strikes Peter across the mouth.]*

*Justice [Pounding the desk, bellowing]*. How dare you strike the prisoner! Turning my court into a beargarden! Let that man be taken away and whipped from the precinct of this court to the Tholsel and back again! *[Leans back and breathes deeply.]* Are you conducting your own defense, Mr. Shanks?

*Shanks*. No lawyer shall speak for me. I shall speak for myself when the time comes.

*Justice*. The time *has* come. The cornered rat can now fight for its life.

*Shanks*. Dispense with your mummery. Have me hanged and be done with it. I do not fear to die for my country.

*Justice [Leaning back]*. "Dispense with your mummery." No, Mr. Shanks, that will not do. "The fornicator in the—" how's this your phrase ran? "The fornicator in the—" Well, whatever it was, it was good. It had a fine ring to it. There was feeling behind it, genuine human feeling. But "Abandon your mummery"—no, that wasn't it. "Dispense with your mummery." Pwa! Try again, Mr. Shanks.

*Shanks*. Buffoon.

*Justice*. Aren't we all, Mr. Shanks, each in his own way?

*Shanks*. I shall take no further part in these scandalous proceedings. Henceforth I shall hold my peace.

*Justice [Throwing back his head and guffawing]*. Henceforth he shall hold his peace!

*Shanks.* The laughter of fools is like the crackling of thorns under a pot.

*Justice [Leaning forward, interested].* Oh—you are a Protestant: you have read the Bible. I had assumed you were a Papist.

*Shanks [Accusing him].* Atheist.

*Justice.* Atheist? Me? Not at all. A devout believer. *[Leaning forward.]* Do you know, I once tried to sell my soul to the Devil?

*Shanks.* Not tried. Succeeded.

*Justice.* Good good good good. You keep your wits about you. But then you're young, Peter, young. Once upon a time I was young like you—

*Shanks.* Who talks platitudes now?

*Justice.* But you shall never be old and copperfaced like me.

*Shanks.* Nor old and villainous. Nor old and dishonest.

*Justice.* Peter, we've all been dishonest since we stopped walking on four legs and started walking on two. *[Leans back.]* Well, you didn't hold your peace for very long, did you? Never mind. Yet in a little while and you shall hold your peace for ever and for aye.

*Shanks.* So shall you.

*Justice.* It is cruel of you to remind me. You have had only twenty years to realize what you're leaving. I've had sixty. My pain is treble yours. *[In a kind tone.]* Guilty, Peter, guilty—?

*Shanks.* If it will facilitate you, I have done all your minions say I have done.

*Justice.* Minions. Oh dear. Your father was either a schoolmaster or a minor poet. Or perhaps both. Let all the accused stand before me.

*[Doyle, Mahon, Kehoe take their place beside Shanks.]*

*Justice.* You have admitted your guilt of one of the most heinous crimes it is possible to commit, a crime against every man, woman, and child in this country. You have tried, by plotting rebellion, to disrupt the established order of things. You have incited men who are ordinarily peaceable and law-abiding to acts of violence and bloodshed.

*Shanks.* To win freedom for our native land.

*Justice.* Your object was to seize into your own obscure hands the power of government and the privileges which go with it. Who desires rebellion? Only the rebellious, who are at bottom the envious. It is no bad thing to strive to improve one's lot. On such ambition depends all human progress. It is open to any man who desires to rise in this world, to overcome the difficulties in his

way. In some cases those difficulties are greater than in others.
The accident of birth may place some of us halfway up to the
summit of human society. But even those who are at the foot of
the hill can climb all the way if they have the will and the energy.

*Shanks.* Are you talking about yourself, Copperfaced Jack?

*Justice [To Shanks with contempt].* The rebel is one who tries to
reach the summit by using the strength and energy of others. He
deludes fools into clearing the path for him. "Fight, my gallant
fellow countrymen," he cries, "to free our beloved country by
overthrowing the tyrant." Meaning, "Fight, my gullible fellow
countrymen to make me—me—your new master. To carry ME
from a backstreet cellar to the palace of kings. Signed, Yours
Faithlessly, the President of the New Republic."

*Shanks.* He is prepared to shed his own blood to the last drop.

*Justice.* The prize is worth the gamble. The pickpocket, the sheep-
stealer, the forger all risk their lives, but not with the damnable
righteousness of the thief who is out to steal a whole country.
There have been times when, sitting in the judgment seat, I would
have said to some petty criminal, were I not bound by the law,
"Go forth a free man. Your offense was no more than a trick of
fate, a momentary lapse, which can be forgiven by men of good
will." But when there stand before me men who have tried to
deceive the credulous multitude with promises of the millen-
nium, of an earthly paradise, then the act of duty becomes an
act of pleasure. Every man may gamble with what belongs to
him, even with his life. But let no man gamble with my life, my
property, in the name of anything, least of all in the name of
patriotism, or of liberty, equality, and fraternity. Nature gives us
no liberty, Mr. Shanks; she laughs at our notions of equality, and
she has set merciful bounds to fraternity. Most brothers dislike
one another. *[Sotto voce.]* I don't like mine anyway. *[Aloud.]* O
ye millions, I do not embrace ye, and I beg ye shall make no
move to embrace me.

*Shanks.* Few will want to do that, Copperfaced Jack.

*Justice.* That is the gibe of a young man or a little man. In your
case there will not be time enough left for you to show whether
you were young or little.

*Shanks.* Dulce et decorum est pro patria mori.

*Justice [Flinging an accusing finger at him].* A schoolmaster! Your
father was a schoolmaster.

*Shanks.* He was not.

*Justice.* Perhaps not in the eyes of the world, Peter, but in the eyes
of God—yes.

*Shanks.* And in the eyes of Copperfaced Jack who thinks he's God.

*Justice [Groaning].* Oh these mechanical smart answers . . . I suppose I perpetrated them too when I was your age. Listen, Mr.
Shanks. You do not give your life for your country by embroiling
it in blood, turmoil, destruction, rapine, murder, robbery, and
then getting your villainous neck strangled in a string. The true
patriot is the man who, dying in his own bed, full of years and
toil, can say, "I leave my country the richer by one new house I
have built, one waste acre I have reclaimed, one new tree I have
planted, even one new picture I have painted or poem I have
written, be they good or bad. No blood has been wantonly shed
by me. I have been the cause of no widow's tears, and no man
is the poorer through any dealing with me." That is the true
patriot.

*Shanks [To the other accused].* What a windbag.

*[The lord chief justice snaps his fingers, and Milligan climbs up
to him and places the black cap on his head. Commotion in the
dock. They all speak together.]*

*Doyle.* Mercy, my lord—mercy! We were promised mercy if we
pleaded guilty.

*Justice.* What mercy would you have had on others if your rebellion
had succeeded?

*Mahon.* I was misled, my lord. I wish to confess and to help the
authorities in every way I can, in exchange for the chance to
make a fresh start. I have information which will be of value to
His Majesty's government.

*Kehoe.* He isn't the only one who has information, my lord.

*Justice.* The only information I want I have—that my name was at
the head of the list of those you were plotting to assassinate.

*Doyle.* Not me, my lord, not me—him. He put your name down—
I didn't. Mercy—mercy—I was promised mercy. I am innocent.
I was led astray—let me live—oh my lord, my lord, mercy—as
you are a Christian gentleman—mercy.

*Kehoe.* Spare me, my lord. I have a wife and family—send me to
jail for as long as you like, but not the rope—not the rope.

*Mahon.* We were told we'd get off if we pleaded guilty. The lousy
lawyers have tricked us.

*[The lord chief justice silences the commotion with a blow of his
fist on the desk.]*

*Justice.* Mr. President of the New Republic, behold your ministry
of all the talents.

*[Peter Shanks has moved apart, and stands cold and proud, his
arms folded across his chest.]*

*Justice.* Thomas Doyle, Michael Mahon, John Kehoe, Peter
Shanks, you have pleaded guilty to the horrible crime of high
treason against the person and lawful power of his sacred majesty. The sentence of the court is that you be taken hence to the
place of public execution, and that you there be hanged by the
neck until you are dead, after which your head shall be cut from
your body and your body quartered and exposed in the public
place for one calendar month. And may the Lord have mercy on
your souls.

*[He waits expectantly, but no chaplain appears to say Amen. He
leans over the side of his chair and shouts "Jenkins!" There is a
flurry of curtains, and a fat and oily clergyman appears from
behind the judicial seat. He unctuously turns up his eyes to the
ceiling, so that the whites are startlingly visible, joins his hands
and intones the word "Amen." With an oily glance at the men
in the dock he stretches his right hand toward them in a sancti-
monious benison, and withdraws. Immediately pandemonium
breaks out in the dock. The three men begin howling and shout-
ing at once. Dark figures come out of the shadows and drag the
men away. Milligan creeps up to the lord chief justice and speaks
to him in a low tone. The lord chief justice nods, and Milligan
creeps away again. Presently, a girl climbs into the dock, the
very picture of terror. She can hardly be more than sixteen. She
is very poorly dressed, and her long dark hair falls untidily
around her shoulders. Her right hand clutches her dress nervously across her bosom. The lord chief justice gazes at her for
some time before he speaks.]*

*Justice.* Mary Neale, you stand where you are because you have
associated with the scoundrels who stood in that dock before
you. What have you to say for yourself?

*Mary [Whispering].* Your Honor—I—I—

*Justice [Thundering].* Speak up, child, speak up.

*[Mary goes white, her eyes close, she sways.]*

*Justice.* Is the girl not represented by counsel? *[Silence.]* Very
likely not. She doesn't look as if she has the money to pay them.
Have her brought to my chambers after the court adjourns.

*[The shadowy figures seize Mary and take her away. The lord
chief justice shuffles papers on his desk, rapidly scrawls his sig-
nature on a few of them, and then throws down the pen wearily.]*

*Justice.* The court is adjourned until one o'clock.

*[The justice rises and descends with slow dignity; the curtains
close over behind him. The lights go up again in his room. He*

*stands awaiting Milligan's aid in unrobing. Milligan comes in carrying the lord chief justice's papers, which he places on the table. While the lord chief justice pulls off his wig, Milligan pours his brandy. He takes the brandy and hands the chain to Milligan, who drapes it around the lay figure.]*

*Justice.* An amusing young blackguard, Peter Shanks. Every bit as conceited as you, Milligan. What a very humble man I am. Never once did I dream of taking a short cut to greatness by leading a rebellion.

*Milligan.* That young fellow will get to the top of a different tree from your lordship.

*Justice.* Don't gibe, Milligan. I hate people who gibe at the misfortunate. I hate bullies.

*[Milligan's grip on the judge's robe, as he takes it off, expresses his loathing of his employer.]*

*Justice [Facing Milligan].* Besides, Milligan, I am not at the top of the tree. I am not yet lord chancellor.

*Milligan.* Not yet, m'lud.

*Justice.* Not ever, Milligan. I was passed over in favor of a young whippersnapper, Milligan, although I licked all the right arses. I licked them, he kicked them, I am where I am, he is where he is. I have always been too humble, Milligan, too humble. *[He holds out his glass to be filled. Milligan fills it.]* Milligan.

*Milligan.* M'lud?

*Justice [Gently taking Milligan by the cravat and slowly shaking him].* Whose arse are the young fellows licking now since they've stopped licking mine?

*Milligan.* I have noticed, m'lud, that much attention is being paid to Mr. Wolfe, the attorney-general.

*[A gust of fury sweeps through the lord chief justice. He flings Milligan away from him. Milligan lies where he falls.]*

*Justice.* Get up, man, get up.

*[But Milligan appears to be hurt. The lord chief justice rushes remorsefully to him.]*

*Justice.* Are you hurt, Anthony? I didn't mean to hurt you.

*[He helps him to rise.]*

*Milligan.* It's all right, m'lud. *[He rubs his leg.]*

*Justice.* Forgive me, forgive me. I do not mean to hurt people. I do not mean to do it. I do it and I—you're all right, aren't you? Here. Drink this. *[Hands him his own glass of brandy.]*

*Milligan.* Thank you no, m'lud.

*Justice.* Go on, man, go on.

*Milligan.* Really no, m'lud.

*Justice.* You have not forgiven me, Anthony. I have lost another friend.

*Milligan.* I'm all right now, m'lud.

*Justice.* Are you sure? I'll fetch the physician?

*Milligan.* No need, m'lud.

*Justice [Putting both hands on Milligan's shoulders].* I'm sorry. You have forgiven me—?

*Milligan.* There is nothing to forgive, m'lud. It was an accident.

*Justice [Flinging away].* Oh Milligan, you disgust me with your hypocritical lies. It was not an accident. It was deliberate. *[Turns to him.]* Damages, Milligan, damages. I shall pay you—well, a guinea. When your wages fall due next quarter, remind me. One guinea. *[Cheerful again.]* So it's Mr. Wolfe the attorney-general, eh? They see the hand of death on me? *[Sighs.]* Oh what would I not give to be Peter Shanks!

*Milligan.* A condemned felon, m'lud?

*Justice.* A young man, Milligan: young, young, young, YOUNG.

*Milligan.* The hangman will soon make him as old as the earth, m'lud.

*Justice.* Oh he could buy back his life quite easily. A few words of information, a pinch of incense on the altar of the false gods, and another fifty years of life are his. Another fifty years, Milligan. And here am I with life leaving me and I leaving life. *[With gathering ferocity.]* It took me fifty-nine years to become what I am now, and everything is being snatched from my hand. I could even bear to give up the chain of office but *[A note of anguish]* not my rose gardens and my trees, and my lovely house at Blackrock. Soon it'll all be someone else's. *[Almost snarling.]* Don't tell me it's the common lot: I've had enough platitudes for one day. *[The anguish grips him again.]* Then every little pain and ache—wondering if this is the beginning of the end. The first clutch of death. *[He rages in silence for a few moments, then the mood changes suddenly; a note of semihysterical merriment enters his voice.]* And there's that damned young fool throwing away his life like an empty bottle. Oh why doesn't the devil exist, Milligan, so that I could sell him my soul for that young fool's fifty years of life? *[Throws himself wearily into his chair.]* Did I ever tell you, Milligan, about the time I tried to sell my soul to the devil?

*Milligan.* It is one of your favorite stories, m'lud.

*Justice [Sits, and leans back with closed eyes and joined hands].*

I was only twelve or thirteen at the time. I wanted to go to London to see all the sights. The desire was purely instinctive.

*Milligan [Offering him brandy].* May I venture to remind your lordship that you wished to see the female prisoner privately.

*Justice.* What female prisoner?

*Milligan.* Mary Neale, m'lud. The young female who is charged with aiding and abetting the rebels.

*Justice.* Have her sent in.

*[The lord chief justice puts on his bob-wig, arranges the folds of his dressing gown more becomingly around him, and seats himself in his armchair in an imposing attitude. Milligan returns with two turnkeys who bring Mary into the room. The three men bow and withdraw, leaving Mary standing nervously in front of the lord chief justice. He looks at her silently; she trembles.]*

*Justice.* Well, child, what have you to say for yourself?

*Mary.* I don't know, your honor.

*Justice.* You're not a rebel, Mary, are you?

*Mary.* Oh no, your honor.

*Justice.* It's not enough to say "Oh no, your honor," when you stand in danger of the rope going around your neck.

*Mary [Whispering].* Have mercy on me, your honor.

*Justice.* What was the nature of your association with those rebels?

*Mary.* I don't understand, your honor.

*Justice.* Come, child. You did associate with them?

*Mary.* Tom Doyle is my cousin, your honor. I have been going to his home ever since I was a little girl.

*Justice.* You knew he was a rebel?

*Mary.* I swear before almighty God, your honor—no.

*Justice.* How am I to believe you?

*Mary.* I'm telling the truth, your honor—on my oath I am.

*Justice.* You wouldn't be here, my child, if you hadn't said and done things which no loyal citizen should say or do. How old are you?

*Mary.* Sixteen, your honor.

*Justice.* Very young to be hanged, my child. But when I was a young man, girls of twelve and thirteen were hanged for stealing a ribbon.

*Mary [Sobbing].* But I've done nothing, your honor—nothing.

*Justice [Fiercely].* You must have done or you wouldn't be here. *[Subsides.]* However, I don't believe that you are as dangerous a rebel as they say. The question is, though, what view will the jury take? *[He walks slowly to the window, Mary looking after him fearfully.]* In certain circumstances I might be able to keep

your case from the jury. *[Without looking around.]* Do you understand me, child?

*Mary [Looking up]*. Do you mean you could get me off?

*Justice*. If I thought you were sincerely repentant—

*Mary*. But I've done nothing, your honor.

*Justice*. Sincerely repentant—then I might have set you free. *[He
turns and looks at her.]*

*Mary [She raises her eyes to his; a hint of insolence creeps into
her voice]*. What do you want me to do?

*Justice [Taking her by the chin]*. What do I want you to do? Answer
the question yourself, my child.

*Mary [A touch more insolent]*. I wouldn't know how to answer
your honor.

*Justice [Fiercely]*. Answer the question.

*Mary [Intimidated]*. I don't know what your honor wants.

*Justice*. Answer the question. *[She is silent. He grips her hair, but
not roughly, and forces her to look at him.]* I know what is in
your mind, your pure clean unsullied mind. That you must open
your gates for me to enter in. *[She begins to whimper.]* Oh Thou
who wast crucified to redeem the souls of pious virgins, look
upon Thy handiwork and be glad. *[He pushes her away and goes
to his chair.]* Every dog and devil in the town has had you. *[She
bows her head and cries piteously.]* That is the truth, eh? Every
dog and devil. *[He stares at her and shifts uncomfortably.]* Oh—
does it matter? It mattered to me when I was your age, but that
was because I was a child-man and did not know what women
are. *[He goes over and puts his arm around her shoulder.]* That
was the time when I could look into a face like yours—but only
from a distance: I was too humble to draw near. I could see in
such a face only beauty, purity, chastity, and innocence—all without any taint of the chamber of horrors that lay behind my own
face. *[Gently he grips her hair and twists her face up to his.]* But
now I know that the horrors behind this—*[Raps his forehead]*
are nothing to the horrors behind that *[Raps her forehead]*. Eh?
*[He puts his face close to hers.]* You would devour me, my dear,
if I let you—eh? Sixteen and sixty. I have often been devoured,
my dear, by sweet innocent buds of girlhood like yourself . . .
when I was thirty-three, when I was thirty-eight, when I was
forty, and forty-four, and even when I was fifty-six. There isn't
much left to devour now—but still enough to tempt you. *[He
puts his lips to hers. She does not shrink.]*

*Mary [Whispering]*. Are you telling me you love me?

*Justice [Staring hard at her]*. I think you *are* a virgin. *[She nods.]*

You are only a child. *[She puts her hand timidly on his breast.]*
Only a child. *[Tenderly.]* Are your father and mother alive? *[She
nods.]* I feel sorry for you—for all that you will have to suffer in
this world—you're so young, and youth is a time of torment and
suffering. I remember, my dear—*[Suddenly he stops, glances at
her hand on his breast, then at her face. He walks over to his
chair. She follows him. He laughs up at her.]* My God: thirty-
three . . . and thirty-eight . . . and forty . . . and forty-four . . .
and fifty-six . . . and now fifty-nine. Go away, my dear. I am too
old to bear any more pain. *[He slumps in his chair, his head
bent. She looks at him uncertainly. He glances up.]* I said go
away. No more pain. *[His head sinks again. She tiptoes to the
door. When he hears her turn the handle, he jerks upright.]*
Where are you going?
*Mary [Startled].* You told me to go away.
*Justice [Rising].* You are a prisoner. You have broken the law of
the land and must pay the penalty. Nevertheless, you shall be set
free. As far as your virtue is concerned, you will leave this room
as you came into it. *[Mary shows no reaction.]* I have a reputation for being severe. But it seems to me that I have always been
more inclined to mercy than the judges who are reputed kind.
But I cannot set you free without more ado. That would be to
do you an injury, my child. Your reckless words and deeds must
not go unpunished—
*Mary.* But I did nothing, your honor, I did nothing.
*Justice.* To let them go unpunished would encourage you to repeat
them. And the next time the judge might not be kind and merciful. You shall be whipped.
*Mary [Terrified].* Send me to the jail instead.
*Justice [Angry].* I save you from being hanged and still you're not
satisfied.
*Mary.* Oh not that . . . please not that—I couldn't bear it—before
all those crowds of people—and they jeering and laughing at me.
And the horrible man who whips you—oh please, your honor,
not that. Send me to jail—although I did nothing.
*Justice [Turning away].* You can be whipped or hanged. Please
yourself.
*Mary [Catching at his dressing gown].* Please—and I'll say a prayer
for your honor night and morning for the rest of my life—I swear
it. If you only know how they laugh and jeer when the clothes
are pulled off your back and—the disgrace, the disgrace.
*Justice [With a sigh].* God forgive me for being a silly foolish old
man. *[As if exasperated.]* You shall be whipped in private with

nobody to see you. Does that satisfy you? *[She hangs her head and says nothing. He flings away angrily.]* This is preposterous. The lord chief justice bandying terms with a presumptuous little bitch from the streets. You shall stand trial. You shall be hanged—and may I be damned through all eternity if ever I surrender again to an impulse of kindliness.

*Mary [In a whisper].* I accept whatever your honor says.

*Justice.* Do you, by God? I am much obliged to you. You're quite sure that you do not expect the lord chief justice to whip you with his own hand?

*Mary [With a quick look at him, which shows her understanding of his intention].* Whatever your honor wishes.

*Justices [Stalking back to his chair and flinging himself into it angrily].* I am a fool. I should have let the law take its course with you. Get out of my sight. *[Mary does not move.]* Get out of my sight.

*Mary [In a whisper].* I will let your honor do whatever you please. *[The lord chief justice appears to be thinking deeply for a moment. Mary watches him closely, but he does not look at her.]*

*Justice.* You will find a Bible on the table. *[Mary goes to table.]* Take it in your right hand and kneel down and say after me: I swear before almighty God.

*Mary [Kneeling].* I swear before almighty God.

*Justice.* That I will never again utter any word.

*Mary.* That I will never again utter any word. Are you going to do it now?

*Justice.* Or perform any action.

*Mary.* Are you going to—

*Justice.* Or perform any action.

*Mary.* Or perform . . . *[She cannot find utterance.].*

*Justice [Putting his hand on her shoulder].* Oh, all right. Don't get into a state. Get up, get up. *[She rises. He clasps her paternally.]* There there. Listen. You promise never to have anything to do with rebels again—? *[Mary nods.]* Then there's an end to it. You shall be whipped and set free. *[Takes the Bible from her and puts it on the table.]* Now go into the room over there and prepare to receive your punishment.

*[She goes into the inner room. He quietly locks the public door, pours himself a brandy and tosses it back. He goes to the cupboard and takes out a bundle of twigs. He makes more than one attempt to follow Mary into the room before he finally goes. The lights dim. After some time the lord chief justice stumbles out*

*of the room, flings away the bundle of twigs, and sinks on the
floor where he writhes and then lies still for a moment. The light
gradually returns to the room. He drags himself up heavily. He
looks ghastly. He searches for the bundle of twigs, finds it and
flings it in the fire. He keeps mumbling to himself as he prowls
restlessly around the room, stopping only to drink more brandy.]*
*Justice.* Oh John Scott, John Scott, why do you do these things?
You fool. You're mad, John Scott. You're an animal. Fifty-nine
years old and you still do these vile things. Hateful. Vile. Bestial.
Why why why why? What drives you to do them? And she
knew—she knew you had been maneuvering her into letting you
do it. Christ have mercy on us. She knew she knew she knew.
They all know. People aren't fools. Those girls talk. They do—
they must. *[He goes over to the inner door, glaring.]* I hate you
hate you hate you. You little whingeing bitch. *[He turns away.]*
There must be other men in the world like you too, John Scott.
*[He listens.]* Sobbing and whimpering and whingeing in there,
you hateful little slut. *[In anguish.]* Oh, you knew you knew you
knew you knew. *[He opens the door and speaks calmly.]* Come
out to me. Come along.
*[Mary comes out. She is sobbing and holding her torn dress up
on her shoulder. He takes her in his arms.]*
*Justice.* Don't cry. For God's sake, don't cry. I had to do it. You
did wrong, you had to be punished. There there. *[He looks at
her shoulders.]* It'll all be healed up by the time you're twice
married.
*Mary [Approaching hysterics].* I want my mother. I want my
mother. Oh, mother mother mother mother. . . .
*Justice [Shaking her].* Quiet. Now come. Pull yourself together. It
wasn't all that bad.
*Mary [Her voice rising].* Get my mother, get my mother, get—
get—get—
*Justice [Shaking her violently].* Hold your tongue.
*[A loud knock at the door.]*
*Justice [Pushing her toward the inner door].* Get in there and keep
quiet. Don't disgrace yourself before other people.
*[He closes the door after her. He makes sure that the bundle of
twigs has been consumed in the fire before he unlocks the other
door. Milligan enters.]*
*Milligan.* Are you all right, m'lud?
*Justice [In complete command of himself].* What do you mean,
Milligan?

*Milligan.* I was knocking at the door for a long time, but your lordship didn't seem to hear. *[He looks curiously around the room.]* Where is she? The female prisoner, m'lud?

*Justice.* In the other room. She has given me most valuable information about these rebel dogs—but keep that to yourself. *[Suddenly.]* What are you staring at me like that for?

*Milligan.* Staring—oh, m'lud—I didn't realize—

*Justice [Furiously].* Am I growing two heads? And what were you sniffing and spying around the door for? *[Pounding the table.]* I will not be spied upon, d'you hear?

*[The lord chief justice suddenly clutches at his chest with a gasp of pain. Milligan watches him impassively. The spasm passes, but the justice, badly shaken, is obliged to totter to his chair, breathing heavily and with difficulty.]*

*Milligan.* The attorney-general begs a moment's interview with your lordship concerning the female prisoner.

*Justice [Flaring up].* What concern is it of his what I say or do with the female prisoner? *[Subsiding.]* Oh, send him in.

*[Milligan goes to the door, bows the attorney-general in, then withdraws, shutting the door. The attorney-general, Arthur Wolfe, is a well-preserved fifty, elegant in figure and dress, quiet and calm.]*

*Wolfe [With a slight bow].* I have to apologize for being a little late for the trial this morning, but your lordship certainly dispatched those rascals very quickly. Now, about this girl—

*Justice.* It was stupid to send a girl like that for trial.

*Wolfe [Stiffly].* I understand you didn't deign to hear any evidence. We have enough to hang her.

*Justice.* I believe you. When I was attorney-general, I could always produce enough evidence to hang any man, woman, or child in the kingdom ten times over.

*Wolfe [Drawing himself up].* Chief justice, I—

*Justice.* Give me any two lines in your handwriting, Mr. Attorney-General, and I'll put the rope around your own neck with them.

*Wolfe.* I take your point, chief justice, but this girl—

*Justice.* Especially those confidential letters you send to the viceroy about me. *[Wolfe looks up startled. The lord chief justice grins.]* How do I know you write letters condemning my handling of certain trials?

*Wolfe [Much confused].* Anything that I have said to his excellency—

*Justice.* My dear Arthur, I wrote the same kind of letters when I was attorney-general. And when you are lord chief justice, the attorney-general will stab you in the back too. It's the way of the world. Now then, sit down and tell me what's the latest gossip about Copperfaced Jack.

*Wolfe.* Who's he?

*Justice.* The brandy is beside you. *[Wolfe shakes his head. He sits.]* Well, what are they saying about Copperfaced Jack? What poor innocent widow is he alleged to have defrauded now? What *[there is a fraction of a second's hesitation]* what new vices has he plunged into?

*Wolfe.* I do not know the gentleman. And from what you say I'm rather glad I don't.

*Justice [Jovially].* Come come, confidence for confidence. Tell me the latest gossip about Copperfaced Jack, and I'll tell you the latest gossip about yourself.

*Wolfe.* I never pay the slightest attention to the gossip about you.

*Justice.* So there is gossip?

*Wolfe.* Is there a man in public life, chief justice, about whom there isn't any?

*Justice.* You may speak freely. It will amuse me.

*Wolfe [Smiling].* Well, what everyone says about you these days is that—well. . . .

*Justice.* Yes?

*Wolfe.* The thing is too foolish to repeat.

*Justice [Chilling].* I have asked you a question, Mr. Attorney-General. You will be good enough to reply.

*Wolfe [Quickly coming to heel].* They say there's no hope of promotion for the next forty years, as your lordship is clearly determined to live to be a hundred.

*Justice [Scowling].* I see.

*Wolfe.* About the female prisoner.

*Justice.* I am discharging her.

*Wolfe.* Chief justice, you can't. The evidence—

*Justice.* Farcical, my dear Arthur, farcical. *[He pulls the bellrope by the fireplace.]*

*Wolfe.* There are eleven witnesses, absolutely unanimous.

*Justice.* Oh Arthur, never have eleven witnesses absolutely unanimous; it shows they've been drilled too well. Have a few discrepancies—just as would occur if they were telling the truth.

*Wolfe.* I understand you have interviewed the girl privately?

*Justice.* She is in the other room writing a full account of her knowledge of the rebels.

*Wolfe.* That's curious. She says she can neither read nor write.

*Justice.* She did not so inform me.

*[Milligan comes in.]*

*Justice.* I am going back into court, Milligan.

*Milligan.* Yes, m'lud.

*Justice [To Wolfe].* You will, I take it, be in time for *this* sitting?

*Wolfe.* I intend to be.

*[Milligan escorts the attorney-general out, closing the door. The lord chief justice clenches and unclenches his fists and babbles to himself again.]*

*Justice.* Oh, they're talking about you, John Scott, they know all about you. They're sniggering in corners about you. *[He beats his fists on his temples, writhing and shriveling before his own self-contempt.]* You fool, you fool, you fool, you fool.

*[Milligan enters with a letter on a salver.]*

*Justice [Calm].* Read it to me, Milligan.

*Milligan.* I am informed it is confidential, m'lud.

*[The lord chief justice opens and reads the letter. He throws it on the table carelessly.]*

*Justice.* Milligan, how often have I told you that letters from the wives or mothers of prisoners are not to be brought to me?

*Milligan.* M'lud, I did not know who it came from. It was handed to me by a servant.

*Justice.* Was it not worth your while to enquire whose servant he was?

*Milligan.* I'm sorry, m'lud.

*Justice.* In this case you needn't be. I haven't seen the lady for thirty years—no, forty years. My first love, Milligan. Oh Eliza Eliza Eliza Eliza. Bring her in. No wait. Get a turnkey to come and take the female prisoner away.

*[Milligan goes. The lord chief justice opens the inner door and beckons Mary out. He looks at her kindly and strokes her hair.]*

*Justice.* Well—?

*Mary [Rubbing her shoulder, a hint of insolence in her voice again].* You hurt me.

*Justice [Jovial].* It hasn't taken you long to recover.

*Mary.* Do you do that to other girls?

*Justice.* Of course not.

*Mary.* I have a feeling you do. You seem to have a lot of practice.

*Justice.* Don't be insolent.

*Mary.* I want to go.

*Justice.* Take care the rope isn't put around your neck.

*Mary [A touch of the vixen].* You said I could go free.

*Justice.* The attorney-general wants to hang you.

*Mary [Angrily].* You said I could go free. Aren't you supposed to be the judge?

*Justice.* You're not afraid of me any longer?

*Mary [Peevish].* You hurt me—deliberately.

[*The lord chief justice puts his hand on her shoulder. She shakes him off. He seems amused.*]

*Mary.* Now let me go.

*Justice.* No. I may change my mind about what is best to do to you.

*Mary.* I'll tell everybody about you. I'll tell them the sort of man you are.

*Justice [Furious.]* I'll swing you, by God. With my own hands I'll swing you.

*Mary [Backing away].* Don't touch me. [*Her voice rises.*] Don't touch me.

*Justice [With hatred].* You are beneath contempt. [*He recovers himself quickly.*] A man loses his magic for a woman the moment he condescends to be kind to her.

*Mary [Peevish again].* Well, you hurt me, so you did. You're cruel. That's what you are: cruel. [*She turns away, mumbling.*] Treating me like that. Don't you know a gentleman is not supposed to hurt a lady? What sort of a mother had you got?

*Justice [Going to her, smiling].* I can't help liking you, my dear. [*She makes no move when he puts his arm around her.*] I suppose I liked you the moment I saw you. And I hate to think that when you go I shan't see you again.

*Mary [Muttering].* Pity about that. [*Pulls away the dress and shows him her shoulder.*] Look at that.

*Justice.* I shall kiss it and make it better. [*She will not let him.*] You forget I have saved you from being hanged.

*Mary [Almost putting out her tongue at him].* You couldn't have me hanged because I didn't do anything.

*Justice.* I am tempted to let you devour me. [*Sighs.*] A man never learns, you know.

[*Milligan knocks and opens the door. He pauses. The turnkey is behind him.*]

*Justice.* It was very wrong of you to tell me you could write, my child. However, I have taken good note of what you told me, and shall bear it in mind when you come before me in court. [*Milligan beckons the turnkey in.*] Do not thank me, my child. It will be enough to lead a good and virtuous life from now on. If you remember me in your prayers, I shall feel well rewarded for what I have done for you.

[*The turnkey bows clumsily to the lord chief justice, and leads Mary off by the arm. The lord chief justice beckons Milligan to his side.*]

*Justice [Whispering].* Nobody—absolutely nobody—is to be let speak with her, either in court or when she leaves court.

*Milligan.* Yes, m'lud. Mistress Shanks is outside, m'lud.

*Justice.* I must put on my armor first.

*[Milligan helps him out of his dressing gown and into his red robe, chain, and wig.]*

*Justice.* She will have put on her best gown for me, Milligan. I too must try to make an impression. *[He sits. Milligan arranges his gown in graceful folds.]* I wish it were six feet longer, Milligan, and that the color were purple. Cover my legs. Legs destroy dignity. The Romans knew that—hence the toga. Nobody can take King George the Third seriously as long as he keeps his legs so much in evidence. If he covered his legs like the Pope, he could go as mad as he liked and nobody would notice. *[Milligan stands back to admire his handiwork.]* Well—?

*Milligan.* The chain, m'lud. . . .

*Justice [Adjusting it].* Like so? *[Milligan nods.]* Admit the public. *[He leans back.]* I sometimes think that in a previous existence I was the Emperor Claudius, the most endearing of the Caesars. *[Milligan has opened the door for Eliza Shanks. The lord chief justice makes no move; he seems lost in thought.]*

*Milligan.* Mistress Shanks, m'lud.

*[The lord chief justice slowly turns his head. Eliza, already nervous, bursts into tears.]*

*Justice.* You desired to see me, madam?

*[Eliza's distress increases. It has its inevitable effect upon the lord chief justice. He becomes uncomfortable, then jumps up and sweeps over to her.]*

*Justice [Taking her hand].* There there, you mustn't cry.

*Eliza.* Mercy, my lord, mercy for my poor misfortunate son.

*[The lord chief justice motions Milligan to leave the room. He does so. The lord chief justice places a chair for her. Late middleage finds Eliza run to flesh. She hasn't really helped herself by dressing youthfully and touching up her complexion.]*

*Justice [Kissing her hand].* Well well, after all these years. . . .

*Eliza.* I know I take a great liberty, my lord—it is presumptuous of me—you have become such a very great man in the world since we last met.

*Justice.* I remain the man I always was.

*Eliza.* Peter is innocent, my lord.

*Justice.* He confessed his guilt. I did what I could to save him from himself—even though I didn't know he was your son. The matter has now passed out of my hands.

*Eliza.* I know that one little word from you—

*Justice.* It is not quite as simple as that, my dear.

*Eliza [Pulling out her handkerchief].* You mean you won't help me—

*Justice.* Eliza, I will help you all I can. *[He sits.]*

*Eliza.* You are a great man—

*Justice.* The law is greater than I.

*Eliza.* You won't let them kill him on me—an innocent boy. I warned him not to listen to those people—

*Justice.* What people?

*Eliza.* Twice and three times his age, they are. Men who could buy and sell you—the real leaders of the rebellion—and walking round as free as the air under your very nose, while my Peter is where he is. Why don't you hang *them,* instead of young boys who haven't had time to grow up into sense? What sense had you got when you were his age, John Scott?

*Justice.* You of all people may well ask that.

*Eliza.* You were foolish and hotheaded—I don't mean any disrespect, my lord, but there was no harm in you. You were a fine open generous lad like Peter. I could show you the letters you wrote me—

*Justice [Sitting up].* Letters?!

*Eliza.* All these years I have kept them. I hadn't the heart to throw them away, even when I married Shanks. I still read them, my lord.

*Justice.* Put the past in the fire, Eliza.

*Eliza.* Oh no, John Scott, I couldn't do that. I mean no disrespect—you are a great man now, but I still think of you as John Scott who—who used to say he was in love with me—I mean no disrespect, my lord.

*Justice.* Letters? Um.

*Eliza.* No man ever sent me letters like yours. You said you would gladly give your life for me—

*Justice.* I meant it at the time.

*Eliza [Pathetic].* You were twenty, my lord, and you said you would gladly give your life for me. You begged me for a tress of my hair, and said it would inspire you all your life.

*Justice.* Did I say that? It doesn't sound like me. I am not in the least sentimental.

*Eliza.* But I never asked you for anything. Even when my husband died and there was all that trouble over the property.

*Justice.* I would have helped you had I known you were in trouble. What you ask of me now is impossible. He has confessed his guilt in open court. The law must take its course.

*Eliza.* He is all I have—

*Justice.* The country is on the brink of rebellion. The government has to act with a hand of iron.

*Eliza.* You said you would do anything for me—

*Justice.* Damnation, you keep harping on what *I* said. What did *you* say? What sort of a dance did *you* lead me in the days of my infatuation?

*Eliza.* It was not my doing, my lord, that you were turned away from our house. My father—

*Justice.* Your father! Did your father lure me into believing that you loved me?

*Eliza.* My lord, I was perfectly sincere—

*Justice.* Sincere! You made a fool of me. You ogled and languished and simpered and pressed my hand under your cloak in church, and I thought I was beloved.

*Eliza.* You were, my lord, you were.

*Justice.* While all the time you were sniggering with your friends over my letters—

*Eliza [Hotly].* I never showed as much as one line—

*Justice.* You lie, madam. Flossie MacDonald was able to tell me what was in them.

*Eliza.* Flossie MacDonald! My God, you wouldn't want to believe the time of day from that bitch.

*Justice.* Your best friend.

*Eliza.* Never.

*Justice.* She told me it was you always led the merry girlish laughter at my red pimply face, with my hands hanging out of the coat that was three times too small for me.

*Eliza.* Lies lies lies lies, all lies.

*Justice.* It was you who joked about my uncle's cast-off shoes upon my feet.

*Eliza.* Lies lies lies. I wanted to marry you.

*Justice.* What?! Boozy Bolger the bailiff's lovely daughter marry the candlemaker's ugly son! What a fool I was to aspire to such greatness. *[Viciously.]* But what were *you* to lead me on when you knew that the whole thing was eternally impossible? I know what I call such women *[drives one hand into the other]*, and I have had the whores whipped from one end of the town to the other.

*Eliza [Sobbing].* I loved you.

*Justice.* If that was love, would to God you had hated me. But I give you this much. That I am what I am today is due to you.

*Eliza [Catching at the straw].* I am proud to hear you say it, John.

*Justice [Fingering his chain and rising].* The collar of gold, Eliza.

I had to learn the old lesson: that gold and power are the only realities in the world. All the rest—love, friendship, goodness, kindness, faith, hope, charity, piety, bravery—pshaw! Illusions. *[He goes to the windows.]*

*Eliza.* I don't know what's got into you, John Scott. You never used to be like this.

*Justice.* As for your son—

*Eliza [Convulsed with sobs].* I never showed a line you wrote to anybody. Flossie had no right to say I did.

*Justice.* Forget about Flossie. I hadn't thought of her for forty years until this came up. Now about Peter—

*Eliza.* All lies, lies. I never joked about you. *[Swinging around and looking earnestly at him.]* You must believe at least that. I never joked about you—never.

*Justice.* It hardly matters now whether you did or not.

*Eliza.* I know I've gone old and I've lost my figure.

*[The lord chief justice is touched. He goes over and lays his hands on her shoulders.]*

*Justice.* You haven't, my dear. Not really. *[She begins to perk up.]* When you came in through the door, I recognized you immediately. You have hardly changed at all.

*Eliza.* I knew you too. But you looked so fierce in your red cloak.

*Justice.* My armor.

*Eliza.* Your what?

*Justice.* My wig. My robe. *[He pulls off his wig and flings it aside.]*

*Eliza [With a half giggle].* Oh John—what have you done with all your lovely hair? You that used to be as black as a crow, with that thick mop of lovely curly hair.

*Justice [Fingering the top of his head].* Damn it, Eliza, I'm nearly sixty. There's many a man completely bald at thirty nowadays.

*Eliza.* I always knew you would grow stout. Even as a boy you were plump. Of course, I know *I* shouldn't talk.

*Justice.* Stand up there and let me see you.

*Eliza.* No, I won't. Don't be silly.

*Justice.* Stand up, I said.

*Eliza.* I don't want you to look at me.

*[He takes her hand and, in spite of some resistance, hauls her to her feet. She is very confused.]*

*Eliza.* Well—aren't you glad you didn't marry the like of that?

*[He walks around her, surveying her. She goes to sit down, but he deftly moves the chair with one hand and saves her from flopping on the floor with the other. She is virtually in his embrace.]*

*Justice.* Old times, eh?

*Eliza.* My goodness, John Scott, but you haven't changed one bit.

*Justice [Both arms around her].* You always had a fine rump, my girl.

*Eliza.* Now, John, behave yourself. Suppose someone came in.

*Justice.* Well, suppose someone came in—?

*Eliza.* It's all very well for you. You never cared what anyone ever said about you—

*Justice.* Oh, didn't I?

*Eliza.* But a woman can't afford to have people talk about her.

*[He unfastens the clasp of his robe and lets it fall to the ground. Eliza, startled, backs away with surprising agility.]*

*Eliza.* Now, John Scott, what are you up to?

*Justice.* Come back here to me.

*Eliza [Sitting primly in her chair].* I'll do no such thing. Put your cloak back on you and sit down in your chair and behave yourself.

*Justice.* I don't like behaving myself, Eliza. *[He defiantly unbuttons his waistcoat and throws it on the floor.]*

*Eliza.* Take that up and put it back on you.

*[He begins to unfasten his braces.]*

*Eliza [Turning her back on him].* Oh—!

*Justice [Grinning].* Why don't you leave the room? Why don't you scream?

*Eliza.* Because I know you're only trying to frighten me.

*Justice.* Are you that easily frightened? *[He stoops to retrieve his waistcoat, wheezing loudly.]*

*Eliza [Swoops on the garment and holds it for him to get into].* That's what happened to my husband. Stooping down to get his pipe and burst a blood vessel. Of course, he was even stouter than you.

*Justice.* So you married a fat man after all. And you used to tell me you liked only thin men.

*Eliza.* He was nice and thin when I married him. *[She picks up the robe.]*

*Justice.* Your son takes after *you* though.

*Eliza.* Maybe. But stubborn as his father. My goodness, the weight of this thing. It must kill you in the hot weather.

*Justice.* I'm used to it. *[He goes to his chair.]* Pull the bell. I'll have them fetch him in to us.

*Eliza [Pulling the bellrope at the mantelpiece].* Yes, get him in. And give him a good telling off. That'll teach him to listen to his mother in future.

*Justice [Gently]*. Eliza, I cannot stop his being hanged—not now.

*Eliza*. Nonsense. If you say he's to be hanged, you can as easily say he's not to be hanged. *[He shakes his head.]* I think you should put on your wig. It makes you look fiercer.

*Justice*. I've told you, the matter is out of my hands.

*Eliza*. How can it be? Aren't you the lord chief justice? Just go out into your court and tell them you have changed your mind.

*[Milligan comes in.]*

*Justice*. Bring in the prisoner, Shanks.

*[Milligan bows and goes.]*

*Justice*. If he were to turn informer—not that I think he will. I know his type. You can hang them ten times over, and they still wouldn't do the sensible thing.

*Eliza*. It'll be different when you speak to him. You see, he was only fourteen when his father died, and boys need a man over them. He was a perfectly good child until he was sixteen, but then something got into him. It was the books. Those accursed books. I got the vicar to talk to him, but poor Mr. Benson might as well have been talking to the wall. Those books should be burned, and the men who wrote them burned along with them.

*[Milligan comes in, followed by two turnkeys escorting Peter Shanks, who is fettered hand and foot.]*

*Shanks [Surprised and angry]*. What are you doing here, Mother?

*Turnkey*. Quiet, until his lordship speaks to you.

*Justice*. Get out, you hangdog curs. All of you.

*[Milligan and the turnkeys go.]*

*Shanks*. Mother, it's no use.

*Eliza*. This is what I've had to put up with the past five years.

*Shanks*. Why in God's name didn't you stay away?

*Justice*. She came in God's name to rob you of your martyr's crown, my boy.

*Shanks*. Mother, not only do you waste your time but you sacrifice your dignity—and mine.

*Eliza*. Be respectful to his lordship.

*Shanks*. Desist, Mother, desist. I command you. *[To the lord chief justice.]* As for you, I know what you want of me. If I turn informer, I shall have the means to start a new life in America.

*Justice*. No, not America. We shall be more merciful than that. Australia.

*Shanks*. You've got my answer, Copperfaced Jack.

*Eliza*. Peter! How dare you to speak to his lordship like that! He could have you flogged for your impertinence, and really I couldn't blame him if he did.

*Justice.* You are very young to die.

*Shanks.* A few years more or less—what does it matter when the cause is honorable?

*Justice.* Death at the end of a rope—honorable?

*Shanks.* More honorable than yours in a featherbed will be.

*Justice.* We know there were other men in this conspiracy—men older than you, and more dangerous.

*Shanks.* No use—no use. I shall not inform.

*Eliza.* Peter, we are only trying to help you.

*Justice [Kindly].* Give us an excuse *not* to hang you, my boy.

*Shanks.* Hang me and ten thousand swords shall spring from their scabbards to avenge my death. Hang me and every drop of my blood shall be a dragon's tooth to rend you and your attendant jackels limb from limb. Hang me and—and—and—be damned to you.

*Eliza.* Go down on your knees and ask his pardon for saying the like of that.

*[Peter is about to refuse angrily when he pauses.]*

*Peter.* Very well. *[He kneels, but without trace of fear or servility.]* I willingly ask your pardon, Copperfaced Jack—if—*if*—I have done you any wrong. *[He rises.]* Are you satisfied, Mother?

*Justice.* I told you so, Eliza.

*Shanks [Starting].* How dare you address my mother in that familiar way? Keep your distance, Copperfaced Jack.

*Justice.* Your mother and I are old friends.

*[Peter stares aghast at Eliza.]*

*Eliza [Uncomfortable].* I had the honor of knowing his lordship when I was young.

*Justice.* Love, Peter. She loved me. Ask her.

*Eliza [Giggling].* My lord, I don't think we need—

*Peter [Shattered].* Oh Mother—to think you could have done this to me.

*Justice.* Such is life, Peter. C'est la vie.

*Shanks.* This red-faced old clown, this bloated mash tub of drink and pig swill, this heap of offal—how could you have ever walked the same side of the street as him? Isn't my cup of bitterness full enough without your adding humiliation to it? Why have I been dragged here to be insulted by this swindler, this rogue, this lecher, this—

*Eliza.* Peter! *[To the lord chief justice.]* I am ashamed—utterly ashamed.

*Shanks.* I take no favors from Copperfaced Jack. Let me be brought back to my cell.

*Justice.* He's an amusing young devil. I'm just wondering could I by any chance have been his father?
*[With a yell Shanks raises his fettered fists and runs at the lord chief justice. Eliza throws herself in front of him. Shanks lowers his fists and steps back.]*
*Justice.* What, Peter! Strike an old man—old enough to be your father?
*Eliza.* Don't be saying these things, John. He wouldn't understand that you're only joking.
*Shanks [Stung].* "John!"
*Justice [Putting his arm around Eliza].* Old friends. Old friends. *[Holds out his hand to Shanks.]* Give me your hand, Eliza's son.
*Shanks [Ignoring the gesture].* Mother, from this moment forth I do not know you.
*Eliza.* A nice way to speak to your own mother. And in front of strangers.
*Shanks [To the lord chief justice].* You can torture me with your tongue as much as you like, but another word out of me you will not get. I have only this to say to you: I see I am dealing with a madman.
*Eliza [Flouncing away to her chair].* Wouldn't he make you sick? I've a good mind to let them hang you. It's down on your knees you should be, thanking me and his lordship for what we're trying to do for you, if only you'd let us.
*Justice.* I see his point, Eliza. Take the martyr's crown away from his otherwise not very distinguished brow—and what's left?
*Eliza.* His father was the same. Would never listen to me. And then when he died, there was all the trouble over the property. Men are such fools.
*Justice [Sardonic].* How true.
*Eliza.* I don't mean men like you, my lord. After all, no fool could have got where you are.
*Shanks [Raising his clenched fists to his forehead].* Oh God, Mother, will you stop?
*Justice.* Be as emotional as you like, but don't rattle your chains so much.
*Shanks [Near tears].* Send me back to my prison cell.
*Eliza.* If you'd only listened to your mother who knows what's good for you, you wouldn't be standing where you are today. *[Whimpers.]* Disgracing the family . . . chains . . . thank heaven your grandfather isn't alive to see it. *[Sobs.]* Oh my lord, you knew our family and how respectable we always were. And now . . . chains! A convict!

*Justice.* Not a convict, dearest Eliza, the president of the new republic, the Lord of the new Earthly Paradise. Though admittedly under something of a cloud at present.

*Eliza.* He had a private tutor after his father died, though God knows I could hardly afford it.

*Shanks.* Great God, Mother, you'll drive me mad.

*Justice [Going to him].* Women always spoil our finest performances, Peter. Mothers particularly.

*Shanks [Shrinking].* Don't touch me.

*[A knock. The attorney-general opens the door.]*

*Wolfe [Stiffly].* I am sorry to intrude but—

*Justice.* Come in, Arthur, I was just about to send for you. Close the door. *[He sits.]* I am considering a new trial for Peter Shanks.

*Shanks [With a vehemence that makes Wolfe jump.].* I want no new trial.

*Wolfe.* This man had confessed.

*Justice.* A new trial this afternoon.

*Wolfe.* Upon what grounds? I shall certainly not consent to a new trial except on proper grounds.

*Justice.* Don't forget yourself, Mr. Attorney-General.

*Wolfe.* Let your lordship not forget the law.

*Justice [Pounding the chair].* I am the law, Mr. Attorney-General.

*Wolfe.* That contention shall be judged elsewhere.

*Justice [Bellowing].* No insolence, or by God you shall know who and what I am.

*Shanks [With much rattling].* Cease your bickering. *[His intervention causes both men to stop and look at him.]* I refuse the offer of a new trial.

*Wolfe [Hardly able to talk].* Chief justice, if you are prepared to allow a condemned traitor to address you like that, I am not.

*Justice.* Quack quack quack, Arthur. Sit down and be quiet.

*[Wolfe turns on his heel and walks out. The lord chief justice strides after him and bellows, "Arrest him! Arrest him!" Confused shouts outside. The lord chief justice returns to his chair. Wolfe is brought in by two turnkeys, with Milligan, betraying not the least surprise, following.]*

*Wolfe [To the turnkeys].* You have dared lay hands on His Majesty's attorney-general.

*Justice.* Contempt of court, Arthur. Now listen to me.

*Wolfe.* I refuse to listen. You have gone out of your mind.

*Shanks.* You see what happens, Mother, when thieves fall out.

*Wolfe.* Mother! Is she his mother?! Now I KNOW you have gone out of your mind.

*Justice [To the turnkeys].* Release Mr. Attorney-General. *[They do so.]* Take away the prisoner, but not beyond the precincts of my court. *[He rises.]* Madam, be so kind as to withdraw.

*[Eliza curtseys to the lord chief justice. All leave except Milligan, who has been motioned to stay.]*

*Justice.* See that Mistress Shanks is allowed to remain with the prisoner, Milligan. Send to the tavern for wine and victuals for them.

*[Milligan bows and goes.]*

*Wolfe.* I respectfully request your lordship's permission to withdraw.

*Justice.* I know I am a hasty man, Arthur, but by God I brook no threats from you or anyone else.

*Wolfe.* I did not threaten you. You threaten the law.

*Justice.* This is a matter that we settle out of court, I think.

*Wolfe.* I am not falling into that trap.

*[The lord chief justice suddenly strikes him across the face. Wolfe reels, partly under the force of the blow, but chiefly from shock. He stares at the lord chief justice with mounting fury, and speaks in a choking voice.]*

*Wolfe.* You are only an old man.

*Justice.* Still young enough to handle a pistol.

*Wolfe.* That may follow.

*Justice.* I had forgotten. *[He takes off his chain of office and throws it into his chair.]* I am now a private gentleman, sir.

*Wolfe.* Very good, Lord Clonmell. A friend of mine shall call upon you.

*Justice [Pulling the bellrope].* I can dispense with ceremonial.

*Wolfe.* So can I.

*Justice.* Then . . . here and now.

*Wolfe.* When I get a pistol, I shall be at your service.

*Justice.* I have pistols here.

*[Milligan comes in.]*

*Justice.* The pistols, Milligan.

*[Milligan takes a case of pistols from the cupboard and places the weapons on the table. Meanwhile the lord chief justice has unfastened his robe and flung it on the chair.]*

*Justice.* My coat, Arthur. It's somewhere over there.

*[Wolfe reluctantly goes to the corner and gets the coat. He has to hold it for the lord chief justice.]*

*Milligan.* The pistols, m'lud—they've been loaded for a long time. The powder may be damp.

*Justice.* Reload.

*Milligan [Reloading the pistols].* Shall your lordship be requiring the services of a friend?

*Justice.* No.

*Wolfe [To the lord chief justice in an undertone].* I shall wait in the meadow two miles beyond the turnpike.

*Justice.* Why walk yourself to death before I kill you? I shall have my court cleared. That place will be as good as any. A new kind of legal duel, eh?

*Wolfe.* If you have such little respect for your own court, I have nothing further to say.

*Justice.* Profaning that temple of truth and eloquence—eh?

*Wolfe.* And justice.

*Milligan.* The pistols are ready, m'lud.

*Justice.* Take your choice, Arthur.

*Wolfe.* As your lordship is the person challenged, you have the right of choice.

*Justice.* Pedant.

*Wolfe.* I insist, my lord.

*Justice.* I waive the right as the pistols are mine.

*[The attorney-general takes up the pistol nearest his hand and hides it under his gown. The lord chief justice takes up his other pistol and thrusts it carelessly under his arm. The two men bow to each other and walk out of the room, the lord chief justice indicating that the attorney-general is to precede him.]*

*Justice [As he goes through the door].* Remain here, Milligan. In case I should become indisposed, break the news to her ladyship as tactfully as you can.

*Milligan.* Yes, m'lud.

*[The lord chief justice goes out, leaving the door open. Milligan quite calmly sits down in his chair and props his feet up on the table. He takes a toothpick from his pocket and begins to use it with gentlemanly elegance. There is dead silence. Then two shots reverberate through the building. Milligan, quite unperturbed, rises and addresses the audience.]*

*Milligan.* My lords, ladies and gentlemen, and others, those shots need not cause you a moment's alarm. Gentlemen who fight duels like this never aim at each other. But that pair are such rotten shots they could have hit each other by accident. So I took the precaution of putting in only a little powder . . . and no bullets.

*[He bows and retires as light vanishes, and the curtain falls.]*

## Act II

*A large yard in Newgate jail, Dublin, where prisoners are herded together during the day, men and women alike, old and young, first offenders and hardened criminals. There is a wall of massive granite blocks at the back, with an arched gateway in the middle, and a smaller gate near it; at left is an open passage leading to another yard. Also to be seen is the front part of a ramshackle wooden shed, which serves as a privy. Some female prisoners, of varying ages, dirty and ragged, are sitting on wooden benches to the left of the main iron gate. They are Rosalind and Viola, a pair of slatterns; Bessie, who is young, buxom, and good-natured; and a couple of others who are no more than slightly animated bundles of rags. In the corner, right, Michael Fennessy, a carpenter, is putting the finishing touches to a black coffin on rough trestles. He is a tall, gaunt man of indeterminate age, of transparent simplicity, with a manner to match. In happier circumstances he might be jolly and good-humored, but his expression is now sad and lonely; even his rare smiles are sad. He works away, clearly oblivious to the chatter around him.*

*Viola [Holding her hands to her ears].* Gawd, Mr. Fennessy, will ye soon be finished hammering at that thing? You have me head splitting.
*Fennessy [Hammering in one more nail].* There, ma'am. I'm finished. There won't be any more hammering now for a bit.
*Bessie.* This place'd get on your nerves.
*Viola.* Sometimes it's all the noise. Sometimes it's all the quietness. Things was never the same since poor oul' Billy-in-the-Bowl was hung.
*Bessie.* It was a tragedy for a fine man like that to be hung, especially when you look at the drips they leave behind.
*Fennessy [Mournful].* I'll be out of your way in three days' time, ma'am.
*Bessie.* Don't worry, Mr. Fennessy, it may never happen.
*Fennessy.* It wouldn't be me luck, ma'am. If they was to do away with hanging, it'd be the day *after* I was hung.
*Viola.* I sometimes wish I was going on the swing-swong myself. It'd be a bit of excitement after sitting here day after day, week after week, month after month. D'ye know what it is, ma'am, I've clean forgot what I'm in jail for?

*Bessie.* I'll try to believe ye.

*Fennessy.* Isn't Mr. Brian Borroo lively enough for you, ma'am?

*Viola.* He's too full of himself. Though he has a gorgeous voice.

*Bessie.* The voice isn't bad. I love the way he sings "The Night Before Larry Was Stretched." Great humor he puts into it. But the filth that comes off his tongue—even when there's ladies present.

*Viola.* I blame his mother. What way did she rear him?

*Bessie.* There's no control over childer nowadays. Dare ye open your mouth to your father and mother when I was a girl and you'd be knocked flying.

*Viola.* Me own father was a very nice man. He was hung for a rebel.

*Bessie.* They don't hang half enough of them. Why don't them fellows go out and do an honest day's work instead of shooting from behind hedges at poor landlords and proper gentlemen? There was this lovely young gentleman I had, and he showed me where he'd been shot by them blackguards. No use he'll ever be now, ma'am, to any poor girl. I nearly cried. Such a gorgeous young gentleman he was, too.

*Rosalind [Mournfully].* I love a man that gives you a bit of a laugh.

*Viola.* Oh Rosalind, I thought you was asleep.

*Rosalind.* I was just thinking with me eyes shut.

*Bessie.* That gorgeous young gentleman what was shot . . . skin like a baby he had.

*Rosalind.* Aye, a laugh and a bit of an oul' song.

*Bessie.* Lovely long, thin legs and as straight as a pole.

*Rosalind.* I mean to say, if ye couldn't have a bit of laugh you'd go mad.

*Viola.* Mr. Fennessy, would you ever trot down to the well and get us a jar of wather. I'm famished with the drooth.

*Fennessy.* Very good, ma'am. *[He goes out.]*

*Rosalind.* Gawd a'mighty, it's inhuman sticking the likes of him on top of us.

*Viola.* Do ye know how he spends the night? On his knees saying prayers for himself.

*Bessie.* You'd be the same if you were going up on the swing-swong in three days.

*Viola.* I would not. God and me parted company many's the long year ago. It was friendly but final.

*Bessie.* Don't be saying things like that. D'ye want us all to be struck dead?

*[Fennessy comes back with a jug of water.]*

*Fennessy.* There's wather for ye now, ma'am.

*Viola [Taking the jug].* If you had the price of a pot of porter, Mr. Fennessy, you could have an hour of joy before you go on the swing-swong.

*Fennessy.* In what way, ma'am?

*Viola [Winking at the others].* Oh, in any way that took your fancy, sir.

*Fennessy.* I don't rightly follow ye, ma'am.

*Bessie.* Ah, leave the poor fella alone.

*Viola.* Gawd pity his poor wife, that's all I say.

*Fennessy.* Why would you say that, ma'am?

*Bessie.* Sing us a bit of an oul' song, Mr. Fennessy.

*Viola.* Jasus no, the only one he knows is "Faith of Our Fathers." *[Sighing.]* Ah, Billy-in-the-Bowl, why aren't ye here with us now?

*Rosalind.* Was Billy really in a bowl?

*Bessie.* He had to be. Both his legs was cut off down to the stumps, so he sat in a little baskety bowl on wheels and begged from the quality.

*Viola.* He'd just about enough of himself left to sit on.

*Bessie.* But he was all there, all the same. Ten children he had.

*Viola.* God love him.

*Bessie.* And a perfect gentleman.

*Viola.* Even the oul' faggots he raped out in Ballybough had to admit that.

*Bessie.* They said he took off his hat.

*Viola.* Which is more nor a certain viscount I used to know did. Wouldn't even take off his dirty boots.

*Rosalind.* Was it for that they hung Billy?—for what he did out in Ballybough?

*Bessie.* A damn shame it was.

*Fennessy.* Fancy hanging a poor man like that and he with no legs. Didn't that good God put enough affliction on him without men adding to it?

*Rosalind.* Justice is justice, Mr. Fennessy.

*Fennessy.* But listen, if Billy-in-the-Bowl had no legs, why didn't those ladies out in Ballybough run away when he went for to attack them?

*Viola.* Gawd, where were *you* brought up at all at all?

*Bessie.* A nice gentleman like you wouldn't understand, Mr. Fennessy.

*Viola.* Some ladies goes outa their way to meet their fate.

*Rosalind.* I wonder is he all that much of an innocent lamb? Hasn't he four childer? So he mustn't use it only for stirring his tay.

*Bessie.* Leave him alone. I only wish there were more like him.

*Viola.* Gawd forbid.

*Fennessy.* I wonder how did they hang a man with no legs? Sure, he couldn't climb up the ladder.

*Viola.* He wasn't asked to. Mr. Galvin rolled him in his bowl up the plank.

*Bessie.* A perfect jintleman is Mr. Galvin.

*Fennessy.* Thou shalt not kill.

*Rosalind [Puzzled].* I beg your parsnips, Mr. Fennessy.

*Fennessy.* Me last words to Mr. Galvin on Monday will be: "Fifth, thou shalt not kill."

*Viola.* Suppose he says back to you, "Seventh, thou shalt not steal—?"

*Fennessy.* I hadn't thought of that. *[He sighs.]* Seventh, thou shalt not steal.

*Bessie.* Ach, you shouldn't have said that to the poor man, and he. . . .

*Viola.* Isn't it the truth?

*Rosalind.* The greater the truth the greater the libel, as me granddad used to say.

*Viola [Haughty].* We're not here for robbing people.

*Rosalind.* It was givin' people too much good value for their money has us here.

*Viola.* Ladies shouldn't be put in here for what they does be doin' in the privacy of their own room.

*Rosalind. Where's* your private room?

*Viola.* Where's *yours?*

*Rosalind.* Did I say I had one? It's anywhere outa the east wind for me.

*Viola [Sneering].* Up ag'in the trees of the Royal Canal?

*Rosalind.* Like yourself, darling.

*Bessie [Restoring the peace].* Sure, them poor oul' trees is more sinned against than sinning.

*[A man is heard singing]*

*Bessie.* Oh, here he comes.

*[Fennessy with a grimace goes back to his coffin-planing. Brian Borroo comes in from the left; he is young, and would be good-looking if he didn't carry a hundredweight of fat and his fine features weren't so often distorted by a sneer. He carries a bucket of whitewash and a brush. He stops in the middle of the room, takes a deep breath, and sings at the top of his voice.*

*Borroo [Singing]*

Sez the daughter to the mother,
"Yes talk is all in vain,
For knights 'n' lords 'n' dukes 'n' earls
Their efforts I disdain.
I'd sooner live a humble life
Where time I would employ
Doing what comes natcherally
Wid my bonny laborin' boy."


*Viola.* Go and do a dance for us, Mr. Borroo. Gawd knows the place needs a bit of livening up. I'll be the band.
*[Viola begins to troll an Irish jig, clapping her hands in rhythm. Borroo folds his arms and executes a step dance with peculiar elegance. While he is dancing, a turnkey marches briskly across the room and in passing gives him a tap of the head with a huge key. Borroo immediately stops and throws himself into a fighting attitude. On seeing the turnkey, he becomes respectful, giving him a little bow.]*
*Borroo.* God save your honor.
*Turnkey [Unlocking the little gate].* You get on with your work.
*Borroo.* Yes, your honor.
  *[Borroo takes up the bucket and brush again, but the moment the turnkey is gone he puts them down.]*
*Borroo.* I'm damned if I will. *[Glowers after the turnkey.]* My God, I hate them crawling, sniveling, sleeky, snuffly bitch's bastards.
*Fennessy.* Ladies present, Mr. Borroo.
*Bessie.* Declare to Gawd, he's crying.
*Borroo.* I'm not crying. It's only water in me eyes. If you got a belt on the head with a great big goddam key, wouldn't *you* get water in your eyes? *[Angry and frustrated, he looks around to see whom he can vent his spleen on. He decides to bait Fennessy.]* Well, Fennessy?
*Fennessy [Mildly].* Yes, Mr. Borroo?
*Borroo.* Whose are ye making today?
*Fennessy.* Me own, Mr. Borroo.
*Borroo.* You're the right eejit to be killing yourself making your own. Let them provide one for you. They can't leave you above ground.
*Fennessy.* They're paying me a shilling for it, and that'll come in handy for me wife.
*Borroo.* Yer widda.
*Fennessy.* Widda—? That's true. God help me, I haven't much to

leave the poor girl except the memory of me short-comings and four children.

*[Peter Shanks, Doyle, Mahon, and Kehoe come through the gateway, guarded by a posse of turnkeys. Only two turnkeys come in with them. Borroo picks up his bucket and brush and stands respectfully to one side. The two turnkeys unlock the prisoners' chains and take the chains away as they go off to the left. When Borroo is sure that the turnkeys are out of earshot, he lays down his bucket and brush, and faces the prisoners, rubbing his hands.]*

*Borroo.* A hundred thousand welcomes to ye.

*Shanks [With a slight bow].* Thank you. *[He bows to the women.]* Good afternoon, ladies. *[The women rise and give him a little curtsey. He turns to Fennessy.]* Good afternoon, friend.

*Bessie [Whispering].* Isn't he the gorgeous young gentleman?

*Fennessy.* Me name's Jack Fennessy, sir, and I'm to be hanged a Monday on the stroke o' noon.

*Shanks.* I grieve to hear it. I am *[Momentous]* Peter Shanks.

*Fennessy.* And what are you in for, sir?

*Shanks [Put out].* Don't you know? *[Recovering his dignity.]* Ah, but of course. In prison you are held incommunicado. Nevertheless, I thought that even in this place the echoes of my name would have sounded. We shall soon lay down our lives for our country.

*Viola [Disgusted].* Rebels, me dear. It's a disgrace putting the likes of them in with respectable women.

*[Doyle has been cowering at the sight of the coffin.]*

*Doyle [Suddenly shrieking].* What's that thing in here for?

*Fennessy.* It's only mine, sir.

*Doyle.* My God—tormenting us like this.

*Shanks [Through his teeth].* Try to be a man, Captain Doyle.

*Doyle.* It's all very well for you to talk, but I'm innocent.

*Shanks [Contemptuous].* Well, go and turn informer and save your neck.

*Doyle [Babbling].* What could I tell them? You never trusted me. You never told me a thing.

*Shanks.* I was wiser than I knew.

*Fennessy.* If the sight of me handiwork is upsetting the young gentleman, perhaps you'd consider taking him down to the yard. I can't go meself. I've been ordered to stay up this end.

*Shanks.* Come along, Captain Doyle; we shall inspect the premises. Your pardon, ladies.

*The Women.* Not at all, sir. You're welcome. Don't mention it.

*[Shanks and his companions go out, left.]*

*Borroo [Spitting].* Wouldn't it make ye throw up? If the rebellion had been a success, them fellows would have been driving round in carriages with a string of lackeys tailing behind them and decent people like meself paying for it all.

*Viola.* There wasn't much spunk in the little fellow, to be sure. But the youth of today is gone soft with fat living and easy money.

*Bessie [Dreamily].* And to think that gorgeous young gentleman is going to be hung.

*[A turnkey comes in briskly from the left. Borroo immediately bends down to pick up his bucket. The turnkey kicks him, nearly sending his head into the bucket. The women scream with laughter.]*

*Turnkey.* Get on with your work, d'ye hear? *[He unlocks the gate, right.]* Well, what are ye waiting for?

*Borroo.* I was just waiting, yer honor, to see if the women were finished going to the jakes till I clean it out. Does any of youse ladies want to see a man about a dog?

*[The women close their eyes and turn away haughtily. The turnkey makes a threatening move toward Borroo.]*

*Turnkey.* Move, d'ye hear me?

*[Borroo goes quickly into the shed with his bucket and brush, and closes the door. The turnkey stands watching the door quietly. After a moment Borroo thrusts out his head.]*

*Borroo.* Is that goddam bitch's bastard—

*[Borroo sees the turnkey and shoots in again, but the turnkey goes into the shed after him. A sound of blows and howls. The turnkey comes out, slamming the door. As he reaches the gate Jack Galvin, the hangman, comes in.]*

*Turnkey.* Good day to you, Mr. Galvin.

*[Galvin is elderly, somewhat stooped, and as lean as a greyhound. His hands and feet seem to be disproportionately big, and the sleeves of his ill-fitting coat are so short that about four inches of wrist are visible. He has small, narrow-set eyes, under bushy grey brows. He will not look people straight in the face, but restlessly and watchfully surveys them through the corner of his eyes. He wears a pair of rusty black gloves with the fingers out of them, which he removes with exaggerated elegance while talking.]*

*Galvin [Meaningfully].* Have they arrived yet, Mr. Smith?

*Turnkey [Nodding toward the left].* Down at the other end. Four of them.

*Galvin [Disappointed].* Only four?

*Turnkey.* God almighty, if the whole country were given over to you to be hung, you still wouldn't be satisfied.

*Galvin [Without humor].* I'd need them all to make a decent living.

*Turnkey.* Maybe you'd like me to go and start up another rebellion to provide you with customers.

*Galvin.* If I didn't take the rough and tough ones off your hands, Mr. Smith, life would be hard for you and your brethren. *[He turns round and rubs his hands together slowly.]* Good day to ye, Mr. Fennessy. Good day to ye, ladies.

*[The women return his greeting with cheerful cordiality and more than a little respect. Galvin saunters slowly toward the left, and peers out at the condemned men. He scratches his ear thoughtfully.]*

*Rosalind [Sympathetic].* Ye have your hands full these days, Mr. Galvin, with all them rebels.

*Galvin [With a sigh].* Hard work, ma'am. But amn't I keeping the country well pacificated and fit for ladies and genkilmen to live in? Though it's a pity the same ladies and genkilmen don't reckonize that the laborer is worthy of his hire.

*[Borroo, brush in hand, opens the door of the shed. As Galvin is behind the door, he doesn't see him for a moment.]*

*Borroo.* Gawd, the stink in there'd choke ye. *[He draws in huge gulps of air. Then his eye falls on Galvin, and he hurriedly goes back into the shed.]*

*Galvin [Scratching his chin].* I only hope I never have to attend to that young man. *[Shaking his head.]* He'd make a very unbecoming end. *[With a glance over his shoulder in the direction of the condemned men.]* Not like these genkilmen down there.

*Rosalind.* That little downy fellow will give ye trouble, Mr. Galvin, with his howling and struggling.

*Galvin.* Devil a bit. It's the likes of him are always the easy jobs. They're fruz stiff with the fright. But it'll be a pleasure to do that same young man. Don't ask me why because I daren't tell you. It's not fit for the ears of ladies to hear.

*Bessie [Knowing he intends to tell them].* If it's not fit for ladies' ears, we better not hear it.

*Galvin.* Too shockin' and scandalous it is.

*[The women say tsk tsk tsk and look meaningfully at one another.]*

*Galvin.* God knows I'm only too well tutored in the ways of the wicked. But when the major who arrested them told me, it rose me hair.

*Viola [Holding her ears].* Don't tell us, Mr. Galvin—for Jasus sake don't tell us.

*Galvin.* The four of them were in this room all be themselves.
*[The women shriek with horror.]*

*Galvin.* And there was the little downy fella—oh, don't ask me to say it.

*Bessie.* Gawd love you, Mr. Galvin, having to hear these things. But I suppose it's yer jooty.

*Galvin.* Me jooty it is. Oftentimes I have to soil me ears, I have to grovel in the dirt, but it's me jooty. *[Lowering his voice.]* The little fella was bending forward over a table and don't ask me where his pantaloons was.
*[The women shriek and cover their faces.]*

*Galvin.* I ax yer pardon for mentioning pantaloons in the presence of ladies—

*Rosalind.* Spare us, Mr. Galvin, spare us.

*Galvin.* Those articles—garments I might call them *[More shrieks]*—were hanging down around his ankles. There he was, bending down as unadorned as the day he was born. *[Shrieks.]* Not as much as a square inch of wool or cotton to cover that which should be hidden from the eyes of man and beast—

*Bessie.* Don't tell us any more, Mr. Galvin, not another word out of ye.

*Galvin.* Sez I to the major, major, sez I, it may be that he was short took. It may be that he had taken opening medicine.

*Bessie.* 'Tis only a kind Christian jintleman'd think the like of that.

*Rosalind.* The poor Gawd'll reward ye for yer charitable mind, Mr. Galvin.

*Galvin.* Short took?!!! sez the major. Opening medicine?!!! sez the major. *[Earnest.]* Wasn't it only me jooty, ladies, to think the good thing? Ah no, sez the major. No, sez he. A pure mind like yours, Mr. Galvin, sir, would naturally think the good thing. *[Momentous.]* But this is just the Bishop of Clogher all over again.
*[The women shriek and squeal.]*

*Viola.* Say another word, Mr. Galvin, and I'll fall fainting to the ground.

*Galvin.* The Bishop of Cloger all over again! Ladies—when those words crept in through the holes of me ears, me hair riz. *[He holds up extended fingers.]* Like that ladies. Stiff as a—

*Rosalind.* Don't tell us: We know only too well.

*Galvin.* Mr. Galvin sir, sez the major, you'll be called upon to perform your painful jooty on these villains. And I'll tell you this, ladies, as long as the good God leaves me the strength of me arm, I'll do me bit to stop them turning poor oul' Dublin into a Sodom and Gomorrah.

*[Feeling he has reached his apotheosis, Galvin strolls over to Fennessy, whom he claps on the shoulder in a comradely manner.]*

*Galvin.* A very mellingcholy occupation for you, Mr. Fennessy.

*Fennessy.* Yessir.

*Galvin.* If the ladies and genkilmen was only left to me and me alone, Mr. Fennessy, I'd be on the pig's back. But them that should be mine is being handed over to the millingtary.

*Bessie.* Oh, the millingtary's a disgrace, Mr. Galvin, a proper disgrace.

*Galvin.* Not trained for the job, ma'am. Butchers. Many's the day since the rebellion started, I've had to stand and look at the millingtary, and shout "Not that way, ye clown—will ye put the knot under the genkilman's ear, not his Adam's apple."

*The Women.* Disgraceful. Croolty, that's what it is. They should leave the job to the proper tradesman.

*Galvin.* What's more, the millingtary only annoys the people. The people hates bad workmanship. And d'ye know? The govermint won't even pay me a livin' wage. D'ye know what me rate works out at? A penny an hour. How's that for a Christian country, Mr. Fennessy? *[He spits in disgust.]* And if you open yer mouth, you're told the millingtary will do it for nothing. *[Confidential.]* What's this you're being done for, Mr. Fennessy? A little touch of forgery, eh?

*Fennessy [Shocked].* O no, sir, nothing like that. *[Shamefaced.]* To tell the truth, sir, I done away with a sheep on Lord Delville's estate.

*Galvin [Almost a screech].* A sheep!!!

*Fennessy [Humbly].* I couldn't stand see me poor childer go hungry, sir.

*Galvin [With throbbing emotion].* Ah no, Mr. Fennessy, you still oughtn't to have done it. I have little ones of me own, but I'd sooner see them dropping down at me feet from the hunger before I'd steal another man's property.

*Fennessy.* It's a hard and bitter world for the poor, sir.

*Galvin [With a sigh].* Won't ye be as well off out of it?

*Fennessy [Almost unconsciously fingering his neck].* Does it hurt much, sir?

*Galvin [Airily].* It needn't.

*[Fennessy stares at him uncomprehending. Bessie goes over and whispers in his ear.]*

*Fennessy [Starting].* Oh, I'm sorry, sir. I didn't understand. *[Reluctantly he takes a coin from his pocket and gives it to Galvin, who registers disgust.]* It's all I've left, sir.

*Galvin.* Outa the sheep? *[Fennessy stands mutely miserable.]* Well, I won't do much damage to me liver drinking that.

*Fennessy [Piteous].* Sure, ye wouldn't be after hurting me, sir?

*Galvin [Brusque].* If the millingtary was doin' ye, it'd be pure hell. But with a proper tradesman looking after ye, you've nothing at all to worry about.

*Bessie.* Give him an aisy drop, Mr. Galvin, and God'll reward ye.

*Galvin [Putting his arm around her].* As aisy and delicate as I'd give yerself, me love. *[He pinches her.]*

*[A turnkey unlocks the gate and comes in dragging Mary Neale. He flings her amongst the women and goes over to the other turnkey.]*

*Second Turnkey.* See everything's all right down in the yard. Copperfaced Jack's on his way.

*[Some excitement among the women as they hear the name.]*

*Galvin.* What's the oul' bastard coming for now? We're not doing any flogging today, are we?

*First Turnkey.* Devil a one.

*Galvin.* Though I thought he was going off the flogging a bit, this while back. Just like her excellency's going off the hangings.

*Second Turnkey.* Women never stick anything for long.

*Galvin.* Her excellency always slips me a guinea for meself. Once she gave me two guineas . . . I was doing a great big bull of a young fellow. "Make it slow," she said. "Make it slow."

*[Borroo comes out of the shed.]*

*Borroo.* Gawd, I'm choking for a breath of air. The stink in there'd kill ye.

*First Turnkey.* Have you finished the whitewashing?

*Borroo.* Yes, your honor.

*[Borroo bows the turnkey into the shed, remaining outside himself, mouthing curses and cocking snoots. He seems to have forgotten about the second turnkey behind him, who raps him smartly on the head with a big key. The women again scream with laughter. The first turnkey comes out of the shed.]*

*Second Turnkey.* Go on—do it to his face now.

*First Turnkey.* Oho—was he up to his little tricks again?

*[The turnkey grips Borroo's ear, twisting it with venomous cruelty, so that Borroo falls to his knees with a howl of anguish.*

*The second turnkey kicks him in the groin. Borroo falls to the ground, writhing and gasping in agony. Mary covers her eyes and turns away. The other women huddle together in fear. Fennessy's eyes narrow and his grip on the chisel in his hand tightens ominously. The first turnkey, with a careless kick at the prostrate figure, goes out again with his companion. When they have gone, Fennessy and the women crowd sympathetically round Brian Borroo. Peter Shanks and his companions come back from the left.]*

*Shanks.* What's wrong?

*Bessie.* They're after beating him up something cruel.

*[With a cry of rage Shanks rushes to the gate, shakes the bars violently, and yells after the turnkeys.]*

*Shanks.* You brutes, you brutes! You damned cowardly brutes! Hellhounds! By God, if we were free men, you wouldn't do that. *[Meanwhile Borroo has been helped up and has been placed sitting on one of the benches, where he huddles, moaning.]*

*Borroo.* Oh, let me be, let me be. Don't move me—just let me be.

*Shanks [Shouting].* Get a physician! Where is the prison doctor? Send for the apothecary.

*First Turnkey.* Hold your tongue.

*[During the commotion, Dr. Jacob Palmer has appeared at the gate. He is one of the very few men in a clean-shaven age who have let their beard grow; but he had close shaved cheeks, and his iron grey goatee and moustaches are trimmed after the style of Charles I. The turnkey opens the gate and stands at a respectful distance from the doctor who, resting elegantly on his staff, bends a dignified gaze upon the group before him.]*

*Shanks.* I know you—you're the viceroy's physician.

*Galvin [Going to Palmer].* Good day to yer honor.

*Shanks [Pointing to Borroo].* Attend that man.

*Palmer.* I am not the prison doctor.

*Shanks [Fiercely].* There's a man in agony. He has been kicked by a damned cowardly turnkey. Are you going to—

*Palmer.* I said I am not the prison doctor.

*Second Turnkey.* Speak when you're spoken to, prisoner.

*Shanks.* I shall see the governor about this. *[He marches out with his companions.]*

*Palmer [To Galvin].* I shall require two bodies this week. *[He takes a pinch of snuff.]*

*Galvin.* Your honor can have your pick of any of the four men that have just gone away.

*Palmer.* One must be female.

*Galvin.* There aren't any females this week, yer honor. There'll be a couple next week, please Gawd.

*Palmer [Looking after Shanks].* That impudent young fellow who spoke to me . . . he can be one.

*Galvin.* Wouldn't you like that big bull of a fellow who was with him?

*Palmer.* Too fat. Fat makes dissection unnecessarily laborous.

*Galvin.* Indeed it must, yer honor. I find that meself when I'm drawing and quartering a man. The carpenter won't be ready till Monday afternoon, but you could have the other fellow tomorrow morning. *[Snapping his fingers.]* Gawd blast it, I nearly forgot. The young fellow's a treason case. He'll have to be drawn and quartered. But I tell you what I'll do. I'll just go through the motions. I won't damage the carcass.

*Palmer.* I trust not. The last two subjects were very badly damaged.

*Galvin [Shaking his head mournfully].* They must have come from the millingtary, yer honor.

*[An excited turnkey runs to the gate.]*

*Third Turnkey.* They're here. *[He rushes away to spread the news.]*
*[The other turnkeys look at each other. The second turnkey nods significantly towards Brian Borroo, who is surrounded by the women. The turnkeys push their way to him and take him gently by the arms.]*

*First Turnkey.* Come along with us, lad.

*Second Turnkey.* Poor fella, are ye after hurting yerself?

*First Turnkey.* Aisy does it, aisy does it.
*[They have got the groaning Borroo to his feet when Shanks and his companions march back.]*

*Shanks.* Where is the governor? I demand to see the governor.

*Second Turnkey.* Hould yer tongue and get to hell out of our way.

*Shanks [Pointing to Palmer].* I shall denounce you for refusing to attend an injured man.

*First Turnkey.* We're taking him away to be attended.

*Shanks.* I shall denounce you for your brutality.

*Second Turnkey.* We'll look after you in a minute, me man. Get out of the way.
*[The lord chief justice appears at the gate with the governor. Milligan is in attendance. Silence. The gate is unlocked and the lord chief justice enters. The women curtsey. Palmer and Galvin and the turnkeys bow deeply. Kehoe, Doyle, and Mahon incline their heads in some show of respect. Only Shanks remains erect.]*

*Justice.* What are *you* doing here, Palmer?

*Palmer [Bowing again].* I am performing a small work of mercy, my lord. Every now and then I visit the prisons to tend the sick.

*Shanks.* Liar and hypocrite.

*[The second turnkey rushes at Shanks.]*

*Justice [Shouting].* Do not touch him.

*[The second turnkey stops dead, and falls back sheepishly.]*

*Shanks [Pointing to Borroo].* That man has been savaged by these brutes. *[Pointing to Palmer.]* He refused to attend him.

*Governor.* Be silent, prisoner. Do not presume to address his lordship.

*Justice.* Be silent yourself, governor. *[To Borroo.]* Is this true? Were you assaulted?

*Governor.* Scandalous accusations, my lord. My officers are most kindly and humane men. I have distinctly laid down regulations—not indeed that they are really necessary—

*Justice [To Borroo].* Is it true? What do you allege against the turnkeys?

*Borroo [Gasping out the words].* Very good men, yer honor—noble, kind and generous men—couldn't ask for better.

*Shanks.* Tell the truth, you fool. Tell him you've been kicked.

*Justice.* Let the witness speak for himself. Has a turnkey kicked you?

*Borroo.* The turnkeys is all very good men, yer honor. I wouldn't complain about them for the world.

*Justice.* Answer the question—did a turnkey kick you?

*Borroo.* Yes, yer honor—but I'm not complaining.

*Justice.* Examine him, Palmer. You, turnkey, what have you to say for yourself?

*First Turnkey.* If yer honor was to believe everything them scoundrels say, it'd be a poor lookout for us.

*Justice.* Did you or did you not kick the prisoner?

*First Turnkey.* I may have brushed the ankle of his leg and I passing him, yer honor. The lazy devil was lying snoring in the sun instead of doing his work. I didn't notice him in me way.

*Justice.* Well, Palmer?

*Palmer.* The prisoner would appear to have received a kick, my lord. A vicious one.

*Justice.* You hear that, governor? The prisoner has been wantonly and viciously assaulted.

*Governor.* I cannot bring myself to believe it, my lord.

*Justice.* I can. *[The Governor shrugs.]* Do not shake your head at me, Mister Governor, or by God I'll give you good reason to shake it. *[Indicating the first and second turnkeys.]* Let those two men be given fifty lashes. Are you in good form for work today, Mr. Galvin?

*Galvin [Bowing]*. I'll do me best, your honor.

*Governor*. My lord, I must protest. I cannot permit my officers—

*Justice*. I give you liberty to share as many of their lashes as you desire.

*Galvin [Sidling up to the lord chief justice]*. Does your honor wish—

*Justice*. No, I do not wish to attend their punishment. Now Mr. Governor, have the yard cleared of everyone except the prisoner Peter Shanks. And fetch a chair for me.

*[The governor passes the instruction to the third turnkey. The lord chief justice, in glancing around at the prisoners, notices Mary Neale. He starts.]*

*Justice*. What is that young woman doing here?

*Governor*. Which one, my lord? *[Mary Neale identifies herself by shrinking back.]* Answer his lordship. What's your name?

*Mary*. Mary Neale.

*Justice*. I discharged you this morning. Why are you here?

*Mary*. They said I stole the money you sent me. I told them to go and ask you.

*Governor*. I remember now, my lord. She is charged with receiving five guineas which were obviously stolen.

*Justice*. The money was not stolen. Let her be released forthwith.

*Governor*. I shall need an official warrant—

*Justice [Flaring up]*. My word is your warrant.

*Governor*. If your lordship will condescend to give me a scrap of paper for the attorney-general.

*Justice*. To hell with the attorney-general. Now clear the place.

*Governor*. For safety's sake I'd better have the prisoner Shanks chained.

*Justice*. I did not order the prisoner Shanks to be chained.

*Governor*. Your lordship is making it extremely difficult for me to preserve discipline.

*Justice*. We have seen the kind of discipline you preserve.

*Governor [Stung]*. I am not accustomed to being addressed in such a tone before my own staff, my lord. *[The lord chief justice glowers.]* I apologize, my lord. *[The the turnkeys.]* Clear the place.

*[The turnkeys clear the prisoners away to the left. Galvin and Palmer take a conspicuous part in helping Borroo off. The third turnkey has returned with a chair for the lord chief justice.]*

*Justice [To the governor].* What are you waiting for?

*Governor.* My lord, it is customary for the governor to be present at all interviews with condemned persons.

*Justice.* My patience is not unlimited.

*[After some hesitation, the governor bows stiffly and goes out.]*

*Justice [Sitting].* Peter Shanks—

*Shanks.* Once and for all, Copperfaced Jack, it is no use.

*Justice.* On reflection I felt that it would be pointless to order a new trial.

*Shanks.* I do not want a new trial. I will not have life on your terms, Copperfaced Jack.

*Justice.* Do you think it matters a farthing to me whether you live or die?

*Shanks.* Why should it? You are not God, no matter what you may think. Oh, I know all about you. I made my mother tell me.

*Justice.* Tell you—everything?

*Shanks.* She did not dare conceal anything from me.

*Justice.* Refresh my memory.

*Shanks.* You were born in a pigsty.

*Justice.* A stable, Peter. There is a precedent.

*Shanks.* Your father begged the fat from my grandfather's kitchenmaid to make candles.

*Justice.* And married the kitchenmaid.

*Shanks.* My mother didn't tell me that.

*Justice.* The poor dear must have had her reasons for omitting that one.

*Shanks.* So you can sit there safe in your satin and your velvet, and you do not impress me in the least.

*[The lord chief justice edges his chair into a shaft of sunlight, but without rising.]*

*Justice.* You will of course forgive me for remaining seated while the president of the new republic has to stand. *[Stretching his legs.]* But I am only a poor old man, Peter, only a poor old man. Why don't you move out into the sun, my boy? It won't shine much longer on either of us.

*Shanks.* I prefer to stand where I am.

*Justice.* In the shade? Peter, I was nearly forty years of age before I plucked up enough courage to take my rightful place in the sun. I have always been too humble. Do you know that I once tried to sell my soul to the Devil?

*Shanks.* Does it matter? He'll soon have it. For a little while honest men will spit upon your grave, and then you'll be forgotten.

*Justice.* And you won't be?

*Shanks.* I shall live in the hearts of my countrymen.

*Justice.* Why?

*Shanks.* Because I gave my life for them.

*Justice.* Did they ask you for it?

*Shanks.* No man has the right to ask for another's life. But when that life is sacrificed for him, let him be grateful.

*Justice.* And if he isn't grateful?

*Shanks.* There is always the ungrateful wretch. But honest men remember to pay their debts.

*Justice.* Provided they are aware of their debts. They may not think they owe you anything. *[Shanks is silent.]* Peter, you and I have many things in common.

*Shanks.* God forbid.

*Justice.* We share a craving for distinction. Let me tell you how I tried to sell my soul to the Devil.

*Shanks.* It was characteristic of you to try to sell what you haven't got.

*Justice [Laughing].* And to someone who didn't exist. *[Enjoys the joke.]* Ah Peter, Peter, what I would sell my soul for today would be to be remembered tomorrow. These last few months I have tasted death so many times I have lost my dread of it. But I cannot lose my dread of being forgotten.

*Shanks.* As the man who sentenced me to die, you shall have a footnote in history.

*Justice.* I'd prefer you to be the footnote in my history. But we could earn our page apiece, my boy. Let me persuade you to recant.

*Shanks.* To recant would be to dishonor my country's cause for fifty years.

*Justice.* Precisely.

*Shanks.* Copperfaced Jack, I no longer hate you. I pity you. You never give up the fight, do you?

*Justice.* While there's life, there's hope.

*Shanks.* You mean, while there's life for me there's hope for you.

*Justice.* Death is *your* only hope, Peter. Die at the right time, and a page of glory in the history books will be yours. Live to a ripe old age, and you will be found out for what you are, and history will dismiss you in a contemptuous paragraph.

*Shanks.* We shall see.

*Justice.* We shan't, that's the pity of it. Listen, Peter. The only point in being a martyr is to be seen to be a martyr. Nine years ago in Paris there were hundreds of martyrs for the revolution, but now they're forgotten because there were too many of them. When everyone's a martyr, no one's a martyr. The only martyrs we remember are those who make themselves memorable. Like that French fool who got himself stabbed in a bath by a pretty young girl—he is among the immortals.

*Shanks.* There is no comparison between—

*Justice [Forceful].* There *is,* Peter, there is. History is shortsighted. You have to dance in front of her and wave your arms and shout to draw her attention. There are too many rebels being hanged just now. You won't be noticed in the crowd.

*Shanks.* You are wrong.

*Justice.* You must go on living for another couple of years, Peter, until there is peace. Then disturb it. You need only start a rebellion in a back street with a dozen drunken rascals. Do something ridiculous. March on a fortress at the head of your drunken troops and for generations your folly will be remembered—but not as folly. For you will have taken care to escape to the mountains. You will have left your drunken dozen to be flogged into sobriety, leaving only yourself to be caught. They will put a price on your head. You will let yourself be captured. You will have carefully rehearsed your speech from the dock and left several copies for posterity. Then you will have the gallows all to yourself. You will be the dream of all actors: the only figure on the stage, and the fool will become the hero.

*Shanks.* Scoffer.

*Justice.* The people will crowd to see you hang. They will dip their handkerchiefs in your martyr's blood, though not one will lift a finger to save you. Future rebels will canonize you and invoke your name, for the only glorious leaders are the leaders who died before they had the chance to lead. The people shall hang a flattering portrait of you on their walls that shall not bear the least resemblance to you, and twenty generations shall call you blessed. Then one day a rebellion will have an accidental success, and you'll have a fine statue. And oh—I nearly forgot. Have a lady in the case. Don't marry her, because there is no romance in marriage. Leave her, a lonely figure at the foot of your cross, to weep not for Jerusalem but for you, and the sentimental bards will make us weep for you both.

*Shanks.* You poor, unhappy, envious man. Not even you could reduce nobility to absurdity.

*Justice [Ironic].* Help me, Peter. A martyr's crown for you. A brief glory for me.

*Shanks.* It's the lack of love has made you what you are.

*Justice.* Then long live the lack of love.

*Shanks.* I understand this because I know what love is.

*Justice.* A mother's love? Now *there's* a blessing, my boy.

*Shanks.* You can only sneer, God help you.

*Justice.* And a wife's love—but only the married know what a blessing *that* is.

*Shanks.* If only you knew how cruel Providence has been to you.

*Justice [Smiling].* I know.

*Shanks.* You don't know. You couldn't unless like me you had loved and had been loved.

*Justice.* So you had a girl in your drama, after all. I underestimated you.

*Shanks.* It is you I have to thank for saving her life.

*Justice.* I have saved no ladies' lives recently that I can recall.

*Shanks.* Mistress Mary Neale.

*Justice.* Neale . . . Neale. . . .

*Shanks.* And a few moments ago you freed her after they had flung her in here again on a trumped-up charge. *[Earnestly.]* I suppose there's a touch of good in you, Lord Clonmell. If so, I honor you for it.

*Justice [Slowly].* Are you mad enough to tell me a thing like this?

*Shanks.* I can respect a good deed even in a foe.

*Justice [Grinning].* Oh you fool, you young fool. *[Shouting.]* Governor! *[To Shanks.]* Fool fool fool fool. *[He rises and walks about, rubbing his hands.]*

*[The governor runs in with drawn sword.]*

*Justice.* That female prisoner whom I ordered you to discharge—

*Governor [Confused].* What prisoner, my lord? *[Looking toward Shanks.]* I thought you were calling for help.

*Justice.* Damn your cheek. Help against *him*?!! Where is that female prisoner? Is she discharged?

*Governor.* You didn't give me much time to do it, my lord. You ordered me to clear the yard and—

*Justice.* Bring her here immediately.

*[The governor goes off angrily.]*

*Justice.* Oh Peter Shanks, Peter Shanks, I could have torn you with red-hot pincers and I wouldn't have got a word out of you. Then in your ridiculous vanity, you put this weapon into my hands.

*Shanks [Moaning].* I might have known. I might have known.

*Justice.* Do you love her?

*Shanks [Feebly defiant].* I do not know the girl. I was making a fool of you to amuse myself.

*Justice.* Do you love her, Mr. President of the new republic?

*Shanks.* I never set eyes on her until a few minutes ago.

*Justice.* Was she to sit at your side in the earthly paradise you had planned for us all?

*Shanks.* It was only a trick. I do not know her.

*Justice.* Thrice have you denied her. Peter, you are well named.

*[The turnkey hauls Mary Neale in and slings her before the lord chief justice. He motions the turnkey to go away.]*

*Justice [After sitting again and surveying them silently].* My child, the prisoner Peter Shanks has told me how things stand between you.

*Shanks [Violently].* I do not know her.

*[Mary Neale looks quickly at him, then lowers her eyes. At this moment the whipping of the turnkeys begins in the upper yard. The victim's shrieks are heard after each stroke.]*

*Justice [After sitting in silence for a few moments].* Governor! Governor!

*[The governor comes in with deliberate slowness.]*

*Justice.* Tell them to stop the flogging till I'm gone. *[The governor hesitates.]* Look lively, man. *[The governor bows and turns to go.]* Send the hangman in to me.

*[The governor goes. Mary Neale fingers her dress nervously. The whipping stops. Galvin hurries in. He has taken off his coat and rolled up his right shirtsleeve. He carries his cat-o'-nine-tails.]*

*Galvin [Bowing almost to the ground].* Yer honor—?

*Justice.* The female prisoner—

*Galvin.* Certainly, yer honor. *[He goes eagerly toward her.]*

*Justice [Bellowing].* Stand back. *[Galvin, surprised and puzzled, does so. The lord chief justice rises slowly, goes to Mary, takes her arm, and gently pushes her against Peter Shanks. He then stands back and surveys them.]* A fool and his love. Peter, an intelligent man always comes to terms with his conscience. A little affectionate word to a conscience and it forgives you everything. Except yours. Your conscience is sickly and stubborn. The flesh is willing but the spirit is weak.

*Mary [Breaking].* Tell him, Peter. Tell him what he wants to know, and he'll let you go.

*Justice.* Don't do that to him, child—not at the eleventh hour. Give him strength. It is at the eleventh hour that strength is needed most.

*Mary [Hysterical].* Tell him, Peter, tell him. *[She kneels to the lord chief justice.]* If I tell you, will you let him go?

*Justice.* Woman, do not filch away that poor man's crown of martyrdom.

*Mary.* It's William O'Sullivan is at the head of it all—

*Justice.* Silence. I do not wish to hear anything. Stand up. *[She does so. He puts his arm around her.]* You would not wish the father of your children to be a coward. *[He puts his free hand on Shanks's shoulder.]* They all marry afterwards, Peter—and usually one of the hated oppressors if they're as pretty as she is. I tell you what. You must let me call my chaplain to marry the pair of ye.

*Shanks [Almost involuntarily].* No.

*[Mary shrinks. She half understands his refusal but is hurt by his vehemence.]*

*Justice [Who has noted her reaction].* Not even that little sacrifice, Peter. Well! And it's not that your death would save the others. Soon they will all stand where you stand.

*Shanks.* You've got to catch them first. They walk in and out of the castle, and his excellency smiles upon them, not knowing who they are.

*Justice.* Oh, there's many a man smiles upon his executioner without knowing it. But not in this case.

*Shanks.* You will see.

*Justice [Takes a slip of paper from his pocket].* William O'Sullivan, innkeeper, Drumcondra Lane. Francis Browner, coachman, Church Street. James Rafter, bootmaker, Aungier Street . . . and so on and so forth.

*Shanks.* Not that trap either. I neither confirm nor deny.

*Justice.* You could tell me nothing I do not already know.

*Shanks.* But I shall not recant.

*[The lord chief justice sits.]*

*Justice.* Galvin.

*[Galvin cringes toward him.]*

*Justice.* I have reason to believe that the female prisoner has hidden a knife under her petticoat. Search her.

*[Galvin pounces on her. She fights him off like a wildcat. He grips her waist, throws her down, and flings himself on her. She cries for help, for mercy. Shanks turns away and is compelled to cover his ears. Some of the prisoners creep back to watch, but do no more than mutter rebelliously to each other. The lord chief justice walks over to the struggling pair and kicks Galvin away. Mary runs to a corner where she huddles, a sobbing, quivering bundle of clothes.]*

*Galvin.* I'm sure there's a knife under her petticoat, yer honor. Will I try again?

*Justice.* Get away. *[Galvin moves away but keeps staring at Mary.]* One word from you, Peter Shanks, would have stopped all that.

Was she not worth it? *[He goes to Mary and puts arm around her.]* In his place, my child, I would have died to save you. *[She accepts the protection of his arms and rests her head on his shoulder.]* Send the governor to me.

*[The governor steps forward from behind the little knot of prisoners.]*

*Governor [Icy].* My lord—?

*Justice.* Let this female prisoner be discharged forthwith as I have ordered.

*Governor [With undisguised triumph].* My lord, Mr. Attorney-General desires to see you. I gather he has received certain commands from his excellency.

*[Mary Neale whispers in the lord chief justice's ear.]*

*Justice.* No, my child. It would be better if you did not stay with me. *[He disengages himself from her and goes to his chair.]* She is free to go.

*Governor.* Mr. Attorney-General—

*Justice.* Can go to the devil. I am finished with the prisoner Shanks.

*Shanks.* I have a favor to ask.

*Justice.* Have you, by God?

*Shanks.* Will you be good enough to have me placed in a cell by myself?

*Justice.* You are free to remain here if you wish. I am a humane man. Only the worst of the worst are put into solitary cells.

*Shanks.* Am I not the worst of the worst?

*Justice.* You cannot claim even that distinction.

*Shanks.* It is my last request to you—my lord.

*Justice [Looking up sharply at the "my lord"].* Very well, Mr. President, a solitary cell if you wish it. *[To the governor.]* Let his mother have free access to him at all times. *[To Shanks.]* Though we shan't force maternal consolation on you if you'd prefer not to have it. Take him away. *[The governor signs to the third turnkey, who takes Shanks by the arm. The attorney-general enters rather melodramatically.]*

*Wolfe.* Where is the prisoner Shanks going, m'lud?

*Justice [Ignoring Wolfe].* Take him away.

*[The governor whispers reassuringly to Wolfe, who nods. As he is brought to the small gate, Peter Shanks turns around.]*

*Shanks [Choking with emotion].* Mary . . . remember.

*Mary [Sullen].* I shall never forget what you made me suffer. And in front of all those people, too.

*[The turnkey has unlocked the gate. He takes Shanks out. The*

*gate is locked again. Wolfe saunters insolently to the lord chief justice.]*

*Wolfe.* As I happen to know of the unusual relationship between your lordship and the mother of a certain condemned felon, I took the precaution of procuring from his excellency a warrant for the immediate execution of the traitors you sentenced this morning.

*Justice.* You are too clever by half, Arthur.

*Wolfe [Handing the warrant to the governor with a flourish].* There's your warrant, Mr. Governor. I shall witness the executions myself.

*Justice.* You shall have to wait a long time, Arthur.

*Wolfe.* No longer than it takes to procure four ropes, m'lud.

*Justice.* The prisoners shall not be put to execution until the high sheriff of this city produces a warrant signed by me.

*Governor [Insolently holding up the warrant].* And this, my lord?

*Justice.* Wipe your arse with it.

*[The prisoners titter but are silenced by a glare from the governor and Wolfe.]*

*Wolfe.* His excellency's orders must be obeyed.

*Justice [Holding out his hand for the warrant; the governor looks uneasily at Wolfe].* Give it to me.

*[The governor hands it over. The lord chief justice glances carelessly at it and tears it up.]*

*Wolfe.* This is outrageous. Mr. Governor, you may proceed to execution. My personal order shall be your warrant.

*Justice.* I have had occasion to observe to you before, Mr. Attorney-General, that my patience is not unlimited.

*Wolfe.* For what you have done you can be impeached ten times over.

*Justice [Springing up].* Arrest him.

*Wolfe.* The man who lays a finger on me will be charged with treason.

*Justice.* I said arrest him. By God, I'll teach you who and what I am. Have I to repeat my orders? Get the yeomanry. The military. Have the jail surrounded. This is contempt. This is—*[His voice falters; he begins to choke.]*

*[Palmer rushes forward and grabs the lord chief justice before he falls. Turnkeys and prisoners crowd around him, and he is helped to his chair. Only Wolfe and the governor remain unmoved.]*

*Governor [To Wolfe].* The problem seems to be solving itself.

*Justice [Slowly and thickly].* Leave this place, Mr. Attorney-General. I have decided that the prisoners shall have a new trial.

*Wolfe.* Not in this world, m'lud. Governor, proceed to execution immediately.

*Justice.* Do not dare.

*Wolfe.* You have seen his excellency's orders.

*[The third turnkey appears at the gate, very excited.]*

*Third Turnkey.* Yer honor, the prisoner Peter Shanks has done himself an injury.

*[General excitement. Everyone instinctively looks toward the lord chief justice.]*

*Justice.* What a very clever thing for that foolish young man to do.

*Wolfe.* Is he dead?

*Third Turnkey.* No, yer honor—but nearly.

*[Mary bursts out crying.]*

*Justice.* He took my advice after all. *[He shakes his head.]* But cutting his throat—no. Stabbing himself through the heart would read better on the page of history.

*Wolfe.* He can't be let escape like this. He must be hanged immediately.

*Governor.* My lord, will it be in order to hang him now?

*Justice.* Master Palmer, you will report to me on the condition of the prisoner Shanks.

*[Palmer bows out.]*

*Governor [To third turnkey].* How in the devil's name did you let a thing like this happen? Why wasn't he under proper guard?

*Third Turnkey.* He had a knife hidden somewhere on him, yer honor.

*Wolfe.* We needn't worry about all this now. The important thing is to have him hanged at once.

*Governor.* Galvin, are you ready in case his lordship permits us go ahead?

*Galvin.* Well, I'm ready, yer honor, and the little swing-swong is ready, but it's hard to do a proper job when a genkilman's in that condition.

*Wolfe.* I don't care what mutilation there is. You won't suffer by it.

*Galvin.* The people won't like it, yer honor.

*Wolfe.* If you wish to hold your job you'd better *do* your job.

*Galvin.* Ask the millingtary, yer honor. Them blackguards don't care what they does. They'd ate him for dinner if they was asked to.

*[Palmer hurries back.]*

*Palmer.* Dead, my lord.

*[A sympathetic murmur runs through the crowd. Mahon comforts the weeping Mary Neale.]*

*Justice.* He is now the page of history. I am the footnote.

*Palmer.* I beg your lordship's pardon—?

*Justice.* Nothing that you'd understand, Master Palmer.

*Wolfe.* Dead or alive, he shall hang in public in accordance with his excellency's orders.

*Justice.* He has glory enough, Mr. Attorney-General. Do not give him more. *[He collapses again. Palmer fusses around him.]*

*Wolfe [Quietly to Milligan].* Is the old fox shamming?

*Milligan [Unmoved].* No, sir. I have seen him take many fits like this. During the last few weeks, they have occurred almost every day.

*Wolfe.* Um—I see.

*Milligan.* May I respectfully beg your kind consideration, sir, if you should be looking for a personal attendant, sir, when—h'm— when your honor is lord chief justice?

*Wolfe [With a faint smile].* I shall bear you in mind, Milligan.

*Milligan.* Thank you, m'lud. *[Suavely.]* A slip of the tongue, sir, but pardonable I'm sure.

*Justice [In a rasping tone].* Milligan.

*Palmer.* Please, my lord—don't put any further strain on yourself by talking. It is essential that your lordship should rest.

*Justice.* It is essential, Master Palmer, that I get out of this fetid hole.

*Palmer.* I respectfully suggest that I attend your lordship to your home.

*Justice.* No. Stay here. *[Milligan has taken up his old place behind the lord chief justice.]* Milligan, the purse. Master Palmer, take the body of the prisoner Shanks into your possession—

*Wolfe.* It shall hang in public.

*Justice.* And deliver it to the crown coroner. *[Grinning at Wolfe.]* Little is the law that I know, Arthur, but you seem to know less. *[To Palmer.]* Let an inquest be held upon it. And Master Palmer—

*Palmer.* My lord—?

*Justice.* No dissection.

*Palmer [Raising his hands].* Oh, my lord, I never—

*Justice.* Make the body as presentable as you can and see it is handed over to his mother with due decorum. Milligan, give him the purse. *[Milligan does so.]* Not a cheap coffin, Master Palmer. Let it have silver mountings. *[He hauls himself up.]* And let the inscription be, "Shanks, First President of the New—" No, don't put that. Just "Peter Shanks, died in youth, the 23rd of May, 1798, To be with Christ, which is far better." *[He perks up.]* How pleasing it is to forgive one's enemies. Good Christians like you, Arthur, miss a lot of fun if only ye knew it.

*Palmer.* I respectfully suggest that your lordship permit yourself to be carried to your coach.

*Justice.* Why?

*Palmer.* Merely a precaution, my lord.

*Justice.* I have never taken precautions. What was the use? I was born unlucky. Here, lend me your stick. *[He begins to go toward the gate, feeble and rather tottery. The third turnkey opens the gate for him. He stops as he is passing Mary Neale, who is still standing with Mahon's protective arm about her.]* What's this he said to you? "Remember." Puh! You have already begun to forget him. Next week you'll find it hard to remember what color his eyes were. *[He thrusts his face close to hers.]* But you won't forget my face quite so easily, eh? *[He moves on, but half turns and winks at her.]* Goodbye, my child. Love me when I am dead.

*Mary.* Take me with you, your honor. *[The lord chief justice looks surprised. His face lights up with pleasure and hope.]* They won't let me out when you go.

*Justice [His face goes blank].* Oh, I see. *[He hides his disappointment under the familiar grin.]* I see. . . .

*Mary.* Please . . . please. *[She would go and touch him if Mahon slackened his grip on her.]*

*[The lord chief justice motions her to go through the open gate. She breaks away from Mahon and scurries through the gate like a frightened animal. As the lord chief justice gazes after her, amused, Wolfe signals Milligan to his side and whispers. The lord chief justice drags himself toward the gate. He misses Milligan and turns. The sight of Milligan and Wolfe whispering rouses him. He draws himself up. His voice is as strong as ever.]*

*Justice.* I am not dead yet, Milligan.

*[Milligan hurries over obsequiously and attends him as he goes through the gate. The turnkeys bow deeply. The prisoners and the others stare after him in silence.]*

# THE FIDDLER AND THE DEAN

An Imaginary Conversation between Swift and Handel

## Characters

*Jonathan Swift*
*George Frederick Handel*
*Laetitia Pilkington*

*Announcer.* "The Fiddler and the Dean," an imaginary reconstruction by John O'Donovan of the conversation at St. Patrick's Deanery, Dublin, in 1742, between Jonathan Swift and George Frederick Handel.
*[Light tapping on a door.]*
*Swift [Testily].* Come in, can't you?
*[The door opens.]*
*Swift.* Oh, it's you again, Mrs. Pilkington.
*Mrs. Pilkington.* I'm sure I have woken you, Mr. Dean. You look as if you were having a little nap.
*Swift.* I was not asleep. I was sitting with my eyes closed so that I could concentrate better on what I was thinking about.
*Mrs. Pilkington.* And what were you thinking about, Mr. Dean?
*Swift.* Nothing that would interest a woman.
*Mrs. Pilkington.* The lion is very cross today.
*Swift.* The lion wishes above all things to be left alone. That wish is within your gratification, madam.
*Mrs. Pilkington.* But you were in such good spirits yesterday.
*Swift.* A man of seventy-five is not obliged to be in good spirits *every* day.
*Mrs. Pilkington.* I had rather hoped to find you in good humor this morning.
*Swift.* I am in no mood today to supply material for your memoirs.
*Mrs. Pilkington.* It isn't my memoirs. I've brought someone to see you.

*Swift.* The Dean of St. Patrick's is not a show to be stared at.

*Mrs. Pilkington.* But I couldn't send him away without seeing you.

*Swift.* Another time, madam, another time.

*Mrs. Pilkington.* But he is a great man, Mr. Dean.

*Swift.* There is no such thing as a great man. I know. I was once myself thought to be one.

*Mrs. Pilkington.* He will be very disappointed, sir.

*Swift.* Better that he be disappointed than disillusioned. I am no longer fit for human intercourse.

*Mrs. Pilkington [Wheedling].* Just two minutes, Mr. Dean.

*Swift.* What bribe did he give you, that you pester me like this?

*Mrs. Pilkington.* None, sir. None—upon my honor.

*Swift.* Upon your honor! Upon Laetitia Pilkington's honor! Who is the fellow?

*Mrs. Pilkington [Triumphantly].* Mr. Handel, sir.

*Swift [Flatly].* Who's he?

*Mrs. Pilkington.* The lion is being *very* perverse. Why, you had us all breaking our sides laughing on Wednesday when you imitated his organ-playing.

*Swift.* Do not remind me of my tomfooleries, madam; they ill become an old man. *[After a pause.]* What did you say his name was?

*Mrs. Pilkington.* Mr. Handel.

*Swift.* Mr. Handel. . . . *[Light breaks.]* Ah, Mr. Handel! The fellow that has the club of fiddlers in Fishamble Street!

*Mrs. Pilkington [Eagerly].* You'll see him then?

*Swift.* Ho! A German and a genius! A prodigy! *[A pause.]* Admit him.

*Mrs. Pilkington [Tingling with excitement].* Yes, Mr. Dean.

*Swift.* By himself. Alone.

*Mrs. Pilkington [Crestfallen].* Oh, Mr. Dean—

*Swift.* By himself.

*[A Pause. The door opens.]*

*Handel [Distant].* Dr. Swift, I value greatly the honor of being received by you.

*Swift.* You are very welcome, Mr. Handel.

*Handel.* I know Dr. Swift's time is precious.

*Swift.* There is little of it left at any rate. I am ripe for the sepulchre. Pray be seated, sir.

*Handel.* I have been some months in Dublin, and have been a long time wishing to pay my respects to you.

*Swift.* You honor me. And how do you like our little town, Mr. Handel?

*Handel.* Oh, a noble city. And the people, they are full of charm and—

*Swift.* Pray favor me with the truth, sir.

*Handel [Surprised].* Oh, but I do admire the town and its people, Dr. Swift. I came here last November and shall stay until next August.

*Swift.* You are wise not to stay long. Ireland is a good cradle for genius but a bad nurse.

*Handel.* You are living proof of the contrary, Dr. Swift.

*Swift.* I could do nothing with Dublin, and Dublin could do nothing with me. I owe even my deanery to English friends, not Irish.

*Handel.* Is it not true, then, that you advised the Irish to burn everything English except coal?

*Swift.* I said that in the hope that it would make the Irish think better of themselves and of the work of their own hands.

*Handel.* I should not have imagined your countrymen needed any encouragement in that direction.

*Swift.* In their heart of hearts they feel themselves the meanest race on earth. Sometimes, I think, not without reason.

*Handel.* I think they are the most fortunate nation, sir. Their beautiful country—

*Swift [Grimly].* Optima terra, pessima gens. Although to give the devils their due, the Irish are clever enough to see themselves for the wretches they are. But the English are astonishingly self-ignorant.

*Handel [Politely].* Really?

*Swift.* I tell you, Mr. Handel, they *are.* But their self-ignorance has given them confidence, and in this world confidence carries all before it. So the English have become the greatest race on earth. The greatest since the Roman. But the nation which has brains enough to see that man is no more than a poor, bare, forked animal—

*Handel.* It was an English poet who made that observation, sir.

*Swift.* Yes, but he wasn't a politician, and it is politics, not poetry, that makes a country. A nation of poets is a futile nation. A nation of politicians is rich and successful.

*Handel.* I do not think that England is any different from—

*Swift [Sweeping him aside].* Yet what are politicians but rascals, thieves, rogues, blackguards, pimps, ponces, bullies, lickspittles, rapscallions, dunces—pscha!

*Handel.* I admire my fellow creatures as little as you do, sir, but I take them as I find them. Otherwise I should go mad with despair.

*Swift.* I am nearly in that condition myself.

*Handel.* We are all of us a little mad in some things. There are times when I sit at my table with music paper in front of me and not an idea in my head; I do really believe that the noting down of musical sounds is the maddest occupation in the whole world.

*Swift.* Then why do you do it?

*Handel.* A professional gentleman has to do his best for to live. *[Anticipating the objection.]* Oh yes, you may say there are other ways. But mad though my occupation may be, it would be even madder for me to do anything else, for it is the thing that I can do best. But you must not think that I always look on the compositions of music as madness. Only now and then when I am tired and sunk in my spirits.

*Swift.* At other times it contents you?

*Handel.* Just as your poems and pamphlets content you.

*Swift.* They did not content me. They merely passed the time. Although now and then I used to flatter myself with the hope that they would make men better.

*Handel [Warmly].* The same hope has encouraged me, Dr. Swift.

*Swift.* I cannot conceive of how music could make men better. I see how it could make them more foolish, because it is a foolish vain thing in itself.

*Handel.* Oh, Dr. Swift—

*Swift.* I would not give a farthing for all the music in the world. For my own part, I would rather say my prayers without it.

*Handel.* Every man praises God in his own way.

*Swift.* I am told you have put music to the words of Holy Scripture. You presume to improve upon God's handiwork, Mr. Handel?

*Handel.* Marble is God's handiwork, Dr. Swift, but the sculptor who carves it improves it.

*Swift.* Not always.

*Handel.* A quibble. You evade my point.

*Swift.* You argue by analogy and thereby miss the point, Mr. Handel. Marble is but marble. The Scriptures are the word of the Almighty.

*Handel.* You hear the voice of the Almighty more distinctly when I increase that word with music.

*Swift.* I do not. I have no ear for music.

*Handel.* But you have, Dr. Swift. For the music of words.

*Swift.* For the fit use of words.

*Handel.* It is the same thing. Notes are the words of music. I have a good feeling for their fitness, like you.

*Swift.* You do not properly distinguish between sense and mere sound.

*Handel.* Good sound *is* good sense.

*Swift.* It might be so in music, if there were any sense in music. "Autumnal maypoles roll and rear their ensigns in the fly of golden rambler roses, raving round and rearing ruefully." That's fine sound. But it is not fine sense. No, Mr. Handel, the man who puts music to the word of God and thinks he is thereby magnifying the Lord is—

*Handel.* May not the Lord be magnified outside your cathedral, Mr. Dean?

*Swift.* If howling is magnifying the Lord, then the dog that bays at the moon is a devotee.

*Handel.* Singers can abuse their voice as well as use it, I know. But—

*Swift.* What is singing but a kind of howling? My cat will make fine music for you by walking up and down the manuals of your harpsichord—indeed I am told some Italian has noted down a tune in that very way.

*Handel.* That is true. Signor Scarlatti has written a Cat's Fugue. But it was a jest.

*Swift.* I think little of the dignity or value of an art that a cat can practise.

*Handel.* I will admit that the cat wrote the fugue when you admit that a horse wrote *Gulliver's Travels.*

*Swift.* Mr. Handel, what rational human being can pretend to listen with interest, not to say pleasure, to the squealing of catgut scraped with horsehair? Or to the shrilling of a man's breath through tubes of wood? Or most ludicrous of all, to the thumping of a sheepskin stretched over a tub? Out yonder in the cathedral is a machine called an organ—

*Handel [Defiantly].* The king of instruments, Dr. Swift.

*Swift.* Very like a king in that fools and knaves pretend to listen enraptured to its pompous foolish drone. Turning up their eyes in ecstasy as the bellows sends wind howling and screeching through its pipes.

*Handel.* What are the words you utter but wind from the bellows of your lungs howling through the pipes of your throat?

*Swift.* Those sounds are natural sounds—

*Handel.* So is a dog barking, an ass braying.

*Swift.* They are above all *rational* sounds, which the barking and braying are not. The sounds which are my words convey sensible ideas and feelings from me to all who hear me.

*Handel.* Art is not rational. It is for the soul, not the mind.

*Swift.* I have no use for such metaphysical distinctions. It is enough that you have to agree with me. Music is not rational. Therefore, one day it will perish.

*Handel.* Emotion will not perish, Dr. Swift, and music is the language of emotion. Oh, if only I had a harpsichord here I could show you. Words will never express emotion as fully and vividly as music will. Music enlarges the meaning of mere words, ennobles them, sends them heavenwards.

*Swift.* Mere assertion, Mr. Handel. Sounds must have sense as bodies must have souls. One without the other is useless. Dead.

*Handel.* Thoughts can exist without words. If my thought is to summon my servant, I can ring a bell or beckon to him, without using one word.

*Swift.* Merely the language of gesture. Could you, by playing a tune on your fiddle, order that servant to go out and buy you a mutton chop?

*Handel.* It is not the purpose of music to send servants for mutton chops, but to express feelings and emotions that cold dry words cannot express adequately.

*Swift.* Your thoughts may interest me, Mr. Handel, but your feelings and emotions do not. They are your own concern.

*Handel.* What if my feeling is one of friendship and respect for you, Dr. Swift?

*Swift.* You'll never cause me to return it by playing a jig on a fiddle at me.

*Handel.* Oh, Dr. Swift, you are not so inaccessible to the pleasures of music as you believe. The singing of birds, the sound of a little river sparkling over stones in the sunshine—you find no beauty in these things?

*Swift.* Of course, I do. But they are natural sounds. The scraping of fiddles is a clumsy artificial sound, and I do not value artifice beyond nature.

*Handel.* Then you admit that singing is a natural sound?

*Swift.* Certainly, if it is the spontaneous expression of one's own feelings, like the singing of birds. But birds are wiser than men. They do not prop a twopenny sheet of music up in front of them, composed by another bird, and solemnly perform it to an avian audience who have paid for the privilege of sitting on the boughs to hear them.

*Handel.* The clothing you wear, Dr. Swift, is not natural.

*Swift.* Not natural but necessary. Man could not live in these inclement islands without it. But I have lived 75 years in these islands without feeling the least need to refresh my spirits with a jig on a fiddle. Now do not try to bully me by invoking your poet and his "man that hath not music in his soul," and so forth.

*Handel.* The poet goes on to point out that the very beasts in the field are moved by the power of music.

*Swift.* Out of your own mouth you condemn yourself. Music is fit only for creatures with no power to understand rational language. Wise men do not waste time discoursing to infants: They let women croon at them. Music has no meaning. So we must agree to differ. Go on, therefore, seeking to refine and exalt the sense with your jigs and hornpipes.

*Handel.* I should prefer to write only operas and oratorios, but fine art for many centuries to come must always be a compromise between what people want and what the artist thinks they should have. At the same time, I firmly hold that the art which does not please many people is useless.

*Swift.* I should have rather thought that it was a useless art which *did* please many people. So long as the human race is what it is, whatever is popular is bound to be bad. Video meliora proboque, deteriora sequor.

*Handel.* Your own *Gulliver's Travels* is popular, Dr. Swift. Is it therefore bad?

*Swift.* I am surprised to hear it is popular.

*Handel [Enthusiastically].* Oh, but everyone reads it, sir. Every gentleman's library has its copy. The very children read it.

*Swift.* Why?

*Handel.* Because—well, because it is an excellent book. It has wit and satire, invention, entertainment, instruction. It tells a capital story—it is so humorous, such a great comedy.

*Swift.* Then it is the most misunderstood book that was ever written. Yet I labored much to make its meaning plain to the dullest reader.

*Handel.* Nobody could mistake your meaning. You held up the mirror, Dr. Swift.

*Swift.* In which men saw every face but their own. Everyone agrees that the entire human race consists of Yahoos with the single exception of himself.

*Handel.* The fault lies in human vanity, not in your handiwork.

*Swift.* In my handiwork, sir, because the book failed in what it set out to do: to pierce the armor of man's self-esteem. If it had done that, it wouldn't be popular. So *Gulliver's Travels* is a useless book. I tell you, Mr. Handel, if your music is good and people still like it, then it is only because they misunderstand it.

*Handel.* True, Dr. Swift. It infuriates me to be praised and for the commonplaces in my work, whilst the good things are ignored or disliked. Of course, there are a handful of friends and connoisseurs who *understand.*

*Swift.* If it wasn't for my own handful of friends, I might have gone out and hanged myself. *[Chuckling.]* I admit that at my age hanging one's self is superfluous.

*Handel.* I pray God we shall both die easily in a comfortable bed.

*Swift.* A necessary prayer, Mr. Handel. Men such as you and I are always in great danger from the Yahoos. We should be thankful they do not understand us: The prophet who is understood is stoned. *[Lightly.]* I was myself stoned here in Dublin.

*Handel.* Impossible!

*Swift.* It is the literal truth.

*Handel.* They must have been mad. Mad with drink, perhaps.

*Swift.* Worse, Mr. Handel, mad with politics.

*Handel.* They appear to have recovered their sanity.

*Swift.* Not so. They have merely changed their party. Toryism is now the fashion—and I hope it will last my time. But never discuss politics in Ireland; it is a subject the Irish do not understand.

*Handel.* It is the commonest subject of conversation here.

*Swift.* People generally talk most about what they know least.

*Handel.* Nowhere more than in music, Dr. Swift. I have little interest in politics myself, and the little I know of it gives me no reason to like it.

*Swift.* Politics is the most important thing in the world.

*Handel.* Not to me.

*Swift.* It governs your life whether you will or no, as much as air and food.

*Handel.* Perhaps. But though you can interest me in air and food, you cannot interest me in politics. Politics has interfered with my music so often that it makes me mad even to think of it.

*Swift.* A thing which can do that is surely a very important thing.

*Handel.* I do believe that you would prefer to have been prime minister rather than the author of *Gulliver's Travels.*

*Swift.* Of course. I then could have done the things I had to be content merely to write about.

*Handel.* What things, Dr. Swift? Make the Yahoos better creatures?

*Swift.* I should have made it harder for them to be so bad as they are. The whole art of government is to frustrate crime and encourage virtue.

*Handel.* I do not think it can be as simple as that.

*Swift.* You are confusing the simple with the easy, Mr. Handel. Simple things are not necessarily easy to do. Simplicity in literature is the hardest effect to achieve: I fancy you may find it the same in your music.

*Handel [Enthusiastically].* Oh, but yes yes yes—simplicity is the thing. There is the musician Sebastian Bach who lives in Leipzig, and friends of mine in Germany praise him to the skies. They have sent me music of his, a set of organ fugues, which have every great quality that music can have except simplicity.

*Swift.* Very well then. What *is* government but the prevention of evil and the encouragement of good?

*Handel.* Who is to say what is evil and what is good? Is Sebastian Bach to lay down the laws of music for me? Worse still—is some rascally minister of state to order me what to write?

*Swift.* These are unreal questions, unreal and frivolous. No minister of state shall ever order musicians to compose a certain type of music, or painters to paint a certain type of picture. I admit that literature risks chains as long as there is a hangman to burn books written for the good of mankind, but the other arts shall remain as free as air.

*Handel.* No no, Dr. Swift, it seems that I think even worse of the Yahoos than you do. Court chamberlains have dared to tell me the kind of music I should write, but I have been able to defy them because my music pleases the King. But when the Prince of Wales becomes King, then—!

*Swift.* That is not government; that is tyranny.

*Handel.* So far as I can see, Dr. Swift, they are merely two names for the same thing. I do not want to be governed; I do not ask to be governed, even by so honest a man as you yourself. I will not suffer any man—not even you, Dr. Swift—to lay down coercively for me what is right or wrong, good or bad. Your Oliver Cromwell said, "I meddle with no man's conscience." That is not enough. He must meddle with no man's person and no man's actions so long as those actions do not interfere with other people's freedom.

*Swift.* And if they do?

*Handel.* Then the aggressor must be forced to mind his own business. That is the only allowable force: to force people to mind their own business.

*Swift.* Under what penalty?

*Handel.* The penalty of being *made* mind their own business.

*Swift.* How do you make them do it?

*Handel.* That, Dr. Swift, is the whole art of government, not what you say about preventing evil and doing good.

*Swift.* Mr. Handel, do you keep a servant in your house?

*Handel.* I know what you are going to say. My reply is that my servant puts himself at my disposal for so many hours in return for my putting so much of my food and money at *his* disposal. The arrangement is voluntary on both sides. If he finds me an unpleasant man, I do not compel him to stay. If the public do not like my music, I do not compel them to listen. Surely the great lesson of *Gulliver's Travels* is that we must not force other people to do our will instead of their own? We may seek to persuade them, to amuse them, please them, instruct them, offer them our services in some things in exchange for their services in others. But we must not violate their will. It is strange to me that you who composed a great parable in praise of freedom and toleration should have yourself always longed for power over other men.

*Swift.* Power to do good, to encourage virtue. Power to maintain public peace and promote public welfare. To see that every farthing of public money was spent with miserly care and the most perfect honesty. To place the best man in the public service, not knaves, flatterers, pimps, jumped-up scullions, or my relatives down to the fourth cousin of my discarded mistress.

*Handel.* Oh, you would have good intentions all right, Dr. Swift; all rulers have good intentions. Only, when you go against the rulers, they flog you, imprison you, hang you—all with the very best of intentions.

*Swift.* Men might be left to govern themselves only if the world was peopled with Handels.

*Handel.* Or Swifts.

*Swift.* Perhaps. But the world is peopled with Yahoos, and these must be governed, for better or for worse, by the few Houyhnhnms that chance to be born.

*Handel.* Remember—you cannot make people good by act of parliament.

*Swift.* I care not whether they are good so long as they act as if they were good.

*Handel.* You mean in accordance with your ideas of what is good.

*Swift.* My ideas of good are the univerally accepted ideas of what is good. All men know the difference between a good deed and a bad one.

*Handel.* You attribute to mortal, fallible men a quality of the gods.

*Swift.* We are talking of men in this world, Mr. Handel, not gods in some other. Men can surely judge men's deeds.

*Handel.* What *is* a good deed, Dr. Swift?

*Swift.* Any deed which is not bad. Could a definition be more tolerant? I have said that the man who causes two blades of grass to grow where only one grew before, is worth more than the whole race of politicians together. I will go further and say that even he who writes an opera deserves well of mankind. It needs no Lycurgus to see that such men are better men than forgers or pickpockets. Do not make a mystery of the difference between good deeds and bad, Mr. Handel. The question of whether Caligula or Michelangelo was the better man is not one that need be debated outside of Bedlam.

*[The bells of St. Patrick's Cathedral have begun to ring.]*

*Handel.* Are the cathedral bells ringing for a service, Mr. Dean?

*Swift.* I do not take the morning service.

*Handel.* Still, I must not intrude further upon your time. And I must return to Fishamble Street—to my club of fiddlers, where you forbade your vicars chorale to foregather with us as songsters, pipers, trumpsters, drummers, drum majors, or in any sonal quality. *[Chuckling.]* A magnificent sentence, Dr. Swift.

*Swift.* Forgive an old man's petulance, Mr. Handel. My vicars are a troublesome lot to control at the best of times, and much given to haunting taverns. Not that there is much else for them to do in this useless, futile city of Dublin.

*Handel.* I like Dublin. *[Sighing.]* Though I could not earn my living here.

*Swift.* Neither could any other man of art. All our best authors go away, you know.

*Handel.* Except the author of *Gulliver's Travels*.

*Swift.* My cathedral supports me, not my pen. Heaven help me if I depended on *that*. I am too old to move from here now, but twenty years ago I would have exchanged my deanery for a minor canon's stall in the smallest English cathedral, if I had the chance.

*Handel.* But why why why? Why do all your best men of art leave?

*Swift.* Because art is urban, and Dublin is the most rural of villages. Besides, the Irish dislike one another.

*Handel.* So do the English and the Germans and the Italians.

*Swift.* But not enough to prevent their working with one another. The Irish, in so far as they will work at all in Ireland, work only against one another. It's what I said before: The Irish see themselves for what they are and refuse to be taken in by one another's artistic effusions. There is another complication. Art requires a certain degree of social intercourse in order to thrive. There must be many marriages of true minds. But there is no real social intercourse between Irishmen and their own country. If one Irishman talks to another, it is only to contradict him for the sake of contradicting him. What the other man thinks is of no interest.

*Handel.* A prophet is not without honor, Dr. Swift . . . I am myself better thought of in London than in Halle, where I was born.

*Swift.* Then Halle is a village like Dublin. London can forgive an author for being born there—nay, they will be proud of him if they can. But you said you must get back to your club of fiddlers. If you will permit me, I will walk up the street with you.

*Handel.* It would be a great honor, Dr. Swift.

*[A door opens.]*

*Swift [Calling].* Martha! Martha! My hat. My best beaver hat. I shall wear my best beaver hat in your honor, Mr. Handel.

*Handel.* I am flattered.

*Swift.* So will the hat be, because it seldom gets an airing nowadays. This way; we can go out by the garden gate and escape Mrs. Pilkington. . . .

*[Bring up the sound of bells, then fade to background street noises.]*

*Swift.* You have, of course, been in the cathedral?

*Handel.* Well—no, I must confess I—er—

*Swift.* Not a churchman, eh?

*Handel.* I am, I hope, a truly religious man. But not a churchman.

*Swift.* The two things seldom go together. But how can you expect me to permit my vicars to sing for a man who is not a churchman?

*Handel.* They do not come to me as vicars but as tenors and basses.

*Swift.* A vicar is a vicar, Mr. Handel.

*Handel.* I am prepared to overlook that, Dr. Swift.

*Swift.* I am not.

*Handel.* Thank God we have not got the author of *Gulliver's Travels* as prime minister. His determination to frustrate evil and do good would earn him a martyr's crown before a month was ended.

*Swift [Chuckling].* You shall have your vicars, Mr. Handel. They shall sing for you until you drive one another into Bedlam.

*Handel.* I am deeply obliged to you, sir. Believe me, they shall have music worthy of your cathedral.

*Swift.* Tell me, Mr. Handel, are you a hard task-master at rehearsals?

*Handel [Carried away immediately].* Oh, but one has to be, Dr. Swift. Leave singers to themselves, and they will play all sorts of tricks with your music. They will put in notes that are not required and leave out notes that cannot be done without. They will sing with too much fervor at this point, and too little at that, and never at the right tempo. The men are bad, but God in Heaven, the women are worse! There is the woman Cuzzoni. Will she sing what I put before her *as* I put it before her? No! She knows better than I how my music should be sung. I have had to threaten to throw her out of the windows before she would do my bidding.

*Swift. Your* bidding?

*Handel [Sweeping on].* Yes. She has a voice—through some jest of Heaven she has a voice—but no feeling in her body from the top of her head to the sole of her foot. I have to hammer each aria into her note by note, and when I have it done for today I know it will be gone tomorrow and I shall have to start all over again.

*Swift.* Why don't you let her sing it her own way?

*Handel [Fiercely].* Because she is a—*[He stops abruptly, having caught the drift of Swift's questions.]* Ha!

*Swift.* It is not enough to meddle with no man's conscience, eh?

*Handel.* She was meddling with my music.

*Swift.* Well, Mr. Handel, we may differ about music, but we are agreed on the necessity of government and—are you married, Mr. Handel?

*Handel.* No.

*Swift.* Then we are agreed about women also.

*Handel.* It's easier to keep one's heart in England than here. Your Irish women are sweeter in looks and in manner than in any other country known to me except Italy.

*Swift.* They are as bad here as anywhere else, my friend.

*Handel.* Oh no, Dr. Swift. In England women use their power much more tyrannically. They are more capricious—

*Swift.* The caprices of womankind are not limited by any climate or nation. They are much more uniform than can be imagined.

*Handel.* Be that as it may, Dr. Swift, I cannot get on without them.

*Swift.* Have you ever tried? Success is easier than you think.

*Handel.* I mean I need them as singers.

*Swift.* I have boys in my cathedral choir that will give you all the high notes you want. And people who are good judges tell me that boys' voices are more pleasing than women's.

*Handel.* I need the women for the stage.

*Swift.* Why? The poet Shakespeare used boys to play women's parts. Indeed, when I was young myself, the custom still lingered on here in Dublin.

*Handel.* If you want to portray women on the stage, it is better to have women actors to do it.

*Swift.* Women will never consent to portray women as they really are: They will only portray what they want men to think they are.

*Handel.* They must portray what the author puts there for them.

*Swift.* You, a man who has worked in the theatre, tell me that!

*Handel [Firmly].* They sing what I put there for them: not more, not less. I see to that.

*Swift.* The question is, what do you put there for them? When I was in London, I used to go to the playhouse and the opera house, but the creatures on the stage were not creatures of nature, certainly not the females.

*Handel.* I admit that art sometimes improves on nature for its own purposes.

*Swift.* These creatures had no relation to nature whatsoever. Even in your best dramas, you dare not portray women as they really are. The actresses would refuse to play the part, and even if they did, the public could not bear to witness them.

*Handel.* How about the play with the Lady Macbeth in it?

*Swift.* A portrait, Mr. Handel, very flattering to women. Women love to think of themselves as the creator of ambition in men, as the manipulator of the lord and master. The Lady Macbeth made a king of her husband, and see what happened to him when she died! So long as your woman figure is superior to your man figure, it matters not a jot whether she be moral or immoral because morality has no meaning for a woman. A woman may have wit: I have known women who were clever and subtle, but I have never know a woman who had a soul or a conscience.

*Handel.* In any church you will find the congregation always has more women than men.

*Swift.* Women's prayers are things done perfectly by rote, as they put on one stocking after another. Their prayers do not come from the soul.

*Handel.* Your calling may make you more expert than I in such matters, but I cannot credit what you say.

*Swift.* Mr. Handel, if you have made money in the theatre, it is because you have flattered women as well as amused them. Try the experiment of writing an opera in which a woman is outwitted by a man, and it will not profit you a sixpenny piece. Oh yes, Mr. Handel, the man may temporarily deceive her by lies and treachery, he may steal from her her fortune and her virtue—such pieces may not be popular, but they will be tolerated. But let him *outwit* her, let him laugh at her, let him show her as the inferior creature, and your piece will be damned for evermore.

*Handel.* Women are neither inferior creatures nor superior. They are just beings just like myself, no better and no worse.

*Swift.* And no different?

*Handel.* There is no difference in human terms that I can see. A bass voice as such is neither better nor worse than a soprano, but the difference, like the other differences between men and women, is useful and interesting.

*Swift [Scornfully].* You can bear to have commerce with women, then?

*Handel.* You would misunderstand me no matter what I said. Let me say that I am not a slave to women.

*Swift.* Empty phrases, Mr. Handel. Do you not resent the indignity of man's subjection to womankind?

*Handel.* The men seem to be willing enough captives.

*Swift.* They might be if women spent their time making cages instead of nets.

*Handel.* But you and I are not in the cage.

*Swift.* I was in the nets more than once.

*Handel.* Clearly you were strong enough to break free.

*Swift.* It is not that I was strong, but that the nets were weak.

*Handel [Impatiently].* You make too much of the matter, Dr. Swift. Why should womankind go to all the trouble of making nets and cages to capture—what? Look at that beggar-woman over there with her dozen children and her poor pitiful starved face. A woman of sorrows. Oh, Dr. Swift, Dr. Swift, if there be any creature in a cage, it is such a woman, not her husband.

*Swift.* It is no mitigation of her crime to say that in ruining her husband she ruined herself too.

*Handel.* Crime? Ruining her husband?

*Swift.* She has put a dozen millstones around that wretch's neck.

*Handel [Firing up].* And you—you, a Christian clergyman, can say that! *[Controlling himself.]* It is not for me to preach charity to a churchman. But that woman with her children has done a noble part in the replenishment of the earth, and I honor her for it.

*Swift.* You can well thank her, Mr. Handel. She is providing your future audience for you.

*Handel [Revolted].* Oh, ignoble! Ignoble!

*Swift:* Fine words butter no parsnips. Neither do fine attitudes.

*Handel.* Dr. Swift, I make no answer to that.

*Swift.* You need have no fear that I will withdraw permission for my vicars to sing for you.

*Handel.* I do not *fear* a thing like that, Dr. Swift.

*Swift [With a little laugh].* Forgive me for teasing you. It is one of our abominable Irish habits. Well, here is Fishamble Street, and I shall not keep you any longer from your club of fiddlers.

*Handel [Rather stiffly].* Thank you for the honor you have done me in receiving me and in walking so far with me. If I have said anything to offend you, pray forgive me.

*Swift [Astonished by the suggestion that he might be offended by an argument].* Offend me? Not in the least Mr. Handel, not in the least. I have enjoyed arguing with you, greatly enjoyed it. And now let me wish you much success with your opera.

*Handel.* Not an opera, a sacred oratorio. *Messiah.*

*Swift.* I still wish you success in your serenading of heaven.

*Handel.* I hope it will be a success, not entirely for my own sake. I am giving all the profits of the performance to the Dublin Charitable Institution.

*Swift.* Indeed?

*[A chink of coins.]*

*Swift.* You remind me of my obligations. Pray take my purse, Mr. Handel, with my apology for its being so light. But I am a poor man in a poor country.

*Handel.* Such poverty is a virtue in yourself and your great country, not a reproach. Do you feel disposed to come in and listen to us for a little while?

*Swift.* If I did, those vicars of mine would be too busy watching me to pay attention to you.

*Handel.* Who would blame them?

*Swift [Jovially].* Wretches and rascals! But I hear your fiddlers scraping away inside. I'll detain you no longer. Good day to you, Mr. Handel.

*Handel.* Good day to you, Dr. Swift.

*[A door opens; the sound of tuning-up can be heard before the closing door cuts off the sound.]*

*Swift [After a moment].* What, Mrs. Pilkington! Have you presumed to follow me?

*Mrs. Pilkington.* I have come to hear Mr. Handel's music.

*Swift.* Let him be, Mrs. Pilkington, and walk back with me to the Deanery. He has too much work to be pestered with questions about what we were saying to each other.

*Mrs. Pilkington.* I should not dare to ask him.

*Swift.* You lie.

*Mrs. Pilkington [Coquettishly].* I should only dare to ask *you,* sir.

*Swift.* Mr. Handel and I talked nonsense, madam. We talked about our illnesses and our aches and our poverty, just as do all old men.

*Mrs. Pilkington.* And what did he—

*Swift.* Ask me no questions, Mrs. Pilkington, and set down no more lies in your memoirs. Just walk along with me in silence—blessed silence. I have had enough of talk for one day.

# THE SHAWS OF SYNGE STREET

## Cast

*George Carr Shaw*, a corn merchant
*Lucinda Elizabeth Shaw*, his wife
*Lucy Shaw*, their daughter
*Walter John Gurly*, a ship's doctor
*Rev. William George Carroll*, the rector of St. Bride's, Dublin
*George John Vandeleur Lee*, a singing teacher
*Joseph Robinson*, a vicar choral
*Matthew Edward McNulty*, a bank clerk
*George Ferdinand Shaw*, a university professor
*Ann Ellen Shaw*, his wife
*Dr. Morgan*
*Patrick Cooke*, a carter
*Sonny*, (G.B.S.)
*Guests*

Acts One, Two and Three take place in Dublin in the 1860s. The Epilogue takes place in London about fifteen years later.

## Act One

*A late afternoon in the 1860s. The drawing room at No. 3 Upper Synge Street (later renumbered 33), Dublin. A smallish room, conventionally furnished. Fireplace with horsehair sofa, right; lace-curtained window, center; door left, with piano against the wall. A small table covered with red plush cloth in the middle of the room. A cabinet with drawers. Oil lamps.*

*George John Lee and Lucy Shaw are engaged in love-play on the sofa. Lee is in his late 30s, not bad-looking; lean, pale, restless, energetic, with glossy black hair and whiskers shaved away to reveal a prominent chin and a straight, resolute mouth. Elegantly dressed, with a poetic cravat. Everything about him is elegant, even*

*the limp (one leg is shorter than the other because of a childhood
accident). He is rapid in speech and decisive in manner.*

*Lucy Shaw, aged 16, is slightly tomboyish but with all the charm
and good looks of her age. She is high-spirited and clever, with a
habit of staring intently at people as she talks to them.*

*A knock at the hall door. Both spring up and tidy themselves.*

*Lucy.* You answer it.

*Lee.* No, you.

*Lucy.* But I'm all . . . *[Frantically she buttons herself up. Another
knock.]* Oh, wait, wait, can't you wait, damn you?

*Lee [Sharply].* Watch your language.

*Lucy.* I'll say it if I like. *[As she goes out.]* Damn, damn, damn,
damn, DAMN.

*[Lee takes out a pocket mirror and comb, checks his appearance
and sits at the table. Lucy returns with Matthew Edward
McNulty, a handsome, curly-headed, ingenuous lad of about her
own age.]*

*Lucy.* It's only Matt McNulty. You made an appointment to hear
his voice.

*Lee [Without rising].* Surely our appointment was for Tuesday.

*McNulty.* Oh Lord, I thought it was today, Mr. Lee. *[He searches
his pockets.]* I could have sworn I had Monday down in my little
book. I have the book . . . I know I have . . . .

*Lee.* It doesn't matter. Lucy, a middle C.

*[Lucy sits at the piano and strikes the note.]*

*Lee.* Sing that note, if you please.

*[McNulty clears his throat and with some embarrassment sings
shakily and off pitch.]*

*Lucy.* Miles too sharp, Matt. Try it again.

*[McNulty does so, again off pitch.]*

*Lee [Annoyed at her interference].* Lucy, just give the note like a
good girl.

*Lucy.* Sorry.

*Lee.* Sing something for me, Mr. McNulty.

*McNulty.* Oh Lord.

*Lee.* Anything you like. "Believe me if all those endearing young
charms."

*[Lucy preludes; McNulty starts, but too high.]*

*Lucy.* Oh, come down, Matt, come down, come down. *[She strikes
a chord.]* Try it at this.

*Lee.* Lucy.

*Lucy.* I'm only trying to help.

*McNulty.* Could I do it without the piano?

*Lee.* If you like.

*[McNulty quavers a few bars until Lee gestures at him to stop.]*

*Lee.* I'm afraid you haven't a voice, Mr. McNulty.

*McNulty.* Oh Lord.

*Lee.* But I shall be able to manufacture one for you.

*McNulty.* Oh, thank you very much.

*Lee.* It will take four years. *[McNulty looks dismayed.]* I cannot turn you into a Lablache in twelve lessons. I teach singing, not yowling.

*McNulty.* There's another thing . . . could I join your Musical Society?

*Lucy.* Sure. If you have the guinea.

*Lee.* When you have learned to sing, I'll consider it.

*McNulty.* I see.

*Lee.* If you decide to take lessons with me—

*McNulty.* Oh, I would love to.

*Lee.* Then come for your first lesson tomorrow at seven. Not here. Come to my house in Harrington Street. *[In dismissal.]* Good afternoon, Mr. McNulty.

*Lucy.* Oh, you're not going, Matt, are you?

*McNulty.* Well . . . .

*Lucy.* Stay and have a cup of tea with us.

*[McNulty looks uneasily at Lee.]*

*Lee.* Mr. McNulty is obviously anxious to get away.

*Lucy.* Are you really?

*Lee [Rising.]* And you have to do your piano practice, Lucy.

*Lucy.* I won't.

*Lee [Taking McNulty's arm lightly and going out].* You'll find the lessons arduous but rewarding. I aim at professional standards. Amateurism is the curse of all serious art . . . .

*[Lucy stands up and tidies her hair. She is smiling to herself. Lee returns, closes the door and stands with his back against it.]*

*Lee.* I see I must put you in your place.

*Lucy.* You and what army?

*Lee.* I need no army.

*Lucy [Glancing through the window].* He's handsome.

*Lee [Coming back to the sofa].* Hmm.

*Lucy.* And young.

*Lee.* You state the obvious.

*Lucy [Taking up a tea-cosy and coming behind Lee].* I'm getting tired of elderly men. *[She plumps the tea-cosy on his head.]* Napoleon.

*Lee [Taking off the tea-cosy carefully].* Put this back where it belongs.

*Lucy [Going back to the piano].* No.

*Lee.* I said put it back.

*Lucy.* And I said no.

*[He slings the tea-cosy away. She fools with the notes.]*

*Lee.* Come over here.

*Lucy.* I'm not in the mood to be pawed.

*Lee.* I told you to come here.

*Lucy.* I'm quite comfortable where I am. *[She jangles more notes.]*

*Lee [On edge].* Stop it. You unmusical bitch.

*Lucy.* Oh, aren't we the perfect gentleman.

*Lee.* Get out.

*Lucy.* It's my house, not yours.

*Lee.* You heard what I said.

*Lucy.* I don't give a damn what you said, George. You're not ordering me about in my own house.

*Lee.* I have not given you permission to call me by my Christian name.

*Lucy.* I don't need your permission, darling George.

*Lee [Rising].* You want me to box your ears again?

*Lucy.* The next time you hit me . . . !

*Lee.* I shall do so as often as you give me cause.

*Lucy.* Just try.

*[He slaps her face several times, but not really hard. She looks for a moment as if she is going to strike him, but merely puts out her tongue.]*

*Lucy.* Yah! Did you enjoy that?

*Lee [Lightly brushing his sleeve].* Thoroughly. Did you?

*[She springs at him and thumps his chest with her fist. He holds her off with ease, until she seizes his hand and bites his thumb. He cries out with pain.]*

*Lee.* You little . . . . *[He doesn't finish the sentence.]*

*Lucy [Throwing her arms around his neck].* Oh George, I've hurt you. I'm sorry.

*Lee [Throwing her off].* Go away.

*Lucy [Her arms around him].* George! I didn't mean it—honestly. *[Sobbing on his chest.]* Oh, George, George, I love you, I love you, I love you. I want to make a present of myself to you.

*Lee [Trying to disengage himself].* I am not in the mood for being pawed.

*Lucy.* Tell me you love me.

*Lee.* I don't.

*Lucy.* You do. *[She kisses him hotly.]* Well—?

*Lee [Roused, but with a certain distaste].* Do you think you're setting my blood on fire?

*Lucy.* I know what I think, darling George.

*Lee [Sitting on the sofa].* You overestimate the pleasure of physical contact with you.

*Lucy.* I don't, darling George. *[Gravely.]* But you get much more fun out of it than I do. Why is that? *[She straightens her stockings and surveys her ankle critically.]* Don't pretend, George. You're not an enoch. Or are you?

*Lee [Puzzled].* A what?

*Lucy.* An enoch. Like the ones in *The Arabian Nights?*

*Lee.* Oh . . . an enoch. Hmm. And how did *you* get hold of that book?

*Lucy.* Aunt Emily gave it to me. She thinks it's a book of fairy stories. *[Earnestly.]* It isn't, you know. *[Plumping down beside him.]* What is an enoch?

*Lee.* I wouldn't know.

*Lucy.* Anyway, you wouldn't be telling me anything that I don't know already. I know about . . . everything. And I'm not telling you who told me.

*Lee.* I have no desire to know.

*Lucy.* The cook from next door. She's not married, but she knows all about it. She did it with the coalman. *[He remains expressionless.]* With the coalman, darling George. And do you know what the coalman told her? That your father hawked coal around the streets.

*Lee [Jumping up].* My father was a gentleman.

*Lucy [Kneeling on the sofa and putting her arms around him].* It doesn't make any difference to me, darling George.

*Lee [Strangely angry].* Do you ever think of your own father?

*Lucy [Defensively].* Well, what about him? He's a gentleman and cousin to a baronet. *[As he tries to disengage himself, she twines her arms more closely about him and makes her tone husky.]* Please kiss the baronet's cousin's daughter, O handsome son of a coalman.

*[He kisses her with increasing passion. Having momentarily yielded, she backs away and dances off.]*

*Lucy [Crowing with laughter].* I won, I won, I won. I made you do it! *[The hall door bangs. Lucy adroitly changes her laughter into an arpeggio. She stands beside the piano making teasing gestures at him with singing arpeggios. Lucinda Elizabeth Shaw comes in. She is in her 30s, not very goodlooking, but dresses and bears herself well enough to be not unattractive. She is in outdoor dress.]*

*Mrs. Shaw.* Run along and practise in your room, Lucy.

*Lucy.* Yes, Mar. *[She goes, blowing a mocking kiss to Lee behind her mother's back.]*

*Mrs. Shaw [Unpinning her hat].* Trouble again.

*Lee.* Your excellent husband?

*Mrs. Shaw.* Somebody picked him out of the gutter in Camden Street and propped him against a lamppost. I met Walter at the corner and asked him to go and fetch him.

*Lee.* Do you mean to say that your splendid brother is sober enough at a quarter after five to be able to take charge of anybody?

*Mrs. Shaw.* Oh, the blind leading the blind. *[She sits on the piano stool.]* I'm so tired of it all. *[Brightening.]* I've another pupil for you. Mr. Neary.

*Lee.* Baritone?

*Mrs. Shaw.* Tenor. What d'ye think of that!

*Lee.* Splendid. I had McNulty here. Hopeless.

*Mrs. Shaw.* I hope you didn't tell him that.

*Lee.* I never hide the truth.

*Mrs. Shaw.* Of course, it's not his voice—it's Lucy.

*Lee.* I suspected that.

*Mrs. Shaw.* But he's a recruit.

*Lee.* It's hard enough trying to keep Lucy's mind on her work without that distraction.

*Mrs. Shaw.* Lee, *is* her voice good enough for you to bother so much about it?

*Lee.* It could be as good as yours if she'd practice properly.

*Mrs. Shaw.* I'll speak to her again.

*Lee.* And she's seeing far too much of that Ellen woman.

*Mrs. Shaw [Angrily].* I told her not to see—oh, what's the use of talking.

*Lee.* It's nothing but "Ellen says this" and "Ellen says that."

*Mrs. Shaw.* Well . . . was the music all right?

*Lee.* What music? . . . Oh, yes, of course.

*Mrs. Shaw.* Didn't you look through it this afternoon? *[She takes up a sheet of music.]* I've simplified the second fiddle part.

*Lee.* Splendid.

*Mrs. Shaw [Hungry for his approbation].* I was up till four this morning doing it for you.

*Lee.* You needn't have done that.

*Mrs. Shaw.* I knew you'd be glad to have it done.

*Lee.* Yes. Yes, indeed. *[He goes to the window.]* I wonder how your excellent husband and your worthy brother are.

*Mrs. Shaw.* I've gone beyond caring. *[She ties up the paper on the table.]*

*Lee.* Talk of the devil.

*Mrs. Shaw.* Are they coming?

*Lee.* The Ellen woman.

*Mrs. Shaw.* We won't answer the door.

*Lee.* We can't do that.

*Mrs. Shaw [Calling upstairs].* Lucy . . . that Ellen woman is at the door. Don't bring her in here.

*[A knock on the hall door.]*

*Lee.* I wonder what she wants.

*Mrs. Shaw.* Oh, bother her. I'm tired. *[She sits on the sofa.]* The late night, of course. I hope you'll like the way I've divided up Act One between piano and strings.

*Lee.* I'm sure I will.

*Mrs. Shaw.* I think the tenor aria should be accompanied only by piano—

*[Lucy comes in.]*

*Lucy.* Oh Mar, Ellen has it. The missing tablecloth. The laundry sent it to *her.* Come along in, Ellen.

*[Ellen comes in. She is an exceptionally pretty and vivacious woman with a radiant smile.]*

*Ellen.* May I?

*[Mrs. Shaw rises.]*

*Ellen.* The laundry is always getting the two Mrs. Shaws mixed up—goodness only knows what things of ours *you* get. I'm really terrified you'll get some of our sheets; the children have them torn to ribbons. *[She holds out her hand to Lee.]* Good afternoon, Mr. Lee.

*Lee.* Good afternoon, madam.

*Ellen.* You *do* know me, don't you? I'm practically your next-door neighbor in Harrington Street.

*Lee.* Indeed.

*Lucy [Putting a cushion on the sofa].* Sit down, Ellen.

*Ellen [To Mrs. Shaw].* May I? *[Mrs. Shaw shrugs. Ellen sits.]* Thank you. I really shouldn't because I'm sure you've lots to do, but I won't stay more than two minutes. And I hope you're not going to keep on calling me Mrs. Shaw. Do call me Ellen.

*Lee [To Lucy].* Tell Mary Kate to bring some tea.

*Lucy.* It's her afternoon off. *[Mocking.]* Didn't you remember? And there isn't any tea in the house.

*Ellen.* It really doesn't matter, if it's me you're thinking about.

*Mrs. Shaw [To Lucy].* Take my purse and go around to the grocer.

*[Lucy goes.]*

*Ellen.* She's an adorable girl. Don't you think so, Mr. Lee?

*Lee.* Quite.

*Ellen [To Mrs. Shaw].* I may call you Lucinda Elizabeth, mayn't I? *[Mrs. Shaw shrugs.]*

*Ellen.* There! I knew we'd be real friends once we got talking. I have so few women friends, you know. *[To Lee.]* The members of my own sex don't seem to like me at all.

*Lee [Examining his fingernails].* Indeed.

*Ellen.* Music is such a great thing for making friends. It's so charming when I pass your window, Mr. Lee, hearing all the singing inside. Your pupils seem to have the loveliest voices. So fresh and young, and so gay.

*Lee.* As you say, madam.

*Ellen [Indomitably].* The children tell me this house is simply full of music. All the operas and oratorios, choruses and all. Even the Roman Catholics come to sing with you.

*Lee.* God has given one or two Romans quite good voices.

*Ellen.* With all that music it must be *such* a happy home, Lucinda Elizabeth. And everyone says your voice is so beautiful.

*Mrs. Shaw.* I owe it all to Mr. Lee. He is a very great genius of music.

*Ellen.* Your husband is fond of music too.

*Mrs. Shaw.* Well . . . .

*Ellen.* I hear he plays the trombone quite beautifully.

*Lee.* And the penny whistle.

*Ellen [With a quick look at him].* How versatile.

*Mrs. Shaw.* You seem to know a lot about us, Mrs. er . . . .

*Ellen.* You promised to call me Ellen. You do know my husband, don't you?

*Mrs. Shaw.* No.

*Ellen.* People sometimes mistake me for his daughter. And when they hear I have five children—! *[Shining at Lee.]* I was married very young.

*Mrs. Shaw.* So was I.

*Ellen.* Sixteen. How old were you, Lucinda Elizabeth? Oh, I've forgotten my manners. Fancy asking a question like that.

*Mrs. Shaw.* I was little older . . . just a little.

*Ellen.* Ferdie is fifteen years older than I. Your husband is a good deal older than you too, isn't he?

*Mrs. Shaw.* A husband *should* be older than his wife.

*Ellen [With a sigh].* But not too much. Funny we should have so much in common, Lucinda Elizabeth. I adore music too. Indeed, I've been trying to pluck up enough courage to ask Mr. Lee to take me as a pupil.

*Mrs. Shaw.* But you're a pupil of Mr. Robinson's—

*Ellen [Smiling].* Oh, you know that!

*Mrs. Shaw.* I must have heard it from the children.

*Ellen.* Children do chatter, don't they? Well, Mr. Lee?

*Lee.* I do not poach on Professor Robinson's territory.

*Ellen.* I know what you think of professors, Mr. Lee. Wouldn't you like to rescue me from a fate worse that death—musically, I mean?

*Lee.* Robinson is harmless.

*Ellen [Archly].* Do you really think so?

*Mrs. Shaw.* Mr. Lee is rather crowded out with pupils just now.

*Ellen.* I heard that you were looking for contraltos for your musical society.

*Mrs. Shaw.* You're a mezzo.

*Ellen.* Did the children tell you that too? I can get down quite comfortably to A flat, Mr. Lee.

*Mrs. Shaw.* Surely you couldn't desert Professor Robinson.

*Ellen.* Mr. Robinson has dozens of pupils.

*Mrs. Shaw.* So has Mr. Lee. But we don't have to decide about this now, do we?

*Ellen.* I *may* live in hope, Mr. Lee—?

*Mrs. Shaw.* I don't think Mr. Lee could promise anything.

*Ellen.* You know you're quite a celebrity in these parts, Mr. Lee.

*Lee.* Indeed?

*Ellen.* They say you are frightfully severe with your pupils—even your lady pupils. Really, I'm quite surprised at my own courage in asking you to take me on.

*Mrs. Shaw.* Mr. Lee expects his pupils to take music seriously. He has no time for frivolous women.

*Ellen.* How masterful. *[To Lee.]* And the whole neighborhood is talking about how you keep your windows wide open even in the depths of winter.

*Mrs. Shaw.* The whole neighborhood seems to have little to talk about.

*Lee.* I believe in fresh air.

*Ellen.* I know you do, Mr. Lee. I can see you walking in the orchard up the road—quite late in the evening too, sometimes, and even when it's raining.

*[Mrs. Shaw grows tense at the mention of the orchard. Lee remains impassive.]*

*Ellen [Smiling angelically at Mrs. Shaw].* I have the most marvelous view from my bedroom window.

*Lee.* The hills must look particularly beautiful.

*Ellen.* Not the hills, Mr. Lee—the orchard. Those lovely cherry trees. And the apple blossoms.

*Mrs. Shaw [Rising nervously].* I must see what's keeping Lucy with the tea.

*Lee.* Please don't worry about it.

*Ellen.* I didn't think the orchard was public, Mr. Lee.

*Lee.* It belongs to one of my pupils.

*Ellen.* I was just wondering. You're the only person I ever see walking in it. You and your friend, I mean.

*Mrs. Shaw [Rising again].* I really must see about the—

*Lee [Gesturing to her to sit down].* If you want some tea, allow me to look after it. Stay and chat to your visitor.
*[He goes out.]*

*Ellen [Gazing after him].* What a pity. His little disability, I mean.

*Mrs. Shaw.* I've quite forgotten about it.

*Ellen.* Yes, it's so easy to. He's such a— *[Searches for a word]* — such an *interesting* man. I notice you call him Lee—no mister or anything. One would imagine that being friends for so long you'd call him George. He calls you Bessie.

*Mrs. Shaw.* I don't like the name George.

*Ellen.* Isn't your husband a George too?

*Mrs. Shaw.* It's not on that account that I dislike it.

*Ellen.* And your son is George as well. *[Smiling.]* But naturally he's called after his father.

*Mrs. Shaw [Looking Ellen straight in the eye].* Naturally. *[A pause, then pointedly.]* One calls one's son after the father when one is sure who the father is.

*Ellen.* Yes, indeed. *[Sighing.]* Yours is such a happy home, Lucinda Elizabeth.

*Mrs. Shaw.* Quite.

*Ellen.* Happier than mine.

*Mrs. Shaw.* Hmm.

*Ellen.* Lucy has told you, hasn't she? Ferdie and I—the old story.

*Mrs. Shaw.* Lucy hasn't mentioned the subject.

*Ellen.* Surely girls tell their mothers everything.

*Mrs. Shaw.* Do they?

*Ellen.* That sort of thing, I mean.
*[Mrs. Shaw shrugs. Ellen suddenly pulls up her sleeve and displays her arm.]*

*Mrs. Shaw [Without surprise or concern].* Your husband?

*Ellen.* The much-respected Professor Ferdinand Shaw, Senior Fellow of Trinity College, beats his wife and sometimes smashes the furniture. Who'd believe it?

*Mrs. Shaw.* Why don't you put ointment on it, or something?

*Ellen [Smiling].* I'm so used to bruises now, Lucinda Elizabeth.

*Mrs. Shaw.* I think there's a liniment somewhere.

[*As Mrs. Shaw rises to get the liniment, Lucy dashes in, bonnet in hand.*]

*Lucy.* Holy Joe wants to see you at the corner.

*Mrs. Shaw.* Lucy, what on earth—

*Lucy.* Sorry, Mar. He's in an awful state—Holy Joe. Chewing his hatband.

*Ellen.* Professor Robinson—?

*Lucy.* Shall I tell him to come in?

*Ellen [Smiling].* Your mamma mightn't—

*Lucy.* Oh, the Mar wouldn't mind—would you, Mar? [*To Ellen.*] Shall I fetch him in?

*Ellen.* I know this is an awful intrusion—

*Lucy.* I'll get him. [*She runs out.*]

*Ellen.* I suppose I'd better explain—

*Mrs. Shaw.* Not at all necessary, I assure you.

*Ellen [Smiling].* My husband and Professor Robinson rather dislike each other, so Professor Robinson avoids coming to the house.

*Mrs. Shaw.* I see.

*Ellen.* It was really the silliest little dispute. But you know what men are like over little things.

*Mrs. Shaw.* Of course.

*Ellen.* Would you have a tuning fork in the house?

*Mrs. Shaw.* Won't the piano do you?

*Ellen.* Oh yes, yes, yes. How silly of me. Really, I hardly know what I'm saying.

*Mrs. Shaw.* I quite understand.

*Ellen [Sighing].* I do wish one of Professor Robinson's pupils had an orchard.

[*Mrs. Shaw flushes and fidgets. Luckily for her, Lucy returns with Joseph Robinson. He is tall, burly, bald, bewhiskered, ruddy, highly strung, slightly absentminded, and very fussy. He is dressed as an artist, Victorian style: flowing cravat, voluminous cloak, broad-brimmed black felt hat. He greets Mrs. Shaw with both hands outstretched, his billowing cloak rocking every light article of furniture as it swirls by.*]

*Robinson.* My dear Mrs. Shaw, this is extraordinarily good of you, it's a fearful intrusion and all that, and I daresay you're up to your eyes getting ready for the evening meal, I understand that being a married man myself, but it's only for a minute, and your

little girl was so pressing—charming little girl too—and it's rather
an important message for—er—our mutual friend.

*Mrs. Shaw [Taking her hands out of his grip].* How d'you do?

*Robinson.* Really lovely weather for the time of year, eh?

*Ellen [Holding out her hand].* Good afternoon, Mr. Robinson.

*Robinson.* Oh dammit, I forgot. Afternoon, dear lady, afternoon.
*[He whirls so suddenly that his cloak nearly knocks over a chair.]*

*Mrs. Shaw.* Do let me take your cloak, Professor.

*Robinson.* Oh no, no, no, please, don't bother. I shan't be staying
more than a minute. *[Nevertheless, he takes off his cloak and
drops it over her arm as if she were the butler.]* Just a word with
our—er—mutual friend.

*Ellen.* I suppose it's the new song you want to try over with me?

*Robinson.* New song? Oh dammit, of course. New song, of course.
yes, that's what it is. We just want to try over a little song.

*Mrs. Shaw.* I presume you'd prefer to be left alone.

*Ellen.* That's sweet of you, Lucinda Elizabeth.

*Robinson.* Very obliging indeed.

*Mrs. Shaw.* You did think of bringing the music with you, Professor
Robinson?

*Robinson.* Oh dammit—

*Ellen.* I know it off by heart, Lucinda Elizabeth. We don't bother
with the music now.
*[Lucy has squatted on the piano with the appearance of one who
is going to enjoy an exciting scene.]*

*Mrs. Shaw.* Lucy . . . .

*Lucy.* I'd like to hear the song.

*Ellen.* Oh, do let's have one run over it in private before we have
an audience.

*Lucy.* All right.
*[She goes out with her mother, Robinson dashing to hold the
door open for them and to bow them out, smiling.]*

*Robinson.* That little bitch needs a good thrashing. That was blackguarding—plain blackguarding.

*Ellen.* Yes, Joe—but what's the matter?

*Robinson.* Fanny has—now remember; hysterics won't help—
Fanny has found out all about us. She's threatening to divorce
me. *[He flops down on the piano stool so clumsily that his elbows
jangle the piano. He springs up.]* This bloody thing left open
too. *[He flings over to another seat.]* She kept screaming "Adulterer," at me.

*Ellen.* Adulterer . . . .

*Robinson.* What's in that word that makes you women roll it around your mouth like damn butterscotch?

*Ellen.* You must try to keep a grip on yourself.

*Robinson.* Keep a grip! Me!! If you knew what I've been through—

*Ellen.* Yes, I know, Joe, but we've got to be calm.

*Robinson.* Calm! Bolting the damn door after the damn horse has gone.

*Ellen.* How on earth did she find out?

*Robinson.* Oh, she always finds out.

*Ellen.* Always finds out? What do you mean by *always* finds out?

*Robinson.* Fanny is after me morning, noon and night. If it isn't over you, it's over somebody else. *[Hastily.]* I mean—

*Ellen.* Do you make love to *all* your pupils?

*Robinson.* Go on. Go on. Carry on from where Fanny left off.

*Ellen.* Well, she can't really be serious about divorcing you.

*Robinson [Springing up].* Dammit, that reminds me what I was rushing to see you about. She has written to your confounded husband.

*Ellen.* Oh no . . . .

*Robinson.* You'll have to do something about that letter, Ellen. Bribe the postman or something. Even if you have to sit up all night watching the letterbox—

*Ellen.* Maybe it's in the letterbox already.

*Robinson.* Not in your afternoon post. I found that out from the postman. Had to give him half a crown.

*Ellen.* Oh my God, I couldn't face home with that hanging over me.

*Robinson.* Dammit, woman, you'll have to.

*Ellen [Going over to him].* Joe—

*Robinson [Backing away].* Be careful, be careful—not here.

*Ellen [Taking his lapel].* Joe, take me away somewhere.

*Robinson.* Take you—?! Are you out of your mind, woman? Where would we go?

*Ellen.* Anywhere.

*Robinson.* Be practical, for God's sake. What would we live on? I couldn't pick up another job as vicar choral just like that. And load myself down with that tribe of children of yours. Dammit, they're your husband's lookout, not mine.

*Ellen.* He's always threatening to take the three boys to live with him in College. So we'd only have the two girls.

*Robinson.* Only the two—oh, my God, woman. Only the—I mean to say—

*Ellen.* They'd be no trouble, Joe. They're as good as gold. And I thought you were so fond of them.

*Robinson [Brusquely].* Of course, I'm fond of them. But going off with another man's wife and family—! I mean it would be kidnapping. He'd have the police after us.

*Ellen.* He wouldn't. He'd be only too glad to get rid of us.

*Robinson.* Well, he just can't get rid of his responsibilities like that. You don't find me trying to get rid of my responsibilities, and they're even heavier than his.

*Ellen [Going back to the sofa].* All right, Joe.

*Robinson.* Am I being unreasonable? Can't you see that I owe it to you to stop you making a fool of yourself? That's what it is. I'm thinking of you, not of myself. Of course, I'd love to go away with you, and leave Fanny and her perpetual howling morning, noon, and night. I love you, Ellen. *[Drawing himself up.]* You may sit there looking like a naughty child that's sulking because it won't be given what it wants, but you'll have to admit that I've shown you how deeply, how profou . . . how recklessly—I've—and how profoundly I've loved you. *[He takes out his cigar case.]* Recklessly, recklessly. I haven't counted the cost. *[He snips the end off the cigar.]* Look at the risks I've taken. A man in my position.

*Ellen [Quietly].* What are we going to do about Fanny?

*Robinson [Stopping in the act of putting the cigar in his mouth].* Fanny . . . my God, Fanny. *[He flings the cigar on the floor.]* Damn Fanny! Now!

*Ellen.* You'd better not leave that thing lying on the floor.

*Robinson [Picking up the cigar, examining it and putting it back carefully in its case].* I swore a hole through a pot never to see you again. That may keep her quiet for an hour or two. But if she goes down to the cathedral and finds I haven't been there, we're sunk.

*Ellen.* We're supposed to be trying out a song. Better play something.

*Robinson.* I'm in no mood for fool-acting now.

*Ellen.* This is not fool-acting, Joe. Give me a note, and I'll sing a few exercises.

*[He moodily plays a chord; she sings arpeggios.]*

*Ellen.* La, la, la, la. *[Sotto voce.]* Do you think we're safe till tomorrow?

*Robinson.* Not with Fanny. *[Chord.]*

*Ellen.* La, la, la, la. You must have had an awful time with her.

*Robinson.* She began firing things at me. *[Pulling up his sleeve.]* Look at that! With the damned poker. My whole arm went numb. I thought I'd never be able to play again. *[Chord.]*

*Ellen.* I could show you many a bruise, Joe. La, la, la, la.

*Robinson.* Men beating women is more natural. *[Chord.]*

*Ellen.* La, la, la, la. *[She kisses him.]*

*Robinson.* Not here, Ellen, not here.

*Ellen [Caressing him].* You poor darling, your nerves must be in ribbons.

*[Voices in the hall. A man is singing lustily.]*

*Robinson.* Great God, he's completely off-key.

*[The voice in the hall starts "Oh Susannah." The door is opened by Dr. Walter Gurly who, with the help of the Rev. William Carroll, is trying to keep George Carr Shaw on his feet. George Carr Shaw, at 56, is slightly built, below middle height, with sparse iron gray hair and beard. Dressed more for comfort than elegance, but neat enough except when falling about drunk. Gurly is a ship's surgeon: a big man, with reddish hair and complexion, and sideburns of Victorian extravagance. He is as boisterous as is consistent with being obviously of gentlemanly breeding. Rev. William George Carroll, Rector of St. Bride's, Dublin, is tall and skeletally thin. He wears a loosely cut frock coat with silk facings and a huge stovepipe hat.]*

*Gurly [Exuberantly].* If it isn't Holy Joe himself? The right man in the right place! Strike up the band there, boy. Broomp, dhroomp, boomp, dhroomp, boomp, dhroomp, boom-boom!

*Shaw [Blowing an imaginary trombone].* Ooom pah pah pah—oom pah pah pah.

*[While Gurly and Shaw are performing, Carroll takes off his hat, brushes it carefully with his sleeve and places it in a safe corner. Robinson rises from the piano, frowning heavily. Gurly, seeing that Ellen is frankly enjoying the minstrelsy, seizes her and begins to dance her about which she enjoys even more frankly. They sing their own music.]*

*Shaw [Lurching towards Carroll].* May I have the pleasure, Willie?

*[He tries to take Carroll into his arms.]*

*Carroll.* Control yourself, man.

*Shaw.* Come on, Willie, a High Church minuet.

*Carroll [Pushing Shaw firmly onto the sofa].* Sit down before you fall and hurt yourself.

*[Lucy appears at the door.]*

*Lucy.* A dance! Hurrah! Come on, Professor! *[She seizes Robinson and begins to whirl him around.]*

*Robinson.* Really, Miss Shaw—preposterous—ridiculous.

*Lucy.* You dance divinely.

*[Ellen and Gurly and Lucy and Robinson bump into one another*

*and go down in a flurry of limbs with shrieks of laughter, except
from Robinson. Shaw whirls Carroll around with a yell of
triumph.]*

*Shaw.* Now who's drunk, Willie! We're the only ones able to stand
on our feet!

*[Mrs. Shaw comes in at the door with Lee close behind her. She
is whitefaced with rage.]*

*Mrs. Shaw.* Even you, Willie!

*Carroll [Very angry].* What do you mean, Lucinda?

*Mrs. Shaw.* I should have expected Professor Robinson at least to
have some respect for my house.

*Robinson.* Dammit it, madam, I—I—*[He stutters to a standstill.]*

*Ellen [Who is lying on Gurly's legs].* Is nobody going to help me
up?

*Gurly.* Don't budge, dear lady. I'm quite comfortable where you
are.

*[Robinson helps Ellen to her feet. Gurly slowly rises and shakes
himself. Lucy has got up by herself.]*

*Carroll.* In justice to myself, Lucinda, let me say—

*Mrs. Shaw.* We'll let the matter drop, Willie, if you please.

*Carroll.* No, Lucinda. You have had your say; I will have mine.

*Mrs. Shaw.* The less said the better.

*Lee.* Precisely.

*Shaw.* Why is the party stopping?

*Mrs. Shaw.* Go to bed.

*Shaw.* I'm not drunk. *[Taking Carroll by the lapels.]* In good form,
Willie, but not drunk. Be honest, Willie. Forget that you're married to my sister, God help you. Speak out boldly as from the
pulpit, Willie.

*Carroll.* You're quite all right, George. Just go and rest yourself.

*Gurly.* Oh, trust a damned clergyman to tell a mealymouthed lie.
You're drunk, George. Rotten stinking drunk just like me.

*Shaw [Slowly taking off his coat].* Brother-in-law or not . . . .

*Gurly [Roaring with laughter].* Listen to him, by God. I found him
holding up a lamp post. Take him home, says Bessie. Sure, says
I. But was I going to take him home half-shot and able to resist?
No. I brought him into Billy Byrne's and made him whole-shot
and as meek as a lamb. I treated you like a king, George, didn't
I?

*Shaw [Putting on his coat again.].* Like a king, Walter. Yes, you
did. Put on the pan, Bessie, and give him a feed of rashers and
eggs.

*Gurly.* Motion proposed and seconded. *[Nudging Robinson.]* What about it, Holy Joe? Rashers and eggs. Better than Bach in B minor, eh?

*[Robinson's saliva flows involuntarily.]*

*Mrs. Shaw.* We'll eat later on. *[To Shaw.]* You come along and sleep it off.

*Gurly.* God, Bessie, you haven't changed. From the time she was that high, always trying to be the boss. Tried it on me once or twice. But I gave her such a hiding that she laid off pretty quickly. D'ye remember that, Bessie?

*Lucy [Her eyes lighting up].* Did you actually beat the Mar, Uncle Walter?

*Gurly.* I gave her such a bang on the back that she said, "Oh, me chest!" *[To Ellen.]* The only way women will respect you. The mailed fist.

*[Ellen giggles.]*

*Mrs. Shaw [To her husband].* Are you coming?

*Shaw [Seizing a flower bowl and dashing it on the ground].* No. I'm head of the house . . . not anyone else.

*Mrs. Shaw [Unmoved].* Help me, Walter.

*Gurly.* Get someone else, Bessie. I've had my fill of him.

*Carroll [Putting his arm around Shaw's shoulders].* I think you ought to rest yourself, George. You're tired. We'll bring you up a plate of bacon and eggs.

*Lucy [Taking her father's arm].* Come on and rest yourself, Papa.

*[Shaw lets himself be led to the door.]*

*Shaw [Passing Lee].* I'm head of this house . . . not anyone else.

*[Carroll and Lucy lead him upstairs, with Mrs. Shaw following.]*

*Gurly [Placing a chair for Ellen].* Apologies, dear lady. *[Abruptly.]* God in heaven, what a commentary on mankind, when one has to apologize for being in good spirits!

*Ellen.* I love good spirits.

*Gurly [Nodding towards Robinson].* He doesn't. *[To Robinson.]* Sit down, you goddam old patriarch and take the weight of those Biblical whiskers off your feet.

*Robinson.* Seeing the condition you're in, I shan't take offence. *[He sits down with dignity.]*

*Gurly.* I don't mind a musician starving the barber in order to look like Beethoven, but when he tries to look like Moses—! Lee, why don't you grow a chinwarmer? You could double your fee. *[He goes over to the cabinet to get a bottle and glasses. As he passes Lee, he drops his voice.]* Look at what you could do with the women—and no one would suspect you of it. *[Holding up the bottle.]* If we wet your whistle, Moses, you won't start climbing up the curtains, will you?

*Robinson.* I am not taking offense.

*Gurly [Offering a glass to Ellen].* Just a leetle, to bring the roses to your cheeks?

*Ellen.* Thank you no, Dr. Gurly. Let it bring the roses to your own.

*Gurly.* It's my nose the roses come to, damn them. *[Offering the glass around.]* It's no use asking *you*, Lee. *[To Robinson.]* Are throaty tenors allowed to have a swig?

*Robinson [Accepting].* Thank you. And by the way, I am *not* a tenor.

*Gurly.* Soprano then?

*Robinson.* A bass, sir.

*Gurly.* Really? *[Filling his own glass.]* I was once in your cathedral, Robinson—years ago: I keep away from hotbeds of virtue nowadays—but I was once down in St. Patrick's, and there was an old chap with a long whisker like yourself in the choir, and he had a voice like a girl. No joke. Sang "Hear my prayer" just like Bessie. I suppose he'd had his thingummyjigs cut off. Art for art's sake. But give me the old banjo every time and the Christy Minstrels. *[He sits down beside Ellen.]*

*Ellen.* I hear you've been away on a long voyage, Dr. Gurly.

*Gurly.* Ship's doctor, you know. This time three months ago I was in the South Sea Islands.

*Ellen.* They say the scenery is very picturesque.

*Gurly.* Well, when the girls are dancing about in their grass skirts—

*Robinson.* Really, Gurly—

*Gurly.* Yes, Moses, are you ready to be filled up again?

*Robinson.* No sir. And I shouldn't have to tell you my name is not Moses.

*Gurly.* Traveling incognito?

*Robinson [Rising].* I have another appointment.

*Gurly.* Oh, sit down, man, and sing us a tune. Or tickle the ivories, and I'll give you a stave myself. I must sing you a little song I picked up in New York.

*Robinson.* I'm afraid I cannot wait.

*Gurly.* Then go and be damned to you.

*[He turns his back on Robinson and speaks to Lee. Ellen signs to Robinson to sit down, and he does after a show of indignant hesitation.]*

*Gurly.* I say, Lee, have you talked Bessie out of her spiritualism yet?

*Ellen [Her interest caught by the word].* Spiritualism? Oh—does Lucinda Elizabeth believe in spirits?

*Gurly.* Oh yes. Her husband drinks 'em, and she talks to 'em. She has a ouija board and all.

*Ellen.* What's that?

*Gurly.* Don't ask me, dear lady. Some damned contraption for calling up spirits from the vasty deep.

*Ellen.* How thrilling. Do they answer her call?

*Gurly.* What the hell would any sane spirit want to talk to Bessie for? I know if I were a spirit and she kept nagging at me, I'd soon tell her where to shove her ouija board.

*Ellen.* Do you believe in spirits, Mr. Lee?

*Lee.* Not unreservedly.

*Gurly.* Dammit, Lee, spirits, ghosts, they're all ba—bosh.

*[Mrs. Shaw returns with Carroll.]*

*Mrs. Shaw.* I believe I owe Professor Robinson an apology. William has explained to me about the disorderliness.

*Gurly.* What disord—oh, you mean the dancing. My God, disorderliness!

*Robinson [Rising].* I'm afraid I must go, Mrs. Shaw.

*Ellen [Rising].* I really must be going too.

*Gurly [Almost pushing her down again].* Oh heavens no. I'll leave you home in a cab.

*Ellen.* I'm only three steps around the corner.

*Gurly.* Then I shall carry you home under my arm like the tasty little morsel you are.

*Robinson.* Really, Gurly, I—I—I—

*Gurly.* Farewell, Moses. And mind the bulrushes as you go out.

*[Robinson bows and stalks out with Mrs. Shaw.]*

*Gurly.* Damn touchy lot, musicians. Hope you're not one of them, dear lady.

*Ellen.* Not exactly, but I'm delighted to say Mr. Lee is taking me on as a pupil.

*Gurly.* You're the lucky devil, Lee. Every time I see him he has six more pretty gals hanging out of him.

*Ellen [Going to the door].* I'll hardly qualify as one of *them.*

*Gurly [Following her].* Fishing, fishing. Naughty little girl, naughty. *[He pinches her. She squeals. They go off laughing.]*

*Carroll [Taking up his hat and brushing it with his sleeve].* It's the children I feel sorry for.

*Lee.* That woman's children?

*Carroll.* And Lucinda's.

*Lee.* It has had no harmful effects on the children here.

*Carroll.* I have noticed things about Lucy.

*Lee.* Indeed?

*Carroll.* She has been reading unsuitable books.

*Lee.* Your wife gave her *The Arabian Nights*.

*Carroll.* Emily didn't understand.

*Lee.* Incidentally, Rector, allow me to congratulate you on your taste in literature. Refreshingly liberal.

*Carroll [Stiffly].* That evil book, sir, was presented to me in all innocence by a lady parishioner. But it was not Lucy's reading the book disturbs me, but that she was consulting my dictionary.

*Lee.* We must ban the dictionary, Rector.

*[Gurly comes back, rubbing his hands gleefully.]*

*Gurly.* Lads, did you ever see such a sweet little bottom?

*Lee.* I should have imagined that as a doctor you would have had your fill of—

*Gurly.* The man who's tired of that is tired of life, old boy.

*Carroll.* I don't think I'm equal to the intellectual pressure of this conversation.

*Gurly.* Oh, we're crushed, crushed, bloody crushed. Worms squashed underfoot by that vicar of Christ Crucified.

*[Carroll goes out.]*

*Gurly.* Well, now that he has given us the pleasure of his absence, let me tell you this one. Got it in New York.

> There was an old man from Chicago,
> Who married a fearful virago;
> When he brought her to bed,
> "Now look here, boy," she said,
> "Get your feet off my—"

*Lee.* Spare me, Gurly.

*Gurly.* So *you* belong to the Confraternity of Holiness, too? There's some excuse for Willie Carroll: he has a dog collar to keep up.

*[Mrs. Shaw comes back.]*

*Gurly.* How about those rashers and eggs, Bessie?

*Mrs. Shaw.* We shan't be eating until half-past seven, Walter. And it will be fish, not rashers and eggs.

*Gurly.* Sister mine, do you know what you can do with your fish?

*[Gurly goes off. Mrs. Shaw sinks onto the sofa, exhausted and despondent. Lee sits on the piano stool with his back to the instrument, after shutting the lid.]*

*Mrs. Shaw.* It's worse it's getting.

*Lee.* Which being translated, signifieth: It's older *we're* getting.

*[Mrs. Shaw turns her head away from him, hurt.]* I didn't mean that unkindly, Bessie. *[He springs up and paces restlessly.]* Oh, when I think of it: Here I am at the age I am, and where have I got to?

*Mrs. Shaw.* There isn't another teacher in the city to touch you! And people are beginning to realize it.

*Lee.* I should like to believe that.

*Mrs. Shaw.* And your book—a second edition for London and all.

*Lee.* Oh, Dublin, Dublin, Dublin. Great God, if I could only get out of it.

*[Lucy comes in with a lighted oil lamp.]*

*Lucy.* I thought you'd like to have this.

*Mrs. Shaw [Irritably].* It's not dark. Oil is dear enough without lamps blazing all over the place when there's no need for them.

*Lucy [Unperturbed].* Sorry, Mar. *[She turns to go.]*

*Mrs. Shaw.* Oh, leave it, leave it.

*Lucy.* I wish you'd make up your mind. *[She places the lamp on the side table and goes to sit down.]*

*Mrs. Shaw.* Run away, Lucy. I have things to discuss with Lee.

*[Lucy goes out, expressionless.]*

*Lee.* Try not to be so irritable with her.

*Mrs. Shaw.* She's quite impossible these days. I don't know *what's* wrong with her.

*Lee.* Sit down.

*[Mrs. Shaw, with an anxious look at him, sits on the sofa.]*

*Lee.* I had intended to keep this for your birthday, but you need something to cheer you up now. *[He takes a key off his key ring.]* You remember that day up on Dalkey Hill—oh, it was two, three years ago—there was a little cottage you said you'd love to live in.

*Mrs. Shaw.* I shall never forget that day.

*Lee.* Nor shall I, Bessie, nor shall I. *[Abruptly.]* Well, it's yours. The cottage. There's the key. *[He drops the key into her lap.]*

*Mrs. Shaw [Almost voiceless].* Mine, Lee?

*Lee.* It'll be nice for the summer. I've sent in the decorators. The place will be ready in a week.

*Mrs. Shaw.* Oh, Lee, Lee—what can I say?

*Lee.* A small token of gratitude. Now there's the more important thing. I'm giving up the house in Harrington Street.

*Mrs. Shaw [Aghast].* You're leaving?

*Lee.* I'm just moving across to Hatch Street.

*Mrs. Shaw [Sinking back in relief].* For a moment I thought it was London.

*Lee.* It will be, some day. But not just yet.

*Mrs. Shaw.* Well, Hatch Street isn't so far away. You'll be able to drop in to see us.

*Lee [Gravely].* Once I move to Hatch Street, I don't ever want to enter this house again. *[She looks almost terror-stricken.]* Great God, Bessie, don't take me so seriously. I was only teasing—I want you to come and live with me. *[She rises slowly, transfigured by joy.]* Say the word, Bessie, and you can come to Hatch Street. There'll be plenty of room for everyone.

*Mrs. Shaw.* Oh . . . for everyone . . . .

*Lee.* Five bedrooms. Everyone should have a separate bedroom.

*Mrs. Shaw [Sinking down again].* Yes, I suppose they should.

*Lee.* You must be prepared for a certain amount of talk, of course.

*Mrs. Shaw.* Let people talk.

*Lee.* Let them by all means. But if and when they do talk, you mustn't try to run away as you did from that Ellen woman this afternoon.

*Mrs. Shaw.* You mean when she said . . . about the orchard?

*Lee.* She was only chancing her arm. She couldn't be certain it was you. But you admitted it by trying to run away.

*Mrs. Shaw.* What right had *she* to talk?

*Lee.* Yes, I wonder what's happened between herself and Robinson that she wants to come to me as a pupil.

*Mrs. Shaw.* To throw people off the scent. They're having an affair, I know they are.

*Lee [Shrugging].* You know Robinson's reputation—

*Mrs. Shaw.* I don't.

*Lee.* Down at the Academy of Music they've had to put glass panels in the girls' classroom because of him.

*Mrs. Shaw [In disgust].* Oh, men are vile. I remember when *he* tried to paw at me with hot clammy hands.

*Lee [Astounded].* Robinson did!

*Mrs. Shaw.* Robinson? *[Stiffening.]* He wouldn't dare.

*Lee.* Oh—your excellent husband.

*Mrs. Shaw [Witheringly].* Ten minutes after we were married. We came out of the church and got into the cab and then—ugh! *[A moment's silence before Lee, carefully casual but watching her closely, speaks.]*

*Lee.* Have you ever mentioned that to Lucy?

*Mrs. Shaw.* Of course not.

*Lee.* Are you sure?

*Mrs. Shaw.* I'm certain. Oh, I may have made some light reference to it. Why do you ask?

*Lee.* No particular reason—except that I've noticed her talking a lot about "pawing." But I dare say she gets plenty of firsthand information on the subject from that Ellen woman.

*Mrs. Shaw.* You're not going to take her as a pupil, are you?

*Lee.* Her five shillings is just as good as anyone else's.

*Mrs. Shaw.* Oh, but you couldn't.

*Lee [Steering her off the subject].* You haven't yet told me if you're coming to Hatch Street.

*Mrs. Shaw [Flinging her arms wide open in ecstacy].* Oh, Lee, Lee, don't you know my answer already? Imagine escaping from this place! I feel I'm sixteen again. Hatch Street will be heaven, heaven, heaven, heaven.

*Lee [Holding out his hand to her].* God knows you deserve a bit of heaven.

*Mrs. Shaw [Taking his hand].* When do we move?

*Lee.* This minute, if you like.

*Mrs. Shaw [Hesitantly].* But the . . . ?

*Lee.* Perfectly simple. I pay rent and rates.

*Mrs. Shaw [With a fleeting touch of shame].* Oh, we couldn't . . . *[Impulsively kissing Lee's hand.]* Oh, Lee, Lee, Lee, I'm going to start crying.

*[Lee, touched, places his hands on her shoulders, and shakes her gently.]*

*Lee.* No, Bessie, you're not.

*[She bursts into tears and weeps contentedly on his breast. A trombone is heard in the hallway outside, blaring out "Oh Susannah." Lee jumps as if stung, and involuntarily claps his hands over his ears. Mrs. Shaw throws herself on the sofa, crying. Shaw opens the door and comes in, brandishing his trombone.]*

*Shaw.* It's freezing upstairs. I'm trying to blow a little warmth into myself. *[Shocked into sobriety at the sight of his wife's tears.]* Oh, you poor girl, what's the matter? *[She repulses him. He turns to Lee.]* I had to do something to cheer myself up today. Our best customer has gone bankrupt.

*Lee.* What difference will that make?

*Shaw [Smiling wryly].* You're quite right, Lee—as usual. It can't make much difference, can it? *[With sudden resolution.]* But I'm not going to go any farther towards the wall than I can help. I'm really going to go after that hospital contract now. 'Tis not in mortals to command success. But we'll do more, Sempronius; we'll deserve it! *[He raises his trombone to his lips and cries wildly.]* In dulci jubilo!

*[Lee snatches the instrument and hurls it through the open door.*
*Shaw, awed by Lee's ferocity, gazes after his trombone.]*
Shaw. Could you not leave me even that?
*[Shaw goes out. Lee and Mrs. Shaw avoid each other's eyes.]*
Curtain.


## Act Two

*Evening. A reception room at No. 1 Hatch Street, a larger and*
*handsomer apartment than that at Synge Street. Two large win-*
*dows right; a single at back; double doors left, but they have been*
*propped open and the apertures draped with plush curtains. Some*
*of the Synge Street furniture has been transferred here, but is*
*supplemented by new pieces more in keeping with the superior*
*apartment. A conversation seat, centre. Side table with decanters,*
*glasses, plates of sandwiches and tea cakes. A gilt mirror between*
*the plush-draped windows. Faint sounds of party conversation*
*from the room on the left. Lee, in evening dress, stands before the*
*mirror, reknotting his bow tie with care. Lucy comes in, very pretty*
*in a white silk dress. She passes Lee almost as if he weren't there,*
*but he catches at her.*

Lucy *[Twisting out of his grasp and patting her dress where he*
    *gripped her]*. Don't paw. It has taken me hours to get myself
    ready.
Lee. I want to see the result.
Lucy *[Springing around]*. Wait'll you see me kill poor Matt
    McNulty stone dead tonight.
Lee. You like your dress?
Lucy. It's the first grown-up one Par has ever bought me.
Lee. So your excellent father bought it, eh?
Lucy. Jolly well about time, too.
    *[Shaw, in evening dress and white gloves, comes in from the*
    *right.]*
Shaw *[To Lucy]*. The guests, my dear, the guests. You should be
    looking after our guests. Where's your Mar?
Lucy. What do you think of your darling daughter?
Shaw *[Putting on his spectacles]*. A credit to me. Ah, poor Matt
    McNulty, poor Matt.
Lee. I trust you are properly grateful to your father for spending
    so much money on you.

*[Shaw winces. Mrs. Shaw bustles in with the maid.]*

*Mrs. Shaw [To Shaw].* Oh, so you're down at last. Go in and try to make yourself pleasant.

*[Lucy takes her father's arm and both go in to the guests.]*

*Mrs. Shaw.* I don't believe we've enough wine for them.

*Lee.* Some of *them* would drink the ocean dry.

*Mrs. Shaw.* We'll have to get more. *[To the maid.]* Take that tray in, and tell Mr. Shaw I want him.

*[As the maid goes out, Gurly comes in, giving her a surreptitious slap in passing. He carries a half-empty wine glass.]*

*Gurly.* Almighty God, Bessie, where did you get this stuff? Might as well give 'em red biddy.

*Mrs. Shaw.* Nobody else is making a fuss about it.

*Gurly.* No, they're just pouring it on the aspidistras, which are dying of alcoholic poisoning, their poor dear little leaves quivering in convulsions.

*[Shaw comes back.]*

*Shaw.* I thought you wanted me to stay with the guests.

*Lee.* I'll go. *[He goes off.]*

*Mrs. Shaw [To Shaw].* Where did you get that wine you brought in this afternoon?

*Gurly.* Oh, it was *you* who got it. You know, since you've turned teetotaller, your taste in drink has gone to hell. *[He holds the glass under Shaw's nose.]* Smell that. You know what that would do to a brass monkey, don't you?

*Mrs. Shaw.* You'll have to go out and get something people can drink.

*Shaw.* I've no money to spare to booze up Mister Lee's pupils.

*Gurly.* Oh, *I'll* do the needful. *[Slapping Shaw on the back.]* You're a decent old bastard when you have to be, damn your eyes.

*Mrs. Shaw.* Take Matt McNulty with you. He'll help you to carry the things.

*Gurly.* I'm not bringing a bloody vineyard, Bessie. *[He goes.]*

*Mrs. Shaw.* Can you do nothing right?

*Shaw [Muttering].* They're not *my* guests.

*[Ellen appears at the curtains, radiantly dressed and very beautiful.]*

*Ellen.* I'm sure you could do with a helping hand, Lucinda Elizabeth.

*Mrs. Shaw.* I can manage, thank you. *[She sweeps past her into the other room.]*

*Ellen.* It's going to be a really wonderful party, Mr. Shaw.

*Shaw [Cheering up immediately]*. Indeed yes. I think we'll have some good fun when things get moving.

*Ellen [Settling herself on the conversation seat and fanning herself]*. It's warm in there.

*Shaw*. I hope you'll favor us with a song.

*Ellen*. I'm afraid my voice wouldn't be much of a treat for you, Mr. Shaw.

*Shaw [Sitting beside her]*. You needn't be so modest, my dear. If you heard some of the caterwauling that goes on down below when Lee is teaching his prize pupils—!

*Ellen*. Your Lucy has the sweetest voice.

*Shaw*. I only hope she's let keep it. Lee and his confounded "Method," you know.

*Ellen*. Tell me, Mr. Shaw, how do you like living with Mr. Lee?

*Shaw [Quickly]*. It's Lee lives with *us,* dear lady. And he's been knocking about here so long now that he's part of the furniture. We even take him to our little place in Dalkey with us. You must come out there some time. Charming little place. Delightful views. Fell in love with the place the minute I saw it, and said to myself, "I'll take this place no matter what it costs." You need a second place when you have a family.

*[Robinson starts singing "Home Sweet Home" in the next room to piano accompaniment.]*

*Shaw [Appreciatively]*. Ah—Professor Robinson has a really magnificent voice. Plenty of body. None of the wishy-washy stuff Lee goes in for.

*Ellen*. Professor Robinson *is* very virile.

*Shaw*. Your husband isn't here tonight?—or is he? Don't think I've ever met him—or have I? So many people in and out of this house, you know.

*Ellen*. My husband is down at something or other in the college. He's always down at the college, pouring over books.

*Shaw*. So am I. Account books.

*[Lee comes in with a pained expression.]*

*Lee*. Do you hear him? Bellowing in there like a wounded bullock.

*Shaw*. He has a voice. A magnificent one.

*Lee*. Then why not go and bask in it?

*Shaw [Rising]*. We were just going to. *[Offers his arm to Ellen.]* Come, dear lady, let's not miss a bit of *real* singing.

*Ellen*. I think I'd prefer to listen to it from out here, Mr. Shaw. But you mustn't deprive yourself on *my* account.

*Shaw [Going to sit down again]*. In that case, I'll—

*Ellen.* No, no, no—you mustn't deny yourself. I should feel so guilty. Besides, I want one little private word with Professor Lee—about music.

*Shaw.* Well . . . . *[He goes, crestfallen.]*

*Lee.* Was he boring you that much?

*Ellen.* I find him charming.

*Lee.* He has the great charm of being another woman's husband.

*Ellen.* Yours is such a different kind of charm. I long to fathom it, but I get little opportunity. You never speak to me.

*Lee.* It's hard to push through the throng around you.

*Ellen [Laughing].* Oh—just silly boys . . . Mr. Lee, will you be so kind as to give me just the smallest finger of cake? *[He goes to the side table.]* And pray have one yourself.

*Lee [Offering her a plate].* Cake is unwholesome. I only eat brown bread.

*Ellen.* Are all your habits so monastic, Mr. Lee?

*Lee.* They're not scandalous enough to make interesting conversation.

*Ellen.* Then choose your own subject. Let me see if you are the brilliant talker they say you are.

*Lee.* Surely you have your fill of brilliance from your excellent husband.

*Ellen.* The professor doesn't shine in private, Mr. Lee.

*Lee.* Nor do I.

*Ellen.* Well, if you won't choose a subject, I suppose I must. Shall we talk about the young lady nearest your heart?

*Lee [Stolidly].* I am, and propose to remain, in single misery.

*Ellen.* How very unfortunate for us poor women. Is it your . . . leg?

*Lee.* One does not offer one's leg in marriage, madam.

*Ellen.* Little things like that can make a man quite attractive. A very beautiful girl I used to know married a hunchback.

*Lee.* "Used" to know? Had you begun to show some interest in her hunchback?

*Ellen.* The lady is now in India.

*Lee.* You must have frightened her dreadfully.

*Ellen.* Would it help you change your opinion if I told you the hunchback treats her most cruelly?

*Lee.* Women seem to have a taste for that sort of thing.

*Ellen.* You speak from personal experience?

*Lee.* From observation.

*Ellen.* Lucy tells me you are curiously fond of smacking her.

*Lee.* The fondness was not on my side.

*Ellen.* Really? Lucy tells me so much about your teaching methods that I am very anxious to become your pupil.

*Lee.* My timetable is full.

*Ellen.* I am told you have lost some pupils lately.

*Lee.* Not lost. I dismissed them.

*Ellen.* I hardly think you object to me because I'm a married woman. After all, some of your pupils are married women. Even those you give private lessons to.

*Lee.* All my lessons are private.

*Ellen.* How very reassuring.

*Lee.* I do not think of my pupils as married or single. Just voices.

*Ellen.* Is that why they leave you?

*Lee.* And go to your friend Professor Robinson.

*Ellen [Crossing to him slowly].* Professor Robinson isn't that much my friend, Mr. Lee. I like friends whom I can *admire*. Men of character. Brains. Ability. Appearance doesn't count so much with me. *[She caresses his cheek; he remains impassive.]* You're positively blushing, Mr. Lee.

*Lee.* I am more used to this kind of assault in the streets at night.

*Ellen [Smiling].* I'm not in the least offended.

*Lee.* Apparently. Why can't you take no for an answer to whatever question you're putting to me?

*Ellen [Softly, as she moves closer to him].* Because it is comically obvious that your body is answering yes. *[Whispering.]* Was that . . . below the belt, George John? *[She kisses him, then stands back and looks quite coolly at him.]*

*Lee.* Why me?

*Ellen.* Why not you? *[A pause.]* Or do you mean you're not interested?

*Lee [His self-confidence ebbing].* What do you want?

*Ellen.* You. *[With a little laugh, she sits on the conversation seat.]* Why do you look so shocked?

*Lee.* Why should you want to trap me?

*Ellen.* Only into my arms. *[She makes a small eloquent gesture. He nervously moves a quarter-step backwards.]* Oh my goodness, don't tell me you're going to go all coy on me.

*Lee [With a brave show of his old masterfulness].* Dear lady, you're not dealing with an inexperienced boy.

*Ellen [Leaning back seductively].* Am I not? *[Her voice becomes soft and husky.]* Or do you prefer . . . girls?

*Lee.* What do you mean?

*Ellen.* Inexperienced girls.

*Lee.* Are you accusing me of—?

*Ellen [Now quite impudently showing that she feels herself mistress of the situation].* Of what, George John? *[He doesn't answer. She rises luxuriously.]* Oh George John, George John, I don't accuse people. I merely ask for information.

*Lee.* Are you trying to extort money from me?

*Ellen [Nettled at last, she turns away angrily].* Now really, Mr. Lee—

*Lee [Quickly and humbly].* I beg your pardon.

*Ellen [Turning, mollified].* Why are you so afraid? *[Realizing he doesn't understand.]* Of women?

*Lee [Drawing himself up and too emphatic to be convincing].* I am not afraid of any mortal woman.

*Ellen [Going over and patting his cheek].* You're terrified of them, George John. Did some woman disappoint you? Or sisters—have you no sisters? That could account for it, you know. I've known several men like you. *[Taking his hand.]* There's no need to be afraid of me—*[Slowly]*—no need to be afraid of me. *[She puts his hand on her breast.]* I am flesh and blood like yourself. *[After a moment she throws his hand away gaily.]* A little shy retiring violet, who shares the passions of—*[She looks intently into his eyes.]*

*Lee [Spellbound].* Cleopatra.

*Ellen [Giggles and sits on the conversation seat].* There! We're getting along famously.

*Lee.* Are we? *[Suddenly he seizes her hand and kisses it.]*

*Ellen.* My goodness, how hard you made me work. *[He tries to pull her up.]* Now now, Mr. Lee, what are you trying to do?

*Lee [Fiercely].* If you love me— *[He has forced her to rise.]*

*Ellen.* I never said I did. *[He is chilled, but retains his grip on her arms. She places an elegant forefinger against his waistcoat and pushes lightly.]* Keep your distance . . . sir. *[He releases her and limps with assumed dignity towards the double doors.]* George John. *[He stops but doesn't look around.]* I shall. *[He half looks around.]* At a more appropriate time. In a more appropriate place. *[She holds out her hand.]* That's a promise.

*Lee [Turning].* A woman's promise.

*Ellen [Laughing].* Oh George John, George John, you must have been badly bitten. Aren't we going to shake hands on it? *[He comes over and kisses her hand lightly.]* Like all men, you are very impatient. You're saying to yourself, why not *now*?

*Lee.* Have you any answer to that question?

*Ellen.* You want me to come to your room—now?

*Lee [A hoarse whisper].* We could.

*[Ellen looks around half apprehensive, half restless. Lee begins to see, with wonder, that she too is roused.]*

*Ellen.* You'd be missed.

*Lee [Hot and eager].* They'd think I'd gone for a walk. They're used to my—my—my ways. *[Drawing her to the other door.]* Quick, while that bloody man is still bellowing.

*Ellen [Only half resisting].* Oh no—it's too risky—ah, George, please don't—it can only be for a moment—*[Almost a sob.]*—ah, George, can't you wait? You have my promise. You—

*[Lee has brought her to the door and opens it, but shuts it quickly.]*

*Lee.* Damnation. *[He pushes her towards the conversation seat.]* Sit down there.

*[She does so. Gurly comes in exuberantly. His doctor's bag bulges with bottles.]*

*Gurly.* Fresh supplies on the way. Starving garrison relieved. *[He takes out bottles of wine and spirits one by one, placing them on the side table.]* You pair look as if you were up to something.

*Ellen [Perfectly equal to the situation].* Goodness, we couldn't hide anything from *you.* Actually, we were planning to elope.

*Gurly [His suspicions completely allayed].* Wonderful, wonderful, wonderful. I hope you'll have time for a glass of port before you go. Wait'll you taste this—ah, a gorgeous wine. Such body. Such blood.

*Ellen.* You'll have us all under the table.

*Gurly.* If I get you under the table, dear lady—! Oh damn, I nearly forgot. Lee, will you tell Lucy her sister's calling for her. *[Lee goes, relieved to be out of the room.]* Poor Yuppy, everyone has forgotten about her tonight, with the party going on.

*Ellen.* Is she sick again, Dr. Gurly?

*Gurly.* The poor child has been in bed for the past week.

*Ellen.* She *is* inclined to be delicate, I believe.

*Gurly.* She'll never comb a grey head. I give her two years at most.

*Ellen.* Oh no!

*Gurly [Taking out the last bottle].* Don't say I said it. They don't realize here she's as bad as she is.

*Ellen.* But surely you should warn them, so they could do something.

*Gurly [Refilling decanters].* It's a hopeless case. Anyway, I prefer to keep out of it. My sister doesn't think I'm much of a doctor. Familiarity, you know. She puts her faith in that fellow Lee.

*Ellen.* How do you mean?

*Gurly.* Didn't you know that Lee fancies himself as a faith healer?

Yes, Bessie once got a pain in her belly, and Lee gave her a dose of salts, and she now worships him as another Hippocrates.
*[Lucy comes in.]*
*Gurly.* Your sister's bawling for you.
*Lucy [Going off right].* Yuppy does pick her moments, doesn't she?
*Gurly.* I don't know why I let my tongue run away like this with you, when I know you'll be babbling it all out to Bessie. Not that I give a tupenny damn.
*Ellen.* You can trust me, Dr. Gurly.
*Gurly.* I'll have to now, whether I like it or not.
*[Mrs. Shaw comes in.]*
*Mrs. Shaw.* Oh—so you *are* back?
*Gurly.* I got down and back in ten minutes. I'm not a bird.
*Mrs. Shaw.* What did you get?
*Gurly.* Six claret, six port, three sherry, and three whiskey.
*Mrs. Shaw.* No brandy?
*Gurly.* They're doing bloody well, Bessie.
*Ellen.* Oh yes indeed, there's plenty of everything. Too much in fact.
*[Robinson appears at the curtains, glass in hand, with some of the guests.]*
*Robinson [Boisterously].* Now, now, now, Mrs. Shaw, you can't run away on us like this. You must sing for us—public demand— "Hear My Prayer." *[The piano in the next room begins to play Mendelssohn's Spring Song. Robinson's face lights up. He thrusts his glass into the hand of the nearest guest.]* Spring is in the air! *[He begins to pirouette, encouraged by laughter and applause by the guests. He seizes Ellen and dances off with her into the next room.]*
*Mrs. Shaw.* If I thought this was the way Joseph Robinson would carry on, one foot across my door he would not have put.
*Gurly.* Bessie, you're the last person in the world who should give a party.
*Mrs. Shaw [Muttering].* An orgy.
*Gurly.* Orgy! Dear God, I've had more fun at a funeral.
*[Lucy puts her head around the door.]*
*Lucy.* Yuppy's spitting blood again—but not much. Will I run over and get the doctor?
*Gurly.* Oh yes, run and get the doctor. There isn't one here, of course.
*Mrs. Shaw [Fussed].* Yes, get the doctor, and tell Yuppy I'll be up to her in a minute—as soon as I possibly can. *[Noticing that*

*Gurly is drinking from a whiskey bottle.]* Will *you* kindly not turn yourself into a beast.

*Gurly.* Beasts drink water; I promise not to be such a beast as to drink any water on this holy and blessed night. Anyway, who the hell is paying for it?

*[Mrs. Shaw puts some decanters on a tray and carries them into the next room. As Gurly is taking another swig from the bottle, a tall thin man in black opens the door. He wears a cape and carries his tall hat in his hand. This is Dr. Ferdinand Shaw, Fellow of Trinity College, Dublin. Although he is not quite as old as Ellen's remarks imply, his sober suit and long straggling beard give him an elderly air.]*

*Gurly [Disliking him at sight].* Who are you?

*Dr. Shaw [Returning Gurly's dislike with interest].* I should not imagine I am a very welcome visitor.

*Gurly.* You state the obvious.

*Dr. Shaw.* The hall door was open.

*Gurly.* Did it follow that you had to come in?

*Dr. Shaw.* My wife, sir. Is she here?

*Gurly.* I neither know nor care.

*Dr. Shaw.* Whom am I addressing?

*Gurly.* A gentleman, and kindly remember it.

*[Dr. Shaw takes a card from his case and holds it out to Gurly who makes no move to accept it.]*

*Dr. Shaw [Replacing his card].* Perhaps I'm wrong in presuming you can read.

*[Before Gurly can retort, there is a loud gust of laughter from the other room, and the curtains belly out as Robinson whirls in, holding Ellen aloft. Ellen starts on seeing her husband and wriggles out of Robinson's grasp. The hubbub dies down quickly. Robinson moves discreetly to the background.]*

*Dr. Shaw.* So this is the aunt you were visiting.

*Ellen.* I'm sure Mr. and Mrs. Shaw would be delighted to welcome you if you wish to stay, Ferdie.

*Dr. Shaw.* This is not the kind of society I am accustomed to frequent.

*Gurly.* Whatever society you frequent, it wouldn't appear to be good society.

*Dr. Shaw.* And what position, pray, do *you* occupy in this menage?

*Ellen.* Ferdie, it would be better if we went home.

*Dr. Shaw.* Silence!

*Gurly.* Shout again, and I'll kick you down the damn stairs.

*Robinson.* Kicking is what he deserves.

*Dr. Shaw [Turning on Robinson].* I shall know how to deal with you presently.

*Robinson.* If it weren't for the respect I have for your wife—

*Dr. Shaw.* Where's your respect for your own wife? You despicable adulterer!

*Robinson.* Hah! I know who *you* have been talking to. *[To the others.]* Taking advantage of the ravings of a sick woman.

*Dr. Shaw.* Not so raving, sir. She was able to tell me where you were to be found.— *[To Ellen]* —and where *you* were to be found too.

*Robinson.* Oh these insinuations! If anybody is interfering with anybody's wife, it's you're interfering with mine.

*Dr. Shaw.* She came to my house this evening.

*[Lee and Mrs. Shaw appear at the curtains.]*

*Lee.* What is all this about?

*Robinson.* This fellow—interfering with my wife—a sick woman—encouraging her ravings about me.

*Dr. Shaw.* You contemptible—

*Robinson.* This is libel. And there's law in the country yet.

*Dr. Shaw.* She told me they hadn't been married one year before he was casting sheep's eyes on—

*Robinson.* Libel. Defamation. I'll take an action against him. You are witnesses.

*Lee [To Dr. Shaw].* Please continue this brawl elsewhere.

*Robinson.* A fine fellow to be preaching. He beats his wife. Yes, you do, and don't deny it. *[To the others.]* With my own eyes I have seen the bruises on her body.

*Gurly [Guffawing].* You lucky devil, Robinson, you lucky devil.

*Robinson.* Her arms, sir, her arms.

*Ellen [Taking her husband's arm].* Ferdie, will you please— *[Dr. Shaw pushes her away violently. She stumbles against the conversation seat.]*

*Robinson [Crowing].* Now you see! The brute! This is the sort of thing she has to suffer every night in the week. Dear, dear lady, are you in pain?

*Dr. Shaw [Exploding].* Great God!

*[Dr. Shaw hurls himself on Robinson. Gurly seizes him from behind and pinions his arms. Lee moves towards the other room.]*

*Gurly.* Don't leave me with this maniac, Lee.

*Lee.* I am merely asking our guests to leave.

*[He goes out, shepherding the guests in front of him. Mrs. Shaw follows.]*

*Dr. Shaw [Panting, but in control of himself].* Will you kindly let
  me go?
*Gurly.* If you undertake to stop behaving like a coalheaver.
  *[He releases him.]*
*Dr. Shaw [Smoothing his clothes].* I have nothing more to say. *[To
  Ellen.]* Get ready and come home.
*Ellen [Sobbing].* I am not going home with you.
*Dr. Shaw.* Don't be silly.
*Ellen.* I am not going home with you, tonight or any other night.
*Gurly.* I'm afraid he *is* your husband.
*Dr. Shaw.* Kindly do not interfere in what doesn't concern you.
*Ellen.* It's no use, Ferdie.
*Dr. Shaw.* I am not discussing my private affairs before a public
  gallery. Come home, Ellen.
*Ellen [Developing signs of hysterics].* No, no, no, I tell you. Go
  away from me.
*Dr. Shaw [Putting his arms around her and speaking command-
  ingly].* Ellen—Ellen—Ellen—stop it now. *[To the others.]* Will
  you leave us for a moment, please?
*Gurly.* Only if the lady wishes us to.
*Dr. Shaw.* Do you realize the woman is my wife?
*Gurly.* She has our sympathy.
*Robinson.* Let's kick him down the stairs.
*Gurly.* By God, I'm tempted to.
*Ellen [Still sobbing, but realizing the situation might grow uglier].*
  Let him have a moment w-w-with me.
*Gurly.* I'm very reluctant to entrust you—
*Ellen. Please.* I'll—I'll be all right.
*Robinson.* Dear lady, we shall remain within call.
  *[Gurly and Robinson go to the other room.]*
*Dr. Shaw.* Now that you've made enough of a show of yourself,
  pull yourself together and come home.
*Ellen.* I'm not going home.
*Dr. Shaw.* I may have been a little hasty, but God knows I have
  enough provocation.
*Ellen.* Leave me alone, Ferdie. That's all I ask.
*Dr. Shaw.* All right, all right, all right. *[More tenderly.]* It seems I
  haven't apologized enough. *[Sweetly reasonable.]* But why have
  I to apologize? Would any other husband put up with what I put
  up with? Who'd blame me if I pitched you and your children into
  the gutter?
*Ellen.* They're your children too.

*Dr. Shaw.* All of them?

*Ellen.* I'll say no more, Ferdie. *[She moves away from him.]*

*Dr. Shaw.* Oh yes, injured innocence, the last refuge of *your* kind. Now listen here, Ellen, I'm coming to the end of my patience.

*Ellen [Rounding on him].* So am I. I am not going to take second place to your wormy old books any longer, Ferdie.

*Dr. Shaw [Withering].* If you want to find reasons for your behavior, find credible ones. You've had your little scene. Now get your hat on and come home.

*Ellen.* I'm not going with you.

*Dr. Shaw [Gripping the back of a chair to restrain himself].* Ellen, if you don't want me to hammer you into a pulp—!

*Ellen [Tauntingly].* You can't do it here, Ferdie.

*[Dr. Shaw's burst of temper passes suddenly. His body sags, all the energy seems to go out of him, and he sinks on a chair with a sigh of weariness.]*

*Dr. Shaw.* Ellen, I'm not *able* for these fights. I'm getting now to the stage where I must have peace and quiet in my home. If you're not prepared to be a wife to me, well and good. God knows, I'm an easy man to get on with if I'm not constantly tormented.

*Ellen [Beginning to recover herself].* Who torments you?

*Dr. Shaw.* Let there be no more argument. Are you coming or are you not? Yes or no.

*Ellen.* No.

*Dr. Shaw.* If you don't come now, you will not cross my door again. I mean that.

*Ellen.* Very well. Send the children to my sister. She wants to take them.

*Dr. Shaw [Rising].* This is my reward for being a good husband. Had I treated you the way some husbands treat their wives, starved you, come home drunk, left you and the children without a ha'penny, I'd have been thought more of.

*Ellen.* When you go on like that, Ferdie, I only want to laugh.

*Dr. Shaw.* That's all you're good for—laugh—you empty-headed little slut. You filthy little—ugh! Oh, Christ in Heaven, when I think how I'm chained to you, you bitch, you streetwalker, you whore, you— *[He lapses into inarticulate growls.]*

*Ellen.* If you're finished throwing bouquets to me, there's just one thing I have to say.

*Dr. Shaw.* I don't want to hear it.

*Ellen.* You're not chained to me. I give you your freedom. *[Proudly.]* I want no man who doesn't want *me*.

*[The facade suddenly cracks. She sobs convulsively.]*

*Dr. Shaw.* Now whine and whinge—oh, you revolt me. How many times have I forgiven you? How many times have I wiped out the past and—

*Ellen.* Wiped out the past!! You've remembered every little thing, and you throw it in my face ten times a day.

*Dr. Shaw.* I do *not*.

*Ellen [Quietly].* Ferdie, you want to go. You want to be free.

*Dr. Shaw.* My God, who's talking!

*Ellen.* You should never have been married.

*Dr. Shaw.* You could sing that if you had a tune to it, my darling.

*Ellen.* You don't want me. Very well. I'll go.

*Dr. Shaw.* You'll go nowhere. You'll come home and be damned to you.

*Ellen.* An irresistible invitation.

*Dr. Shaw.* Going around complaining that I'm fifteen years older than you—don't think I haven't heard about it. Though that doesn't stop you flinging yourself at that old lecher who's thirty years older than you. Now—come on, before I do something I'll be sorry for.

*Ellen.* No.

*Dr. Shaw.* For the last time—

*Ellen.* No.

*[He turns on his heel and goes off, banging the door. Robinson slithers in, mournfully shaking his head.]*

*Robinson.* So that's what's biting him. I'm thirty years older than you, am I? The venomous blackguard!

*Ellen.* Well, I've done it at last. What's going to happen to me now?

*Robinson.* Now, now, now, my dear, don't talk like that. You mustn't do anything rash. You can't break up your home. Marriage ties are sacred. He'll have cooled down tomorrow, and then you can go back and patch things up. Even Fanny doesn't remain at boiling point for more than a day.

*Ellen.* Not this time, Joe. I've broken free, and I'm going to stay free.

*Robinson.* Free to do what? Starve?

*Ellen.* Probably. I have six shillings in my purse—that's all.

*Robinson.* You have good friends—staunch friends—and we'll all rally around. But of course we won't be able to *do* anything—I mean, do anything much.

*Ellen.* Do you think they'd let me stay here for tonight?

*Robinson.* They'll have to. I can't bring you over to *my* place.

*Ellen.* Oh, Fanny would enjoy that.

*Robinson.* Anyway, it's your husband's duty to support you, whether you're living with him or not.

*Ellen.* I dare say he'll give me something. Ferdie's not mean about money. *[Smiling.]* I'm not asking you for anything, Joe.

*Robinson.* Anything I'm in a position to give, I'll give you with pleasure. But I've heavy expenses. Living in Fitzwilliam Street . . . and the doctor three and four times a week for Fanny. Not that there's anything the matter with her. She just works herself up over nothing. *[With a sense of intolerable grievance].* It would be physically impossible for me to do what she says I do. A different woman every—ah, no matter.

*Ellen.* Poor Joe.

*Robinson.* At *my* age. And it's interfering dreadfully with my singing. After a session with Fanny, I simply *cannot* stay in tune. I keep going sharp.

*[Mrs. Shaw and Lee come back.]*

*Ellen.* Lucinda Elizabeth, how can I tell you how sorry I am—

*Mrs. Shaw.* There's nothing can be done about it now.

*Lee.* Has he gone?

*Robinson.* Oh, yes, I got rid of him. *[He sits.]*

*Lee [To Ellen].* I take it you're not going home tonight.

*Ellen.* I'd sooner walk around the streets.

*Lee.* I'm sure we can offer you hospitality.

*Mrs. Shaw [Coldly].* Well, if she wishes to stay . . . .

*Ellen.* Oh, Lucinda Elizabeth, this is too kind of you.

*Mrs. Shaw.* You'll have to share with Lucy, I'm afraid.

*[Shaw and Lucy come to the landing door with Dr. Morgan. Morgan is stout and with a hearty manner.]*

*Shaw.* Dr. Morgan has been up with Yuppy.

*Morgan [Rubbing his hands].* Nothing to worry about—nothing in the world to worry about. Our young friend has a touch of a cough, and there's a hint of a drop of blood, but nothing that need alarm you.

*Lee [Sitting on the conversation seat].* What can you expect? The doors of her room kept hermetically sealed. And living on this confounded white bread.

*Morgan [Surprised by Lee's vehemence].* My dear sir, I don't see how either circumstance has any bearing on the case.

*Lee.* Naturally you don't. If people lived sensibly, you'd starve.

*Morgan [His hackles rising].* I'm afraid I haven't the pleasure . . . .

*Mrs. Shaw.* Mr. Lee is a very dear friend of our family.

*Morgan.* Mr. Lee . . . *[Remembering.]* Ah, Mr. Lee, the singing master! *[His contempt becomes open.]* Your face was familiar, but I couldn't place you for the moment. You run a club for singers and fiddlers, don't you?

*Lee.* Come on, Doctor, let us have your diagnosis.

*Morgan [Turning his back on Lee and addressing Shaw].* There's absolutely nothing to worry about, Mr. Shaw. I could recommend a change of air and scenery—a few months in the country would do our little friend a world of good.

*Mrs. Shaw.* We have a summer place at Dalkey.

*Morgan.* Sea air—a little too sharp. Country air is what I had in mind. Perhaps your august relation at Rathfarnham—perhaps Sir Robert might offer the hospitality of Bushy Park to—?

*Shaw.* I'll have a word with Sir Robert about it. But if you think Dalkey would be all right, it would certainly be more convenient.

*Morgan.* Oh, sea air will do quite well. We can at least try the experiment.

*Lee.* If your experiment fails, Doctor, won't it be rather hard on the poor girl?

*Morgan [With a half-glance at Lee].* I am merely a qualified physician. I haven't the inestimable medical advantage of knowing about doh rah me fah so.

*Lee.* I shall be glad to instruct you at any time.

*Morgan.* Doubtless, I believe you are not overburdened with pupils. *[To Mrs. Shaw.]* As I told you, there's nothing to worry about. Change of air . . . plenty of nourishment . . . juicy steaks . . . build up her strength. *[He offers his hand.]*

*Mrs. Shaw [Shaking hands].* Goodnight, Doctor, and thank you.

*Lee.* Don't forget to pay the man. The most important part of the treatment.

*Morgan.* In your treatment, perhaps; not in mine.

*Lee [Reddening].* Oh, pay the fellow and let him go.

*Shaw [After unconvincingly feeling his pocket].* I say, Lee, could you—er— *[Lee contemptuously throws over his purse.]* Thank you. This will save me going upstairs. When I changed my suit this evening, I left all my money in my other pocket.

*[While Shaw is fumbling in the purse, Morgan turns to Mrs. Shaw and starts drawing on his gloves in half-suppressed anger.]*

*Morgan.* We'll soon have our little friend on her feet again. *[Making conversation.]* That was an appalling business tonight.

*Shaw [Handing him some money].* Somebody in the river again?

*Morgan [Putting the money in his own purse].* No. A woman threw herself out of a window.

*Ellen.* How awful! Was she badly hurt?

*Morgan.* Killed. From the fourth floor. I practically saw it happening myself. Poor creature—out of her mind.

*Shaw.* Where did it happen, Doctor?

*Morgan.* Just across the road. Fitzwilliam Street.

*Robinson [Looking up].* Fitzwilliam Street?

*Morgan.* Yes, number three.

*[Dead silence in the room. Every head turns slowly towards Robinson, who rises, quivering.]*

*Morgan [Hesitantly].* A Mrs. Robinson it was.

*[Deep-drawn sound of horror and terror comes gurgling out of Robinson's throat. He tries to speak but cannot; when the words finally come, they are just a babble.]*

*Robinson.* It wasn't my fault . . . you heard him say she was out of her mind . . . she was always threatening to do it . . . .

*Morgan [Aghast].* Good heavens—is this—Mr. Robinson?

*Robinson [Clutching his head].* What am I to do—what am I to do? *[He mumbles inarticulately. Morgan and Shaw hurry over to comfort him. Lee rises.]* It must have been an accident . . . an accident. She had no worries. I was a good husband to her. She wanted for nothing. Oh, what am I going to do? What am I going to do?

*Lee.* We had better go over to the house immediately.

*Robinson.* I couldn't—I couldn't.

*Lee.* Somebody will go with you.

*Shaw.* I will.

*Mrs. Shaw.* I will too.

*Ellen.* So will I . . . if it wouldn't be wrong of me.

*[Mrs. Shaw goes out. Ellen follows her.]*

*Lee [Handing a glass of whiskey to Robinson].* Take this.

*Robinson [Hardly touching it to his lips].* Nobody can blame me. I did my best for her. *[He hands the glass to Morgan.]*

*Morgan.* Of course, you did, my dear Mr. Robinson. And may I say I hadn't the least idea you were—

*Shaw.* Of course not, of course not.

*Morgan.* And will you please accept my deepest—er—

*Robinson.* She didn't—she didn't say anything before she—?

*Morgan.* The poor lady was dead before anyone reached her.

*Robinson.* They sometimes leave notes. It mustn't get into the papers. They couldn't put it in without my permission. *[Closing his eyes.]* Such dreadful publicity! *[With renewed horror.]* Will there be an inquest?

*Morgan.* Well—but you need have no fears, Mr. Robinson. These things are always conducted with the utmost sympathy for the feelings of relatives. It was a tragedy. What can anyone feel for you except the profoundest sympathy?

*Shaw.* Indeed, indeed, indeed.

*Morgan.* And now, my dear sir, you must look to yourself. You must take great care—a heavy affliction has fallen upon you, but you must not allow yourself to go to pieces. *[Holding out the glass of whiskey.]* Try and take another mouthful—come, come, you owe it to yourself—you must bear up, Mr. Robinson. There— that's it—and another mouthful. Is there any—hmm—any family?

*Shaw.* No.

*Morgan.* A blessing from God.

*Robinson.* She couldn't have any children.

*Shaw [Deeply touched].* The poor, poor creature.

*Morgan. [Almost buoyant].* As I said, a blessing from God. Had you been left with half a dozen—responsibilities—you'd be—oh, a blessing, a blessing. *[Robinson, his eyes glistening, clasps Morgan's hand impulsively.]* Another mouthful, dear sir, try another mouthful. You must try to take care of yourself.

*[Mrs. Shaw and Ellen return in outdoor dress.]*

*Shaw [Taking Robinson's arm].* It won't be such an ordeal with friends around you.

*Lucy [Nervously].* Is everyone going?

*Lee.* I'll stay here with you.

*Mrs. Shaw.* Yes, please do. *[To Lucy.]* We shan't be very long.

*[Mrs. Shaw, Ellen and Robinson, who is supported on either side by Shaw and Morgan, go out.]*

*Lee.* Well, that poor woman is better off dead than having to put up with such a blackguard.

*Lucy [Putting her hand to her forehead].* Imagine her being able to *do* it—to actually *do* it.

*Lee.* It's a happy release for everyone concerned. *[He puts his arm around her shoulder.]* Now, now, don't work yourself into a state over this business. When death is about, life doesn't bear thinking of.

*Lucy [Pushing his arm away].* I'll go up and sit with Yuppy.

*Lee.* The less you are with your sister, the better. It's contagious. *[Lucy glances at him contemptuously.]* You are young, Lucy, and don't understand the risks. *[He draws her towards the conversation seat.]* Come, I'll cheer you up.

*Lucy.* I don't want to be cheered up.

*Lee [Pulling her round to face him].* Now, now, now—

*Lucy [Breaking away from him]*. Keep your hands off me.

*Lee*. My dear Lucy—

*Lucy [Viciously]*. I wish you'd get somebody your own age and leave me alone.

*Lee [Stiffening]*. I have something to say to you.

*Lucy*. I don't want to hear it.

*Lee [Commandingly]*. Sit down, Lucy.

*Lucy*. I'm not afraid of you any longer.

*Lee*. I never wanted you to be afraid of me.

*Lucy*. All right, all right. Now let's leave it at that.

*Lee*. Have I done anything to you?

*Lucy*. You bore me.

*Lee*. Everyone will bore you sooner or later. There have been times when you have bored me.

*Lucy*. Have I? Oh, thank you.

*Lee [With momentary dislike]*. I sometimes wonder why I ever condescended to speak a word to you.

*Lucy [Going]*. Nobody's asking you to condescend any more.

*Lee [Taking her arm]*. I'm not going to fight with you. Come.

*Lucy [Pushing him away so violently that he staggers]*. Don't start pawing me, I tell you.

*Lee [With cold anger]*. Take care, Lucy. Be civil at least. Remember whose house you are in.

*Lucy*. It's as much our house as yours, and if you don't like that you know what to do about it.

*Lee [Angry]*. Who's paying the rent? Who's paying the rates? Who's paying the quack to come and spout his damned nonsense about your sister?

*Lucy*. If you weren't snug and comfortable, you wouldn't stay.

*Lee*. Who put that dress on your back?

*[Lucy receives this like a blow.]*

*Lucy [Slowly]*. Was it—?

*Lee [A little ashamed]*. I don't want to make a song and dance about it.

*[In a gust of fury, Lucy rips her sleeve.]*

*Lee*. If you want to be melodramatic, do it with something a little less expensive.

*Lucy*. I'm giving it back to you.

*Lee*. I can't wear it.

*Lucy*. It might come in handy the next time you're seducing a pupil.

*Lee [Disgusted]*. If that's the sort of remark you're going to fling around—!

*Lucy*. Isn't it true?

*Lee.* Has it come to this between us now?

*Lucy.* You're old enough to be my father. I was only a child when— *[She stops.]*

Lee. When what?

*Lucy.* I want to go now.

*Lee.* I told you I want to talk to you.

*Lucy.* I'm tired.

*Lee.* It's strange . . . you seem to go out of your way to make me dislike you, despise you, yet you cannot completely kill my old tenderness for you. *[He takes her arm to lead her to a chair.]* Sit down and— *[She shakes him off and stands silent, making it clear that she is staying only because forced.]* You're like all women: Something in you drives you to torment yourself. *[Moving around as he talks, but keeping a watchful eye on her.]* You think happiness is around the corner, you poor dear, but it isn't. Such happiness as you can hope to have in this world is always beside you. Take it, enjoy it, and move on.

*Lucy.* Do you mind if I move on now?

*Lee.* The present, Lucy, the present. One should always make the best of the few lovely moments that come to us. We were both of us wise to snatch at such moments while they were within our reach.

*Lucy.* And now if you're finished preaching—

*Lee.* You're tormenting yourself needlessly, my dear.

*Lucy.* I told you I want to go.

*Lee.* Why?

*Lucy.* There's no why about it. I just want to go. I must go up to Yuppy.

*Lee.* Oh, Yuppy can— *[He stops as he hears voices below and the hall door shutting.]*

*Lucy [With a mocking grin].* They're back.

*Lee [Moving away from her and dropping his voice].* It would be better if you stayed.

*Lucy [Not dropping her voice correspondingly].* Better for who?

*Lee [Looking at her with sudden cold hatred].* Get out. Go to hell.

*Lucy [Dancing over to him and chucking him under the chin].* Not to please you, I won't, darling George.

*[Lee flings away to the most distant chair from Lucy, and flops angrily in it. Lucy arranges herself in a demure posture in the middle of the room as Mr. and Mrs. Shaw and Ellen come in. Lee rises.]*

*Mrs. Shaw [Unpinning her hat].* We hadn't far to go. The bereaved husband collapsed at the corner.

*Ellen.* They've taken him off to the hospital.

*Shaw.* In the state he's in, I wouldn't be surprised if he jumped out of the window himself.

*Mrs. Shaw.* He might—if the devil himself were behind him, and he had six inches to jump.

*Ellen [Putting an arm around Lucy].* All this must have been a terrible shock to you, darling.

*Lee.* Lucy has much sensibility.

*Mrs. Shaw.* She's beginning to get a taste of what life is like. Well, I suppose you had better take our—guest—upstairs and show her where she'll be sleeping. I'll be up in a moment. *[Lucy and Ellen go out.]* Oh, Lee, I was never so mortified in all my life, as about tonight. We'll have another party for you. *[Taking off her coat.]* We can't very well have it at the moment, I suppose, but in a month or six weeks perhaps.

*Lee [Abruptly].* Bessie, I've made up my mind.

*Mrs. Shaw [Alarmed].* What's wrong?

*Lee.* The time has come for me to go to London. For too long I have been made a convenience of here.

*Mrs. Shaw [Reddening].* Who has been making a convenience of you?

*Lee.* The whole of Dublin has been. They have taken all and given nothing.

*Shaw [Coming forward; the others had almost forgotten he was there].* I've always felt London was your proper sphere.

*Lee [Dryly].* You won't press me to stay?

*Shaw.* Hang it, no. I shan't stand in your way. *[Brightening up with every word.]* We'll miss your little contribution to the exchequer, of course. But we'll manage. I'm going to put all thoughts of self aside. We shan't try to hang onto you, Lee. At a time like this, it's help you need, not hindrance. And—and— *[His voice trails off as he sees his wife's face.]*

*Lee.* Thank you. I value your good wishes.

*Shaw [In a soberer tone].* Needless to say, I'm sorry you have to go. We've pegged along here very comfortably all these years. We shall miss you. You were just one of the family. The house won't be the same without you.

*Lee.* You'll keep on this house?

*Shaw [Quickly].* Oh, of course. It would be unthinkable to go back to Synge Street.

*Lee.* Of course.

*Mrs. Shaw [In complete self-command].* When are you going?

*Lee [avoiding her gaze].* The sooner the better.

*Mrs. Shaw.* Is it—is it what happened tonight is making you go?

*Lee.* Oh, no. Or perhaps it *was* what happened tonight. But you know it's been in my mind for a long time. *[Briskly.]* However, we needn't talk any more about it tonight.

*Mrs. Shaw.* How about your November concert?

*Lee [Shrugging].* Perhaps my next concert will be in London. The Albert Hall.

*Shaw.* You don't think the Albert Hall is a bit ambitious?

*Lee [Drawing himself up].* I shall give a gala performance there in the presence of the Queen, and I'll pack the place with princes and princesses and dukes and duchesses.

*Shaw.* You're sure they'll come?

*Lee.* They'll be getting free seats. Goodnight. *[He goes off to bed.]*

*Shaw [Flopping in the nearest chair].* Well, my dear, I hate to say I told you so, but I've always warned you that Mister Lee thinks only of Mister Lee. *[She doesn't answer.]* It was just like his cheek, you know, talking about being made a convenience of. That was a knock at us—or at me. However, I let it pass. I'm very glad you didn't let him get away with it though, asking him who was making a convenience of him, I mean. I'm jolly sure Dublin doesn't give two hoots about him. Dublin has paid him well. I don't see that he has anything to complain about.

*Mrs. Shaw.* Are you quite finished?

*Shaw.* Hang it, Bessie, don't take it out on *me*. It's not my fault that he's going. *[Sighing.]* Besides there's always the chance that he may not go at all.

*Mrs. Shaw.* He's not like some people. He means what he says.

*Shaw.* By the way, did you notice Lucy seemed very . . . oh, I don't know . . . but I don't think she's been looking at all well these last few months. *[He wanders to the table and picks up a bottle.]*

*Mrs. Shaw [Half over her shoulder].* Leave that alone.

*Shaw.* You know I don't touch it now.

*Mrs. Shaw.* Yes, after it nearly killed you. *[Rising and pacing around the room like a tigress.]* Not even the money to buy a glass of wine for my friends, nor to pay the doctor for my daughter. Everything you could load on to that unfortunate man's shoulders you did. Is it any wonder he's going?

*Shaw.* Extraordinary how you can't see through that fellow.

*Mrs. Shaw.* Stabbing him in the back again. What'll happen to us when he goes?

*Shaw.* We'll get along as we did before. I'll be getting that hospital contract.

*Mrs. Shaw.* How long have I been hearing about that hospital contract?

*Shaw [Coming over and laying a hand on her shoulder].* Whatever you do, don't depend on *him.*

*Mrs. Shaw.* After my father and you, I depend on no man.

*Shaw [With a sigh].* Oh, all right, all right, all right, I suppose I shall have to climb down again. I'll have a word with him in the morning, and I'll ask him to stay.

*Mrs. Shaw.* You needn't interfere in what doesn't concern you. If he goes, he goes.

*[She sweeps out. Left to himself, Shaw momentarily seems to be about to dash something to the ground in fury, but his temper evaporates, and he almost cheerfully pours out a glass of whiskey and raises it as if proposing a toast.]*

*Shaw.* Bon voyage! *[He pours the whiskey on the nearest plant.]*

*Curtain.*


## Act Three

*The same, six months later. The room has been stripped of furniture and hangings, and is empty except for a wooden crate, a traveling bag, a bandbox, and a few small parcels on the floor near the door. The double doors are slightly ajar. Mrs. Shaw is giving her last instructions to Patrick Cooke, a furniture mover. Shaw hovers in the background.*

*Mrs. Shaw.* I don't want any mistakes—it's no use coming to me afterwards and saying, "Oh, but I thought . . . ."

*Cooke.* It's all right, missis, there won't be any mistakes.

*Mrs. Shaw.* I want my luggage down two hours before the boat goes.

*Cooke.* I've already told you, Missis—

*Mrs. Shaw.* My husband's things can go up to his new lodgings in Harcourt Street later.

*Shaw.* Don't forget to come back for the piano for my son.

*Mrs. Shaw.* The piano will do tomorrow; all you want tonight is your bed.

*Shaw.* I thought he might as well make one go of it.

*[Carroll comes to the door.]*

*Carroll [Gazing around].* Bless my soul, what a very quick clearance!

*Shaw.* Yes, isn't it?

*[Cooke slips away, touching his hat to the rector.]*

*Mrs. Shaw.* We can't afford to let the grass grow under our feet, William.

*Carroll.* So you're really off to London. I couldn't believe it when I heard it.

*Mrs. Shaw.* It has to be. A fine thing at *my* time of life, when I have my family reared, and I should be able to rest and enjoy myself. Now I have to go out and face the world on my own.

*Carroll.* Is it absolutely necessary to break up the home?

*Mrs. Shaw.* We have no choice. We just can't afford to stay here by ourselves.

*Carroll.* But what on earth are you going to do in London?

*Mrs. Shaw.* Teach music. What Lee taught me, I shall teach others.

*Carroll.* That fellow brought bad luck into the family from the day—

*Mrs. Shaw.* He's doing wonderfully well, William. Daughters of the London nobility come to him now—at a guinea a lesson. He has Alderman Sir Timothy Heathcoat's niece and—

*Carroll.* How long will it last?

*Mrs. Shaw.* Do you know where he's living? Park Lane. Park Lane, William. He has bought a house just two doors down from the Marquess of Londonderry.

*Shaw [Muttering].* How delightful for the Marquess.

*Mrs. Shaw.* I hardly imagine that your friend Professor Robinson and Company will be very pleased to hear about *that.* When they had him here, they didn't appreciate him.

*Carroll.* I have not heard anyone bemoaning him.

*[Lucy comes in with Ellen.]*

*Ellen.* So you're going, after all!

*Mrs. Shaw.* Yes.

*Ellen.* We're going to miss you—really we are. Soon there won't be any of the old circle left at all. *[To Shaw.]* And you have to stay behind on your own?

*Shaw [Cheerfully].* Just for the moment, just for the moment. Can't leave my business, you know.

*Ellen [Shaking hands with Carroll].* How do you do, Rector?

*Carroll.* How d'you do? Did we pass each other on the way?

*Ellen.* You sailed past me with your head in the air.

*Carroll.* I mustn't have recognized you.

*Ellen.* I'm getting used to being not recognized by my friends, now that I'm separated from my husband.

*Carroll [Shocked at the insinuation].* I assure you—

*Ellen.* Oh, I wasn't meaning you, Rector. *[Smiling all around.]* Nor my good friends here.

*Shaw.* I'm afraid we can't even offer you a cup of tea—

*Mrs. Shaw.* Everything's packed and gone.

*Shaw.* But we can offer you a seat. *[He leads Ellen to the crate.]*

*Ellen [Curtseying].* Thank you kindly, sir. Well, you won't be too lonely, having your son to stay on with you.

*Shaw.* And Lucy.

*Carroll.* But I thought that Lucy— *[Turning to Lucy.]* I understood you were going with your mama.

*Lucy.* The Mar changed her mind at the last minute.

*Mrs. Shaw.* She will follow later on. I've got to get a roof over my head first.

*Ellen.* I'm sure Mr. Lee will be a great help to you in that, Lucinda Elizabeth. *[To the others.]* He looks as if he's going to do quite well over there. He has rented a house in Park Lane.

*Mrs. Shaw.* Not rented. Bought.

*Ellen.* Are you sure, Lucinda Elizabeth? Rented, he told me.

*Mrs. Shaw [Frowning].* He told *you*?

*Ellen.* I called to see him when I was over in London.

*Mrs. Shaw [Confused].* I didn't know you were over in London.

*Ellen.* I just went over to see if I could manage to live there—on my alimony. It's so much gayer than Dublin. But it's very expensive. The rents—oh dear.

*Shaw.* Yes, I have rather been wondering how Lee is managing to pay his Park Lane palace.

*Ellen.* He has it let out in single rooms. He just keeps one room for himself—the music room. *[Seeing that Carroll is murmuring something to Shaw and that Lucy has drifted over to the window, she casually adds for Mrs. Shaw's benefit.]* And a bedroom, of course. A sweet little room just behind the music room, with a perfectly charming view of the Park in the early morning.

*[Mrs. Shaw stiffens.]*

*Shaw [To Ellen].* Well, it's nice to know that Dublin isn't going to lose you, after all.

*[Ellen and Mrs. Shaw continue to stare at each other.]*

*Ellen [To Shaw, smiling].* You were saying, Mr. Shaw—?

*Shaw.* It's nice to know that Dublin won't be losing you, after all.

*Ellen.* Oh, Dublin doesn't want me at my price. I'm nearly as bad as a divorcee. I can only live now where I am not known; I'm afraid it's Liverpool for me.

*Shaw [Soberly].* We spent our honeymoon in Liverpool.

*Ellen.* I know it isn't exactly Paris. But I'll give it a try.

*[Robinson appears at the door. He is in deep mourning.]*

*Robinson.* Aaah, so it's true. Dear oh dear oh dear oh dear, who would have thought it would come to this? *[To Mrs. Shaw.]* Dear dear lady, you have my profoundest sympathy. *[He kisses her hand.]* The reports are fearfully confused. Some say he has left debts of £5000 behind him. Others say—

*Shaw.* Who has left *what* behind him?

*Robinson.* Oh—have you come back again?

*Shaw.* I was never away.

*Robinson.* It's all over Dublin that you've gone bankrupt to the tune of £5000 and—well, you don't appear to have fled to the Continent.

*Carroll.* I trust, Mr. Robinson, that if you hear any more of these atrocious stories you'll scotch them. My brother-in-law has *not* run away, and is perfectly solvent.

*Robinson.* I'm glad to hear that. Usually, though, there's no smoke without fire. And it's so distressing to hear of any trouble between husband and wife. Since God called to Himself my own little darling in that awful accident, I haven't known what it is to smile. *[Beaming at Ellen.]* Aaah, dear lady, I'm forgetting my manners. *[He kisses her hand and pats it.]* How are you keeping, how are you keeping? I saw your husband at the College sports the other day. *[To the others.]* You wouldn't think the ruffian had a care in the world. Aaah, men may laugh, but women must weep. Perhaps I am touching open wounds, but I do so only in a spirit of comradely sympathy. *[Bowing his head.]* I know what it is to suffer. *[Cheerfully.]* Well, my dear Shaw, I am very happy—really very happy to find that things aren't as bad with you as I'd heard. *[In a lower tone.]* I take it that Mrs. Shaw is leaving you.

*Carroll.* Really, Robinson, we've no right to cross-question people about their—

*Robinson.* My dear Rector, I didn't realize you'd heard me. I am not just being inquisitive. You yourself have asked me to scotch false stories. But if I'm to do that, I must know the facts.

*Mrs. Shaw.* Gossip doesn't worry me, Mr. Robinson.

*Robinson.* Nor me. I never listen to it. Never.

*Mrs. Shaw [In dismissal].* It was very kind of you to come to see me.

*Robinson.* Don't mention it. If I'd missed seeing you, I'd never have forgiven myself. It has all been so sudden though.

*Mrs. Shaw.* When one makes up one's mind, one should act immediately. Now I'm afraid I must get ready to go.

*Carroll.* The boat doesn't leave till seven.

*Mrs. Shaw.* The sooner I'm on board, the better. I'll try to get some sleep before the sea gets rough.

*Ellen.* We'll all go down and give you a good send-off.

*Mrs. Shaw [Quickly].* Oh, please no.

*Robinson.* No trouble at all. We'll be only too delighted to see you off. *[Hastily.]* I mean it'll be no . . . well, you know what I mean.

*Mrs. Shaw.* I'd prefer you didn't.

*Robinson.* But we simply couldn't let you—

*Ellen.* Lucinda Elizabeth might prefer just to have her family with her, Mr. Robinson.

*Robinson.* Oh, of course of course of course of course.

*Mrs. Shaw.* I would prefer nobody came at all—not even my family. I hate fussy leavetakings. We'll say good-bye to one another here, and Lucy will come in the cab with me.

*Robinson.* Yes, I suppose that's very . . . sensible. And poor little Lucy here. You must be very, very sad, my dear. *[Patting her cheek.]* My, what a pretty little thing you're growing into. What lovely coloring. And how are you getting along with your lessons now that our friend Lee has vanished? You must come to *me,* my dear.

*Lucy.* Must I?

*Robinson.* Don't bother to thank me, my dear; it'll be a pleasure. *[Beaming at Shaw.]* Don't worry. I'm not thinking about money. *[Sonny begins to play the Prelude to Act 3 of "Lohengrin" on the piano in the next room.]*

*Mrs. Shaw [Jarred].* Oh Lucy, tell Sonny not to be banging away at the piano. Really, my nerves couldn't stand it just now.

*[Lucy obeys.]*

*Shaw.* The poor lad is only trying to keep up his spirits. He's very upset about your going.

*Mrs. Shaw.* I might as well be only crossing the road as far as he's concerned.

*[The piano stops.]*

*Ellen [Impulsively].* Let's go in and cheer him up. Come along, Professor.

*Robinson [Following her].* I hope he's not going to play any more of that dreadful modern music. Wagner . . . Berlioz . . . they just don't seem to be able to write a simple, heartfelt little melody.

*[Robinson and Ellen go into the other room. Lucy comes back.]*

*Mrs. Shaw.* If people could only be got to mind their own business.

*Carroll [Stiffly].* I beg your pardon. I had not meant to intrude.

*Mrs. Shaw.* Not you, William. You're one of the family. But these are just poking around to see what information they can get. Come along, Lucy. Help me to get the other things down.

*Carroll.* You are far too early, Bessie.

*Mrs. Shaw.* I still have a great deal to do. I have to go to the doctor and collect Yuppy. I sent her over to get some medicine to make her strong for the journey. *[She goes out, right, with Lucy.]*

*Carroll.* George, I'm really worried about this business. I thought that after that fellow had taken himself off to London she'd have settled down. *[Shaw shakes his head.]* You must put your foot down. She must not go.

*Shaw.* I can't stop her, Willie. Apart from everything else, the financial situation is—well!

*Carroll [Forcefully].* She can't desert the ship at the first squall.

*Shaw.* It isn't the first squall, Willie.

*Carroll.* Don't pounce on a word, George. You know perfectly well what I mean. She took you on for better or for worse. It's her duty to stay at your side.

*Shaw.* My dear Willie, this is only a temporary measure.

*Carroll.* You cannot fool me with your temporary measures, George. You know Bessie. If she goes, she will put up with any hardship sooner than come back and admit she was wrong. And you're far too old to pull up your roots here and try to make a fresh start in London.

*Shaw.* Oh, I wouldn't say that, Willie.

*Carroll.* Forgive me for being blunt, George, but how far is that fellow Lee behind all this?

*Shaw [With a touch of hauteur].* He has nothing whatsoever to do with it.

*Carroll.* I know he is sending back word here about how he is conquering London, but I know for a fact he is doing no such thing. And he never will. How could he? A man with absolutely no academic qualifications, hardly able to read music, not able to play any instrument perfectly—how in the name of heaven could a man like that impose himself on a great metropolis as a music teacher?

*Shaw [Shrugging].* He's a bit of a genius in his own way, you have to admit that.

*Carroll.* A genius? A windbag. A charlatan.

*Shaw.* He may not be completely the fine bird, but he has a few fine feathers.

*Carroll.* He bluffed his way through Dublin. He will not bluff very far in London.

*Shaw.* I think you're a bit hard on him. Even Sonny says that he is—

*Carroll.* Don't talk to me about Sonny and Lee. *[Grimly.]* Whenever I see that poor boy, I see Lee all over again.

*Shaw.* What do you mean by that, Willie?

*Carroll.* Lee stole your own son from you, and that I cannot and will not forgive.

*Shaw [Shrugging].* Oh—!

*Carroll.* He undermined your position as a father, as the head of this family. Sonny idolized him. That foolish boy made himself Lee's echo, his ghost, his alter ego. Sonny thinks like Lee. He talks like Lee, in a voice like Lee's. He parts his hair in the middle like Lee. He dresses like Lee. He eats like Lee. I have seen him in the street pretending to have a limp so that he could even walk like Lee.

*Shaw.* I've always thought the trouble with Sonny is that he's so very much like myself, poor fellow. Bessie is always pointing out the awful resemblances between us.

*Carroll [Almost pityingly].* Indeed?

*Shaw.* Of course, Sonny hasn't much respect for me. How could he have? —he has never heard me well spoken of. But maybe one day he will understand and forgive me.

*Carroll.* Forgive you? Forgive you what, pray?

*Shaw.* For not having a few fine feathers.

*Carroll [Flinging away].* I have never heard such tosh in my life. Listen, man, are you going to stand there and do nothing while your wife walks off?

*Shaw.* Her mind is made up.

*Carroll.* Her mind is ma— *[Violently.]* Are you master in this house or are you not? *[He hastily drops his voice as he remembers the people in the next room.]* People will talk. And some of the mud is bound to stick on me too, as a member of the family. If there's any scandal, I can say goodbye to a bishopric.

*Shaw [Stiffly].* I don't see what there is for people to talk about.

*Carroll.* Didn't you hear Robinson at it a few minutes ago?

*Shaw [Contemptuously].* Oh, him . . . .

*Carroll.* I felt it was my duty to speak to him some time ago about seeing so much of that woman in there. And what did he say? "I see no more of her than you sister-in-law sees of Mr. Lee."

*Shaw.* Robinson should talk. *[With mounting anger.]* Did you hear him offering lessons to Lucy? Over my dead body will she go to him. I know the sort of lessons he'd give her.

*Carroll [Subsiding].* We may be unjust to him. He's engaged.

*Shaw.* Engaged! You mean there's some other woman ready to take him after he drove his first wife to kill herself?

*Carroll.* We have no right to assume he did such a thing.

*Shaw.* Oh, you can get away with anything when you're in with the right people. I might have known it when they came around to me looking for the five guineas for the Robinson whitewashing fund.

*Carroll.* The what?

*Shaw.* The Fanny Robinson Memorial Fund. "To aid distressed music mistresses."

*[Matt McNulty comes to the door, stopping uncertainly as he sees Carroll.]*

*Carroll [Shaking hands].* How do you do, Mr. McNulty? *[Turning again to Shaw.]* Well, since you won't have it any other way, George, so it be. I'll say goodbye to Bessie. *[Pausing at the door.]* Hadn't you better come over and spend the evening with us?

*Shaw.* Thanks, Willie, but I have to stay here and look after the shifting of my boxes and things.

*[Carroll goes. Shaw turns to McNulty in a peculiarly embarrassed way.]*

*Shaw.* Well, Matt—?

*McNulty [Equally embarrassed].* I managed that little job all right, Mr. Shaw.

*Shaw.* I really shouldn't have asked you, my boy.

*McNulty.* Not at all. I'd never been in a pawnbroker's before. It was a bit of an experience. *[Taking out some money.]* I got four pounds and sixpence for it.

*Shaw [Wincing].* Oh, dear . . . .

*McNulty.* He wouldn't go a penny more.

*Shaw.* That watch cost me twenty guineas, Matt. *[Sighing.]* I had money in those days. I was expecting at least £10 for it.

*McNulty.* There's the ticket. You won't get your watch back without that.

*Shaw.* I shall stick this on the end of my watchchain. *[He does so.]* Now let's hope nobody asks me the time.

*McNulty [Impulsively].* Take my watch, Mr. Shaw. Please. I can do without it.

*Shaw.* Oh, you're a real Irishman, Matt; you want to give everything away. Thanks, my boy. I appreciate the offer.

*[Ellen and Robinson come back.]*

*Robinson.* I must say that young shaver is taking it all very calmly.

*Ellen.* Oh no, he's very upset about it all. Trying to cheer himself up at the piano. I know exactly how he feels. Did you see the way he kept twisting the edge of his coat all the time he was talking?

Robinson. All young fellows twiddle their hands. No sense or response. He has his nerves in rags with all that modern music. Stick to Handel. Stick to Handel. Since my poor little Fanny was called home, Handel has been my only consolation. [Closing his eyes.] I play the D minor organ concerto twice a day. Heavenly work. So soothing. [He sings soulfully.] Da—dee—deeee . . . .

[Mrs. Shaw, in outdoor dress and carrying her hat, comes back with Lucy. Lucy holds a small tin cash box.]

Mrs. Shaw. It's dreadful not to have even a spare inch of mirror to put one's hat on with.

Ellen. Can I help?

Mrs. Shaw. No, no, I'll manage. [Frankly dismissing them.] Well, we must say goodbye.

Ellen. Yes, we mustn't delay you. Goodbye, dear Lucinda Elizabeth. Safe journey. And do write and tell us all the news. [She kisses Mrs. Shaw on the cheek.] Well, Mr. Robinson, shall we make a move?

Robinson. Oh . . . well . . . er . . . er . . . perhaps if you were to go first, dear lady. It might be better if we weren't seen leaving together. People's tongues, you know. Vile insinuations.

Ellen. Of course. How thoughtless of me. Goodbye, all.

Robinson [Whispering as he goes to the door with her]. I'll meet you at the bridge.

[Ellen goes, and Robinson moves back into the room, shaking his head mournfully.]

Robinson. Tragedy, tragedy, that poor woman. What a mess she has made of her life. One feels so sorry for her.

Shaw. It's nice of you to comfort her as you do.

Robinson. We must be Christian, my dear Shaw, Christian.

Mrs. Shaw [To Shaw]. Have you ordered the cab?

Shaw. I didn't know what time you were going.

[Mrs. Shaw makes an impatient exclamation.]

McNulty. I'll run up to Harcourt Street Station and get one down in a jiffy. [He goes out.]

Robinson. Oh, these leavetakings . . . always a time for sorrow. Well, you're lucky it's not Liverpool you're going to, like our poor friend. When I think of that poor girl having to go to live there, my heart bleeds.

Mrs. Shaw. Don't fret yourself, Mr. Robinson.

[Robinson shakes his head.]

Mrs. Shaw. The population of Liverpool does not consist entirely of women.

*Robinson.* Hmm . . . well . . . I'll say goodbye. Bon voyage, dear lady. *[He kisses her hand.]* Bon voyage. Goodbye goodbye goodbye. *[At the door.]* And don't forget to give my kindest regards to—Mr. Lee. *[He goes.]*

*Mrs. Shaw.* Well, are there any *more* of them here to bid me farewell? *[She puts on her hat.]* I'm so fussed now I can hardly remember what I have to do. Oh yes—Sonny. I have to say goodbye to *him.*

*[She goes into the next room. Lucy hurries over to her father and grips his arm.]*

*Lucy.* Oh Par, make her stay—make her stay.

*Shaw.* It's no use, pet.

*Lucy.* Then why don't we all go to London?

*Shaw.* Later perhaps. *[He mumbles.]* Just a temporary measure.

*Lucy.* Don't let her go down to the boat by herself. You come down too—don't mind what she says. Maybe she'll change her mind at the last minute.

*Shaw.* I—I wouldn't like to go against her, my pet. *[He pats her arm, accidentally knocking the cash box out of her grasp. Its contents spill on the floor.]* What on earth is all that?

*Lucy [Gathering the things up].* It's her box of keepsakes. She left it on the mantelpiece upstairs so that she wouldn't forget it and then walked off without it. You know Mar. *[She hands him a piece of cloth.]* Do you recognize that?

*Shaw.* Looks like a baby's cap. *[He hands it back.]*

*Lucy.* Sonny's. She never bothered keeping *my* baby cap. Or even Yuppy's. Only Sonny's. That and your letters.

*Shaw.* Mine—?

*Lucy.* Yours are the only letters she ever kept. *[A little spasm tightens Shaw's mouth.]* I've seen her crying over them when she thought no one was looking.

*[She puts the box on top of the traveling bag. She moves over to a shadowy corner as Mrs. Shaw returns.]*

*Mrs. Shaw [Talking back to Sonny].* . . . . if you want anything, write to me at once. And make sure your shirts are well aired before you put them on. *[To Lucy.]* Have you got everything ready for me? *[She moves towards the door.]* I hope young Matt McNulty won't be long with that cab.

*Lucy.* Aren't you going to say goodbye to Par?

*Mrs. Shaw [Stopping short on her way to the door and turning].* Oh, of course. I nearly forgot.

*Lucy [Handing her the box].* You left it upstairs.

*Mrs. Shaw.* I did?

*[Lucy goes. Mrs. Shaw and her husband stand looking at each*

*other uneasily for a moment. In the next room Sonny begins to play "La ci darem" but it sounds very remote and ghostly.]*

*Mrs. Shaw.* I daresay we'll see each other again soon.

*Shaw [Mumbling].* Oh, surely. Temporary measure . . . temporary measure. In a way, it's a pity you feel you have to go now, because—

*Mrs. Shaw.* There's no question about it. I just have to, and that's that.

*Shaw.* What I meant was . . . I'm practically certain of the hospital contract.

*Mrs. Shaw.* Hmm.

*Shaw.* Things cannot keep going down and down; they're bound to go up some time. Anyhow, there'll be a bit of money stirring soon, and I'll be able to get over and see you.

*Mrs. Shaw.* Well—

*Shaw.* Only for a day or two.

*Mrs. Shaw.* Perhaps when I've got things fixed up, but not for the moment.

*Shaw.* I haven't got the fare anyway, my dear. Though I'm sure I could borrow it from Sonny. He's very thrifty. Not like me, eh?

*Mrs. Shaw [Drawing on her gloves].* Things are bound to be at sixes and sevens for the first few months. Settling into whatever house I get . . . looking after pupils . . . It's going to be very hard for me.

*Shaw.* Yes, indeed.

*Mrs. Shaw. You'll* be all right. Sonny is settled. Mr. Townshend says there's no reason why he shouldn't be head clerk some day if he works hard.

*Shaw.* He's a steady lad.

*Mrs. Shaw.* I can only say that I hope so.

*Shaw [With an upsurge of tenderness].* Are you sure you'll be all right over there?

*Mrs. Shaw.* Of course.

*Shaw.* Can you depend on Lee to do all he says he will? He has his own way to make.

*Mrs. Shaw.* He'll make it.

*Shaw.* Anyway you—you know you can always come back.

*Mrs. Shaw.* Never.

*Shaw.* Well, I suppose I mustn't delay you any longer.

*Mrs. Shaw.* Yes, and you'd better get up to Harcourt Street as quickly as possible.

*Shaw.* I can't go without the boxes.

*Mrs. Shaw.* I suppose not. *[She checks the contents of the tin box.]*

*Shaw [With an attempt at lightheartedness].* Anything of value in that?

*Mrs. Shaw.* Nothing. Just a few papers and things. They're not really important.

*Shaw [Holding out some money].* A gift at parting, my dear. Excuse the peculiarity of the amount . . . four pounds six and six.

*Mrs. Shaw [Suspiciously].* Were did you get all this?

*Shaw.* Somebody paid their account for once. Half for you, half for me.

*Mrs. Shaw [Slipping the money into the box].* Every little bit helps. But I can't stand here gossiping all night. What time is it?

*Shaw [Checking an involuntary movement towards his pocket].* I'm afraid my watch has stopped.

*Mrs. Shaw.* Tch tch. It just needed that.

*[A horse cab draws up outside.]*

*Shaw.* Sounds like your cab, my dear.

*Mrs. Shaw [Holding out her hand].* I'll say goodbye.

*Shaw [Taking her hand but staring at his boots].* I'll be able to send you a pound a week.

*Mrs. Shaw.* It will be useful.

*Shaw.* Goodbye, my dear.

*[He raises his eyes to hers, unable to speak, then nods and kisses her cheek. She walks to the door, erect and determined. Shaw moves slowly to the window and stares out, raising a hand in farewell, as she is heard driving off. Sonny has stopped playing, and the house is absolutely silent. The room is quite dark by now, except for a shaft of light through the window from the setting sun. Sonny comes in from the other room, holding a lighted lamp.]*

*Shaw.* She's gone, Sonny.

*[Sonny walks to the door, then pauses as if going to say something. But he changes his mind and goes out. With the light of the lamp gone, the room seems darker than ever. Shaw turns and stares out after his wife.]*

*Curtain*


## Epilogue

*Fifteen years later. The sitting room at No. 36 Osnaburgh Street, London. A plainly furnished room with fireplace right, and door at back, somewhat right of center. A gas lamp in a bracket over the mantelpiece lights up only that part of the room near it, leaving the far corner of the room in deep shadow. Mrs. Shaw, a little stouter and greyer, with her face set in granite lines, is sitting over her ouija board at the fireplace. The firelight flickers on her face. She is alone.*

Mrs. Shaw *[Very softly]*. Yuppy . . . Yuppy . . . come, my darling . . . Yuppy . . . I want to thank you for the drawings: They are very lovely. *[She seems to listen.]* Yes, I know your brother scoffs at them. He scoffs at everything. *[The sound of a girl singing "Oh, had I the wings of a dove" can be heard very faintly.]* Oh, you are singing again . . . thank you, my darling Yuppy, thank you. It is so lonely on this side now. I cannot trust anybody. They have all failed me. *[She listens.]* Darling, darling Yuppy. Your voice is even lovelier now than it was when you were on this side.

*[She continues to listen in perfect contentment for a few minutes, then voices are heard outside, but she does not appear to notice them. Lucy opens the door. She is in outdoor dress.]*

Lucy. Oh Mar, we have a visitor. *[Mrs. Shaw makes no response.]* Mar, can you hear me? *[She coughs.]*

Mrs. Shaw *[Without turning around]*. You may bring your visitor in, Lucy.

Lucy *[To the person in the hall]*. Come along, dear. The Mar is not completely over on the other side—just about half and half.

*[Ellen, lovelier than ever, and most brilliantly dressed, comes in. She hurries over to Mrs. Shaw, both hands outstretched.]*

Ellen. Oh, my dear Lucinda Elizabeth, how lovely to see you again—and how well you're looking!

Mrs. Shaw *[Rising and submitting to Ellen's kiss on the cheek without response]*. How do you do?

Ellen. You *do* remember me, don't you?

Mrs. Shaw. Of course.

Ellen. You haven't changed a bit—I'd know you anywhere. Have I changed at all?

Mrs. Shaw *[With an ironic glance at Ellen's clothes]*. Apparently not.

Lucy *[Taking off her coat and throwing it on a chair]*. Sit down and make yourself as comfortable as you can—we're rather rough and ready, as you can see. *[She coughs.]* Give me your cloak.

*Ellen.* No darling, I'll just loosen it. I really can't stay more than a
few moments. *[She sits.]*

*Lucy.* Ellen, you can't just walk in and walk out like this, when we
haven't seen you for fifteen years.

*Ellen [To Mrs. Shaw].* Wasn't it amazing? Lucy and I recognized
each other immediately.

*Lucy.* I saw you before you saw me.

*Ellen.* Not really. I saw you crossing the—

*Lucy.* Oh, indeed yes: You were staring at that tall policeman who
was—

*Ellen [Laughing].* Was I really! But he was rather a fine figure of
a man, wasn't he now?

*Mrs. Shaw [Coldly].* Are you still living in Dublin?

*Ellen.* Well no, I have been traveling rather about, you know.

*Lucy.* But she's crossing over to Dublin tonight for a long visit.

*Ellen.* I have all my railway seats and cabins and things booked—
what a pity: I should so loved to stay with you for the evening.

*Mrs. Shaw.* I understood you had been living in Dublin.

*Ellen.* Oh dear no, I've been wandering all over the earth. But I
always did want to travel, you know.

*Lucy.* Darling, I positively have my fill of traveling these days. You
know I'm on tour in musical comedy.

*Ellen.* Yes yes, indeed, somebody did tell me. You're doing wonderfully—leading lady and all that.

*Lucy.* Leading lady in a No. 2 company, my dear—a fate worse
than death. Lodging houses—nasty little hotels—cold—and
damp. *[She coughs.]*

*Ellen.* That's a shocking cold you have, Lucy. You really should go
to bed till it clears up—that's what I always do.

*Lucy [With a smile].* It will never clear up, Ellen.

*Ellen.* What do you mean? *[The words are out of her mouth before
she realizes what Lucy does mean.]*

*Lucy [Cheerfully].* Oh, I'm not dying or anything like that. As a
matter of fact, I feel extraordinarily well. And I *have* lasted ten
years longer than Yuppy. The doctors tell me—at a half a guinea
a time—that I shall keep on living until I die. It's so comforting
of them. And well worth the half guinea.

*Ellen.* Lucy, my darling, do you think that—in the circumstances—
it's wise of you to—well—to do the sort of work you're doing?

*Lucy.* One must live, Ellen. Although I do not officiously strive to
keep alive. But I often feel that if by pressing a little button I
could die quickly and painlessly, I'd press it.

*Ellen.* What you need is a good long holiday by the sea, my dear. And I'm going to see that you get it.

*Lucy.* Sweet of you, Ellen, but you've enough to do with your few pounds without doing the Good Samaritan.

*Ellen.* Oh, I've lots of oil and tuppences burning a hole in my purse, Lucy—and—I'm not offending you, am I?

*Lucy.* Not in the least, my dear. *[She begins to prepare tea.]*

*Ellen.* You mustn't look so awfully disapproving, Lucinda Elizabeth. *[Gaily.]* I'm quite a respectable member of the community now, really I am.

*Mrs. Shaw.* I presume so.

*Ellen.* You haven't heard about my legacy?

*Lucy.* Now don't tell us a long-lost cousin died and left you a fortune.

*Ellen.* That's just what the long-lost cousin did, my dear. But surely I wrote and told you all about it?

*Mrs. Shaw.* We got some postcards addressed from various parts of the world, saying "Having a wonderful time." And I have no reason to doubt but that you were.

*Ellen.* I'm a shocking correspondent, I know I am. But my legacy—it was a cousin of ours in Italy that nobody had ever heard of. And he died and left millions and millions, which the lawyers divided up equally between myself and my three cousins. Oh, I'm a perfect capitalist, I can assure you.

*Lucy [Holding out both hands to Ellen].* Oh, Ellen, Ellen, I really am glad. There isn't a soul in the world I'd sooner see well off than you.

*Ellen.* Thanks, my pet. It came just in the nick of time. I was stranded in Liverpool—down to my last sixpence—when the lawyer's letter came. I thought it was a hoax. But it wasn't. So now, how about letting me give you at least what these theatre people are giving you—

*Lucy.* But I love the work, Ellen. I'm quite happy at it.

*Mrs. Shaw.* Why tell lies about it?

*Ellen [Quickly].* Yes—your mamma is quite right. You don't have to pretend to *me*. Anyway, I'm not going to take any more nonsense from you. I know that if our cases were reversed you'd do the same for me. So there.

*Lucy.* No, thanks, dear old Ellen. Anyway, it wouldn't do my husband's character any good to know that I had a tame good Samaritan.

*Ellen [Astonished].* Your husband? But I didn't—why, congratulations, my pet. When did all this take place?

*Lucy.* Eighteen months ago.

*Ellen.* Why, that's just when I fell into all my millions. Well, let's be honest and say thousands. And so you are married! *[To Mrs. Shaw.]* I never thought she'd condescend to any man, you know. *[To Lucy.]* And have you any—

*Lucy [Curtly].* No. No family.

*Ellen.* And are you gorgeously snug and happy?

*Lucy.* Oh, rapturously. Go on, Mar: say "Why tell lies about it?"

*Mrs. Shaw.* Marriage is Dead Sea Fruit.

*Lucy.* Trust Mar to put in the cheerful word.

*Ellen.* It does take a little while to settle down, you know. The first few years are the worst. Is your husband anyone I know?

*Lucy.* No.

*Mrs. Shaw.* Don't be too sure of *that*, Lucy.

*Ellen [Laughing heartily].* Touché!

*Lucy.* Charles Butterfield.

*Ellen.* Charles Butterfield . . . *[Turning to Mrs. Shaw.]* No, not guilty, dearest Lucinda Elizabeth.

*Lucy.* I wouldn't wish him on my worst enemy.

*Ellen.* Oh, Lucy, Lucy, you were always very hard on the men, poor things. What's he like?

*Lucy.* George Bernard says his face looks as if it had been carved out of a bladder of lard.

*Ellen [Laughing].* Oh, the dear save us! And how is your brother— dear, dear Sonny, isn't that what you used to call him?

*Lucy.* There he is—thirty years of age: no job, no prospects, turning an odd shilling writing in the papers, and walking about in a raggy suit preaching Socialism at street corners.

*Ellen [Shocked].* Preaching Socialism! Oh no! *[Brightening.]* Oh well—perhaps he'll get sense.

*Lucy.* If he hasn't got it at thirty, he'll never get it.

*Ellen.* It must be such an awful disappointment to you, Lucinda Elizabeth. And how is our musical friend?

*Mrs. Shaw.* What musical friend?

*Ellen.* Why, Mr. Lee, of course.

*Mrs. Shaw.* Mr. Lee is very well, I presume.

*Lucy.* Oh, go on, Mar, tell Ellen all about Lee. She's worth listening to when she gets going on Lee. *[Ellen turns expectantly to Mrs. Shaw.]*

*Mrs. Shaw.* He remains in good health, I understand.

*Ellen.* You don't see him very often then?

*Mrs. Shaw.* I have not seen the gentleman for some time.

*Ellen.* What on earth happened? Oh, but I mustn't ask rude questions like that.

*Lucy.* Go on, Mar, say your piece about charlatan, imposter, black-
guard, scoundrel, voice wrecker—
*Ellen [All agog].* Oh, I can't believe it.
*Lucy [Pouring tea].* Go on, Mar, tell her what happened.
*Mrs. Shaw.* Nothing happened.
*Ellen [Dryly].* Is that why you fell out?
*Lucy.* Don't make such a mystery of it, Mar. It was all over me,
Ellen.
*Mrs. Shaw.* I do not expect Mrs.—our visitor—will be interested
in these trifles.
*Lucy.* It was all over me, Ellen. Lee made improper advances to
me just before I was married—
*Mrs. Shaw.* These trifles cannot be of the least interest to—
*Lucy.* Fortunately, the Mar came home much earlier than expected,
and walked into the room before things became too difficult.
*Ellen [Soberly].* I'm glad I know, because I really had thought of
calling on Mr. Lee the next time I was passing through London.
*Mrs. Shaw [With her most granite expression].* Now you tell your
friend about that other creature?
*Ellen.* What other creature?
*Lucy [Stiffly].* We don't have to go into all the details.
*Mrs. Shaw.* Tell her about that other creature, Lucy.
*Lucy [Reluctantly].* There's nothing to it, Ellen. We don't go to
Lee's place now, but George Bernard still keeps in touch. And
one evening there, a little while ago, when he went to play the
piano at one of Lee's rehearsals, well—
*Ellen [Smiling].* Mr. Lee was entertaining another of his lady
pupils?
*Mrs. Shaw.* The housemaid.
*Ellen [Shocked].* Oh dear—has he descended as low as that?
*Mrs. Shaw.* He has descended very low in every way.
*Lucy [Quietly].* I really don't know how he keeps going.
*Ellen [With a touch of kindly concern].* His health isn't so good?
*Lucy.* Oh, his health is all right. But he's getting a bit on in years
now. He's not far off sixty.
*Mrs. Shaw.* Fifty-five.
*Ellen.* Well, I suppose we're not all that young ourselves, either.
*Mrs. Shaw [With satisfaction].* He has no pupils left.
*Ellen.* No pupils?
*Mrs. Shaw.* He is now peddling cures for clergyman's sore throat.
*Ellen [Genuinely touched].* Oh, the poor man—what a comedown.
*Mrs. Shaw.* He is now a charlatan and a humbug.

*Ellen.* And where does the poor fellow live?

*Lucy.* He's still in Park Lane. Goodness knows how he manages to hang on.

*Ellen.* What an awful end for such a genius.

*Mrs. Shaw [Almost spitting].* Genius—shah!

*Ellen.* And your father—? He's still living in Dublin?

*Lucy [Sipping her tea].* Poor Par died last April twelve months.

*Ellen.* I'm really sorry to hear it. He was such a nice man. *[To Mrs. Shaw.]* Were you with him when he . . . ?

*Mrs. Shaw.* No.

*Lucy.* The Mar hadn't seen him since she left Dublin. Except for that few days he came over here. And your own husband?

*Ellen.* Ferdie is flourishing—or so I hear. I'm sorry to say I haven't seen him for years, but then so long as he has his books, he doesn't encourage visits from me.

*[The conversation flags. Over in the shadowy corner of the room a vague greenish shape becomes dimly discernible. As the shape gradually resolves itself into the likeness of old Shaw, Mrs. Shaw slowly lays down her cup and half rises from her chair.]*

*Lucy.* Oh dear me, Mar, are you off again?

*Mrs. Shaw.* They are coming. *[She turns to her ouija board.]*

*Lucy.* These are Mar's pals, the family ghosts. They're coming to visit her again.

*Ellen [Uncomfortably].* Ghosts?

*Lucy.* Yes. They talk to her and draw the most weird and wonderful designs for her, and write on her ouija board, and do all sorts of things.

*Ellen [Staring in fascination].* That's the ouija board?

*Lucy.* Don't ask me how it works. So far as I can see, the Mar does all the drawing and writing herself.

*Mrs. Shaw [Tonelessly].* Yuppy is singing. *[The girl's voice is faintly heard.]*

*Ellen [Frightened, catching at Lucy's arm].* Oh my God, Lucy—I hear it—I hear a girl singing.

*Lucy [Laughing].* It's only young Mollie Concannon next door. Go out on to the landing there, and you'll hear her quite plainly. The walls of these houses are like matchboard: every sound carries. Just go over to the door, and you'll see.

*Ellen.* Thanks, pet, I'll take your word for it.

*Lucy.* Now Mar, don't go off again, please. Not when we have visitors.

*Mrs. Shaw.* Your father is here.

*Lucy.* Well, say I was asking for him, and tell him to keep his woolly vests on him in this awful weather. Now you send him a message, Ellen.

*Ellen.* Me? Oh—er—tell him I send my love.

*Shaw [Smiling and rubbing his hands].* Why, that's uncommonly kind of you, dear lady. My love to you too.

*Ellen [Her cup and saucer rattling in her hand].* Oh, my goodness—

*Lucy.* What's the matter, Ellen?

*Ellen.* I don't know. I got a most peculiar feeling that time. *[With a nervous laugh.]* You wouldn't want to let your imagination run away with you, would you?

*[Mrs. Shaw's expression becomes puzzled. Ellen stares at her in frightened fascination, and nudges Lucy to look too.]*

*Mrs. Shaw [Whispering].* I do not understand. I do not understand.

*[Over amongst the shadows Shaw too turns with a puzzled look, for there is another shape becoming dimly visible—that of Lee.]*

*Shaw [Aggrieved].* Hang it all, Lee, what are you doing here?

*Lee.* I don't know. I haven't quite got used to the new circumstances yet. But I heard people talking about me over in this direction so I thought I'd come and hear what they were saying.

*Ellen.* I simply can't get poor Mr. Lee out of my head. What you tell me disturbs me very much. To think that a man of such great— *[With a glance towards Mrs. Shaw.]* —of course, I'm not a good judge, I know, but he did seem to me a really great genius in music. And to think he has hit such bad times.

*Lee.* Who'd been telling her I hit bad times? I never complained.

*Shaw.* There's nothing to be ashamed about bad times. I had them myself for the last forty years of my life. You only had them for a few years.

*Lee.* That's all you know about it.

*Shaw.* By the way, when did you pass over? It couldn't have been very long ago.

*Lee [Looking at his watch].* Eight minutes ago, to be exact.

*Shaw.* Well, well. And had you much trouble?

*Lee.* Not really.

*Shaw [Complacently].* Oh, I had an awful time—dreadful—shocking.

*Lee [Dryly].* You would.

*Shaw.* You can sneer away, Lee, but let me tell you the doctors all said they simply couldn't understand how I managed to hold out—on the other side, I mean.

*Lee.* The story I heard was that you died quite peacefully and happily, with your landlady weeping over you as if you were her own husband.

*Shaw.* Hang it, Lee, I should know whether I died peacefully or not. My sufferings were—you've no idea what I went through.

*Lee.* You were rotten with drink, of course.

*Shaw [Indignantly].* I was no such thing. And whether I was or not, I lasted a hang sight longer than you. I was seventy-three.

*Lee.* Seventy-two.

*Shaw [Hotly].* Seventy-three—I was in my seventy-third year. You were only fifty-five.

*Lee [Angrily].* Fifty-six.

*Shaw.* You can't fool me. You always said you were exactly the same age as Bessie, and she's only fifty-five and a bit. *[He turns towards his wife.]* Isn't that right, Bessie?

*Mrs. Shaw.* Does it matter?

*Ellen [Gently].* Does what matter, Lucinda Elizabeth?

*Mrs. Shaw.* Age.

*Lucy.* You mustn't mind the Mar. When she gets talking to her spirits, you can get neither rhyme nor reason out of her.

*Mrs. Shaw.* Lee is here.

*Lucy.* Tell him to take himself off again.

*Lee [Quietly].* Do you really mean that, Lucy?

*Lucy [With almost a cry of pain].* No! *[Her mother turns slowly and stares at her.]*

*Ellen [Puzzled].* I beg your pardon, dear—no what?

*Lucy.* I didn't mean to say anything. Let me give you some more tea. *[She pours the tea with a shaking hand.]*

*Shaw [To Lee].* So you had a nice easy passing, eh? I suppose you had everything carefully planned as usual.

*Lee.* As a matter of fact, I hadn't. If I had known, I would have arranged things better. I hadn't been feeling at all well this afternoon.

*Shaw.* What! Not well! With all the brown bread and fresh air!

*Lee [Speaking more to Mrs. Shaw].* But this evening I felt somewhat better and went down to Leicester Square to have dinner with some friends. But after dinner I got a pain in my chest—I had to take an omnibus up Regent Street. When I got home, I started to go to bed and just when I had put my arm through my nightshirt—phut! I just crumpled up on the floor. Nobody knows I'm there yet.

*Shaw.* Not even the housemaid—? Won't she be coming up to you in a minute? *[Lee involuntarily lays his finger on his lips and looks anxiously towards the women.]* My dear fellow, they know all about it. *[Chuckling with satisfaction.]* All about it. They were telling Ellen about it just before I came in.

*Lee [With a touch of anger].* Damned women! Have they nothing else to gossip about?

*Shaw.* Oh, it doesn't matter a hoot now. But I must say, you managed your little business very nicely. Sounds like the heart, doesn't it?

*Lee.* That's what it was.

*Shaw.* Still, I didn't expect to find you after me so soon. *[Gesturing towards Mrs. Shaw.]* And how quickly she spotted you were coming. *[Suddenly serious.]* I say, Lee, do you think there really can be anything to this spiritualism business?

*Lee.* I'm not sure yet. Do you come here often?

*Shaw.* Every night.

*Lee.* Liar.

*Shaw.* Well . . . almost every night. Some nights I have other engagements. *[Hastily changing the subject.]* But I was telling you, Lee, about the dreadful time I had passing over. I started getting bad on the Tuesday—oh no, it was really on the Sunday. You see—

*Lee [Looking at Ellen].* That woman looks even lovelier than when I last saw her.

*Shaw.* Ahah, Lee, up to your old tricks again, eh? Really, you know, for a man in your present situation to be leering at women—and by the same token, now that I have you here and now that I know what I know, let me say it was damned mean of you to be carrying on the way you did with my daughter—with my two daughters, in fact. *[Lee throws an anxious glance at Mrs. Shaw, but she remains granite-faced.]* Lucy I suspected, but when I heard that you had Yuppy after you as well—!

*Lee.* Yuppy is here?

*Mrs. Shaw.* She is singing.

*Lee [Shaking his head].* That's not Yuppy. That's a soprano. Yuppy was a mezzo like yourself, Bessie, and that girl's voice is not as well-trained as Yuppy's was.

*Shaw.* Though you say it yourself, who shouldn't. As a matter of fact, Lee, you're quite right. It's a girl from next door, and I keep telling Bessie so, but she won't believe me. Yuppy has got dreadfully standoffish since she passed over. Simply refused to know the family. Lucy will go the same way when her time comes.

*Lee.* You were always a parcel of damned snobs. *[He looks uneasily at his watch.]*

*Shaw.* Thinking about that little housemaid coming up to your room, eh?

*Mrs. Shaw [Angrily].* Why do you have to mention that abominable creature?

*Shaw [Chuckling].* Now now now, Bessie, you can't blame me for getting a little of my own back. *[To Lee.]* What's worrying you, Lee? Does it matter whether it's the housemaid finds you on the floor, or somebody else?

*Lee [Embarrassed].* It's my leg. When I fell, my leg . . . remained on show. I remember trying to pull my nightshirt over it . . . but I couldn't move.

*Shaw.* Hang it, we all knew you had a gammy leg. You don't think that people didn't notice, do you? *[Lee turns his head away.]* Oh, come come come, Lee, don't be so infernally touchy. Anyway, you can't do anything about it now.

*Ellen [Laying down her teacup and rising].* Well, I really must be going.

*Lucy.* We haven't had much of a chat.

*Ellen [Glancing towards Mrs. Shaw].* Some other time, perhaps. I'm sure our chattering would disturb your mamma. By the way, dear, what's this the number of Mr. Lee's house is? Park Lane, number—

*Lee [Fiercely].* Don't *you* go there, madam.

*Ellen [Hastily].* It doesn't matter, I've changed my mind. *[Holding out her hand to Mrs. Shaw.]* Well, I must be off. It was lovely to see you again, Lucinda Elizabeth—and thank you so much for the tea.

*Mrs. Shaw [Barely touching her hand].* Goodbye.

*Lucy.* I'm sorry about the way the Mar is going on, but when she takes one of these fits on her you might as well just be talking to the wall. *[Putting on her cloak.]* I'll come to the station with you.

*Ellen.* No no, darling, and you with—with your cold.

*Lucy.* I don't mind the night air at all. Quite used to it, coming home from the theatre. *[They move towards the door, Ellen passing quite close to Lee and Shaw.]*

*Ellen [Shivering].* It's quite chilly when you move away from the fire, isn't it? *[She reaches the door and pauses.]* Oh yes—it *is* a girl singing next door. You know, Lucy, just for a little while I was really beginning to think . . . . *[With a last glance towards Mrs. Shaw.]* Goodbye again, dear Lucinda Elizabeth, goodbye.

*Lucy.* I shan't be too long, Mar. *[Mrs. Shaw makes no response; Lucy smiles at Ellen and shrugs.]* You see . . . ! *[They go.]*

*Shaw.* A fine-looking woman, that.

*Mrs. Shaw.* Is it necessary to insult me?

*Shaw.* Hang it all, Bessie, you insulted me often enough, the Lord knows. But she *is* a fine looking woman, you can't deny that.

*Lee.* Come come, Shaw, you don't need to say these things right out.

*Shaw.* It's better than your way of saying one thing and thinking another.

*Lee.* And you so brokenhearted when Bessie followed me to London—or so Lucy told me anyway.

*Shaw [Warmly].* I *was* brokenhearted. Really, truly, sincerely, genuinely brokenhearted. But hang it, a man can't keep on being really and truly and genuinely brokenhearted for nearly twenty-five years. I got over it. Oh yes, I did feel a bit low again after that time I came over here for a few days—you remember, Bessie, I was over here for a week. Hang it, you should remember that time too, Lee. I called on you at Park Lane, and we both spent a bad quarter of an hour, not knowing what to say to each other. And now here I am, and here you are, and there she is. Just like old times, eh? [Quietly.] Except that you're only imagining us, Bessie.

*Lee.* How can you be so cruel, Shaw? Leave her her last remaining bit of happiness.

*Shaw.* Gammon, Lee; you don't take anyone in with that stuff here. [He prepares to go.] Well, times flies even in eternity. I must be off. Oh, by the way, I must say it *was* rather nice the way you tried to help Sonny along by getting him odd jobs in journalism and so forth. [Chuckling.] But then, of course, you may have had your own good reasons . . . or think you had.

Lee. You needn't go on my account. I'll take myself off.

*Shaw [Grinning].* Looking for Yuppy, eh?

*Lee.* As a matter of fact, I merely want to have a look around. I am a newcomer.

*Shaw.* Ah yes, yes of course. [Expansively.] You'll find it quite all right here. There are some surprisingly interesting people knocking about.

*Lee [Eagerly].* Is Mozart here?

*Shaw [Scratching his head].* Couldn't say offhand. Certainly not in my set. I keep away from all those classical music merchants. You gave me my bellyful of them, you know. But wait now . . . Mozart . . . let me see. Is he a plump little man in a red coat? Very pronounced German accent? Um, that set keep pretty much to themselves, but I think I'd be able to set you off in their general direction.

*Lee.* I am very much obliged to you. So long as there's no danger of bumping into old Joe Robinson; I don't feel quite up to him just now.

*Shaw.* Hang it, old Joe hasn't come here yet, and neither has Gurly nor Willie Carroll.

*Lee.* One should be thankful for big mercies.

*Shaw.* Old Robinson is still going strong, you know. Had his first son—his first legitimate son—when he was nearly eighty.

*Lee.* A pleasant surprise.

*Shaw.* Yes, he was beginning to think there was something the matter with his new wife. *[He takes Lee's arm and begins to lead him away. Both seem to have forgotten about Mrs. Shaw.]* Come along, and I'll see if I can find Mozart for you.

*Mrs. Shaw [Rising and stretching out her hands beseechingly].* No—don't go.

*Shaw.* Hang it all, Bessie, be reasonable. You can't expect me to stay here every night. In the circumstances, I think it is jolly decent of me to come as often as I do.

*Mrs. Shaw.* Don't leave me alone—why don't you bring me Yuppy? She hasn't come to me at all since she went over.

*Shaw [Patiently].* Now now now, my dear Bessie, I have told you again and again that it's no use. Yuppy just will not come. She has got into a new set—damn social climbers, if you ask me—and she just won't come. I say, Lee, what time is it? Saturday night is music night at the Rose and Crown—not your kind of music, but mine. *[Lowering his voice.]* And the drink here is unbelievably good. Lashings of it—and not a penny to pay. As for hangovers, nothing worth mentioning. Just a slight fur on the tongue now and again if you really go beyond the beyonds. But that's all.

*Mrs. Shaw.* Don't go, don't go.

*Shaw.* See you later, Bessie. Come along, Lee, come along.

*[He vanishes.]*

*Mrs. Shaw [With almost a sob].* It's so lonely.

*[Lee, about to follow Shaw, hesitates.]*

*Shaw [In the distance].* Hurry on, Lee; I'm not going to wait for you.

*[Mrs. Shaw half turns and looks at Lee. This decides him. He slowly limps forward into the room and sits on a chair, leaning back and folding his arms across his breast.]*

*Lee [Quietly]*. All right, Bessie; I'll stay.
*[Her hands slowly fall to her sides; she closes her eyes and sits down with a faint smile softening the granite of her face.]*

*Curtain*

# CARLOTTA

### Cast

*GBS (George Bernard Shaw)*
*Charlotte,* his wife
Lucy, his sister
*Mrs. Patrick Campbell,* the actress

    *Charlotte Frances Shaw is sitting on a two-seater couch, half dozing. Beside her is a small table. On it are a copy of the* Times, *a book and, an opened box of chocolates. There is a ladder-backed chair nearby.*
    *Outside in the entrance hall, GBS is singing, to his own not very skillful accompaniment, Handel's "O Ruddier Than the Cherry." He reaches the end of a verse.*

*Charlotte [Opening her eyes].* That will do very nicely, thank you.
    *[Her hand drifts automatically to the chocolate box, extracts a chocolate and puts it in her mouth.]*
    *[GBS comes in.]*
*GBS.* I was going to finish off with some Verdi.
*Charlotte.* He'll keep till tomorrow evening. I don't want you to tire yourself.
*GBS.* I'm not in the least tired.
*Charlotte.* You're not to stay up late tonight.
*GBS.* I never stay up late. I doubt if I've stayed up late ten times in the past forty years. You've seen to that. *[He begins to drift around the room idly.]*
*Charlotte.* I heard you prowling around down here last night at twelve o'clock.
*GBS.* I merely came down to check that the doors were locked.
*Charlotte.* You were *told* not to interfere with the doors after the housekeeper has locked them for the night.
*GBS.* Our housekeeper is a paragon, but even she can make mistakes.

*Charlotte.* We always know when you've locked the doors at night, GBS. In the morning they're all wide open.

*GBS.* I offer no explanation of this mystery.

*Charlotte.* It's a wonder the whole place wasn't burgled.

*GBS.* On the contrary, an open door is the surest safeguard against burglary. The burglar creeps up to the back door. It is open. "How strange," he says. He creeps around to the side door. It, too, is open. Aha, a trap! He tries the front door. Open! He panics. "Dear God, they're waiting on me in there." He flies. Our household goods and chattels remain inviolate.

*Charlotte.* That would make a good scene for your next play.

*GBS.* No doubt. But burglars don't make interesting characters. Burglars are depressingly conventional. They keep doing the same things in the same way for the same reasons. They lack the vital element of surprise.

*Charlotte.* We don't want them to surprise us here. Leave locking the doors to the housekeeper.

*GBS.* My mother never went to bed before midnight.

*Charlotte.* I am not interested in what your mother did.

*GBS [Chuckling and rubbing his hands together].* That's exactly what she used to say about *you*. And in exactly the same tone of voice.

*Charlotte.* I never gave your mother any cause to dislike me.

*GBS.* True. You merely accused her of letting me die because of her neglect.

*Charlotte.* And *weren't* you nearly dying in those wretched lodgings?

*[The lighting changes. Charlotte rises and moves forward. She has become younger, more vigorous.]*

*GBS [In the background].* Mamma, may I present Miss Charlotte Payne-Townshend.

*Charlotte [Overawed in spite of herself, inclines her head politely].* Good afternoon, Mrs. Shaw.

*GBS [Coming forward to the corner of the stage, facing the audience directly and muttering].* You could have said "How d'you do?" or "How nice to meet you at last; I've heard so much about you from your son."

*[GBS is now standing in his narrating position. Charlotte's lighting is brighter and broader. She gazes around her in obvious distaste, even shock.]*

*GBS [As before].* Oh yes, the place *was* shabby and dusty and ill-kept. But hang it all, my mother had only forty pounds a year.

You had four thousand, and it was easy for you to keep your house a hundred times better than she kept hers.

*Charlotte [Politely].* Oh yes, of course, Mrs. Shaw, I quite understand that you have to go out now, but there'll be many opportunities in the future for us to sit down and have a chat—

*GBS.* She was sixty-eight and still had to go out to earn her living teaching singing in a girl's school.

*Charlotte [Almost archly].* Besides, Mrs. Shaw, there's at least one subject *[Glancing towards GBS]* about which we'll have lots and lots to talk—

*GBS [Grimly].* Over my dead body will the pair of you sit and gossip about *me. [To the heavens.]* Oh, why was I not a foundling?! Why was I not orphaned at an early age—and the earlier the better.

*Charlotte.* Ah, so you call him *George.* I always thought he was Bernard.

*GBS.* Ha!

*Charlotte.* And you called him Sonny when he was a little boy. . . .

*GBS [Anguished].* Sweet God! *[In an strangulated voice]:* Mamma, you'll be late for the afternoon class.

*Charlotte.* Yes, of course, Mrs. Shaw, I mustn't detain you another moment. *[She keeps smiling politely until Shaw's mother has gone. Then the expression of distaste and horror returns abruptly.]* You can't go on living in a place like this. I will not allow it.

*GBS [Shrugging].* Where else can I go?

*Charlotte.* You must spend the rest of the summer in the country.

*GBS.* The country? Mud, manure—cowdung. Pigs. Mad bulls. Fox hunters. Farmers.

*Charlotte.* Don't be silly. I'm taking you out of this place—and *now.* There's a very nice country rectory to be let for the summer months at Saxmundham—

*GBS.* A rectory? Out of the question.

*Charlotte.* Oh, you and your atheism. . . .

*GBS.* No atheist I. I am a mystic. But no country rectory, even with you there. *Especially* with you there.

*Charlotte [Bridling].* And what, pray, do you mean by *that?*

*GBS.* You look so respectable they'd mistake you for a clergyman's wife.

*Charlotte.* I don't care *what* people say.

*GBS.* Neither do I. It's what they do that bothers me. My correspondence would be addressed to the Rev. Bernard Shaw.

*Charlotte [Impatiently]*. Then drop it into the wastepaper basket. I wish you wouldn't keep on creating difficulties.

*GBS*. Not so cross, Charlotte. You are speaking to a dying man.

*Charlotte [Uneasily]*. You mustn't say things like that. You're not dying.

*GBS*. Oh, but I am. I have been dying at the rate of sixty minutes an hour ever since I was born.

*Charlotte*. You'll live to be a hundred and see us all down.

*GBS*. God forbid.

*Charlotte*. But first I'll have to take you out of this place. Ugh. The dirt. The grime.

*GBS*. Dirt, grime, That's what comes of living in London.

*Charlotte*. *I* can live in London without it.

*GBS*. Yes, with more servants to look after you than Queen Victoria has.

*Charlotte*. Utter nonsense.

*GBS*. The last time I was in your flat I counted a hundred and forty-seven servants.

*Charlotte*. I have *three*. And one of them merely comes in the mornings.

*GBS*. There were a hundred and forty-seven. Every time I went to put my arms around you, they came pouring in through the door, swarming down the chimney, erupting through the windows, crawling out from under the sofa, materializing through the floorboards—

*Charlotte*. Emily merely brought in the tea.

*GBS*. Damn Emily—and doubly damn the tea.

*Charlotte [Sharply]*. George.

*GBS [Wincing]*. Don't George me. I hate George.

*Charlotte*. But George is what your mother calls you.

*GBS*. That's another reason I don't wish to be Georged. Oh, I know all the little tricks you women use to bring a man to heel. Find out what silly name he was called by his mother and his sisters, and call him that. It will make him feel small and insignificant.

*Charlotte [Mildly]*. Very well, Bernard then.

*GBS*. Not much of an improvement.

*Charlotte [Rebelliously]*. I am not going to call you Shaw like Beatrice Webb and May Morris. It's not ladylike.

*GBS*. But I *am* Shaw. Anyone can be George. Anyone can be Bernard. Anyone can be William, but there's only one Shakespeare. There shall be only one Shaw.

*Charlotte*. And do you propose to call me Payne-Townshend?

*GBS.* Too much of a mouthful. No. I think you shall be P-T.

*Charlotte.* Miss?

*GBS.* P-T if you insist. Pee-Tee? On second thoughts I shall call you Charlotte. I like Charlotte. Shaw . . . Charlotte . . . Shaw . . . Charlotte. *[Almost dreamily.]* Shaw . . . Charlotte. *[Holding out his hand.]* You see? Our names proclaim that we were made for each other.

*Charlotte [Softly, as she kneels by the couch and takes the invisible hand].* I shall call you GBS.

*GBS.* Perfectly acceptable. I still reserve the right to call you Dearest, Belovedest.

*Charlotte [Dryly].* But not before company.

*GBS.* "Madam" before company. *[A pause.]* Is Beatrice Webb company?

*Charlotte.* Why do you ask?

*GBS.* Because when Beatrice is around, I shall call you my little apple dumpling, my honey bunch, my peaches and cream, my heart's delight.

*Charlotte [Settling a cushion under his head].* No wonder Beatrice doesn't like you.

*GBS.* Beatrice Webb is madly in love with me.

*Charlotte.* Beatrice doesn't care a fig for anybody except her husband. All the same, one could wish she wasn't quite so demonstrative.

*GBS.* Oh, she keeps plumping herself into Sidney's lap in front of everybody merely to annoy, and because she knows it teases.

*Charlotte.* It certainly annoys *me*.

*GBS.* Actually it's meant to tease *you* and annoy *Sidney*.

*Charlotte [Rising and moving away, irritated].* I do wish you wouldn't contradict everything I say.

*GBS.* Don't take offence so easily.

*Charlotte.* Why should she want to *annoy* Sidney? Teasing a man I can understand. *[Almost sniffling.]* Some women find that kind of thing amusing.

*GBS [Patiently].* There is no point in teasing a husband. Any passion a wife arouses in a husband he can readily satisfy at her expense.

*Charlotte. Must* you be so explicit?

*GBS [Ignoring the interruption].* But *annoying* a husband is a different matter. It's the one amusement a wife never tires of.

*Charlotte.* Why should any sensible woman want to annoy her husband?

*GBS.* Sensible women do it even more than the foolish.

*Charlotte.* But why? Why? Why? I have you cornered. I'm not going to let you escape.

*GBS [In thrilling tones].* But dearest Charlotte, I don't *want* to escape you. I've been throwing myself at you, begging you to capture me, imploring you to make me a prisoner-of-war . . . the sex war.

*Charlotte [Melted, moving towards him, then stopping].* I'm not going to be taken in any more by your soft talk.

*GBS [Exuberantly].* Splendid! I'm so glad you've slung that answer at me. I should have despised you if you'd fallen for my revolting sentimentality. If there's anything more disgusting than to see a woman clinging to a man, it's to see a man clinging to a woman. Let us plough through the waves side by side, like twin battleships.

*Charlotte.* I'm not sure I like being a battleship.

*GBS.* But you are a person to be reckoned with. That makes you a kind of battleship.

*Charlotte.* I have no desire to be a person who is to be reckoned with. I am quite happy to be a lady and to behave like a lady insofar as I can.

*GBS [With burlesque wildness].* Kiss me—for God's sake.

*Charlotte.* Why should I—for anybody's sake?

*GBS.* Because you can't kiss me and behave like a lady at the same time.

*Charlotte.* George, you are an infernal flirt.

*GBS.* Payne-Townshend, your cheek is very tempting. Waft it, please, within reach of my lips.

*Charlotte [Almost impatient].* It's very hard to be cross with you.

*GBS.* It's impossible. I'm dying. I am virtually an angel. You can't be cross with an angel.

*Charlotte [Hurrying over and kneeling beside the couch].* You are not to be saying things like that. Not even in jest. Mocking is catching.

*GBS.* Do you know, I haven't heard anybody say "mocking is catching" since I left Ireland twenty-three years ago.

*Charlotte.* Are you forgetting that *I* was born and bred in Cork?

*GBS.* A place I was never in . . . Cork.

*Charlotte.* Perhaps I shall bring you there some day. Our house is rather nice. Eighteenth century. Large airy rooms. Beautiful woods. And all Roscarbery spread out before you.

*GBS.* Beloved woman, anything you want you can do with me. Except for one thing. Never for any reason, or any pretext, shall

I ever set foot in Ireland again. Not even *you* will be able to get me back to that damnable country.

*Charlotte.* We shall see.

*GBS.* Weren't you miserable there as a child?

*Charlotte.* There was happiness too.

*GBS.* I had a devil of a childhood.

*Charlotte.* No happy moments?

*GBS.* There are a few, of course. Even in the condemned cell there must be one or two comparatively happy moments.

*Charlotte [Melting].* You may kiss me if you want to.

*GBS [Softly].* I very much want to.

*Charlotte.* On the lips if you like.

*GBS.* Well no, the cheek will do. I must remember my precarious health.

*Charlotte [Seizes his invisible head between her hands and kisses his mouth resoundingly. Rises and walks away to hide her embarrassment].* There. That won't kill you.

*GBS [Plaintively].* It nearly did.

*Charlotte [Brushing her dress].* My goodness, the dust in this place. *[Gesturing around.]* When did any of this furniture last get a rub of polish?

*GBS [Solemnly].* They drink the furniture polish in this house.

*Charlotte [Freezing].* They what?!!!

*GBS. And* the methylated spirits.

*Charlotte.* Your mother?!!

*GBS.* Good heavens no. And not my sister, either. My aunt.

*Charlotte [Almost voiceless].* Your aunt?!!! Furniture polish?!!

*GBS.* Only when she runs out of methylated spirits.

*Charlotte.* I don't believe a word of this.

*GBS.* Properly speaking, she is only my step-aunt. My mother's half-sister.

*Charlotte.* And she's in this house?!

*GBS.* We don't put her on display—for obvious reasons. Though I'll say this much for her: If she could afford it, she'd drink only eau de cologne.

*Charlotte [Shaking her head vigorously].* This is another of your fairy stories.

*GBS.* The truth, I assure you. As a girl in Ireland, my aunt started on wine. She pilfered it from her father's cellar—he was my grandfather. When he locked up the decanter, she got porter from the servants. Then whiskey. Then poteen. By this time no man would touch her; not one of her five sisters would allow her into their houses. So she followed us over here to London, and my mother took her in. Where else had she to go? She hadn't a penny to buy whiskey or gin, so she raided my sister's bedroom and drank her bottle of eau de cologne. Then she discovered methylated spirits in the scullery. When she finished that, she started on the furniture polish.

*Charlotte.* Is nobody *doing* anything for the unfortunate woman?

*GBS.* What *can* be done? She's past praying for. Now if you're planning to send her a case of the choicest champagne, you'll only be wasting your money. She'll run down to the shop at the corner to exchange it for a half-dozen bottles of furniture polish.

*Charlotte.* But this is dreadful.

*GBS.* Not really. Is there any significant difference between a bottle of malt whiskey and a bottle of furniture polish? The world is full of people like my aunt who cannot face life without an anaesthetic. Does it greatly matter which anaesthetic they use? *[Pointing upwards: Charlotte glances upwards too.]* She's upstairs, lying in her bed, probably senseless. *[Pointing to his left.]* A few miles away in Leyton, my uncle Walter is probably on *his* bed too, senseless from whiskey. Neither of them can last much longer, and when they go they will neither be missed in this world or noticed in the next.

*Charlotte [Staring at him, fascinated].* Beatrice Webb is right. You haven't any heart at all.

*GBS.* Heartless? Heartless because on the rack of this tough world I would not stretch them out longer? Do you imagine either of them would thank me if I tried to?

*Charlotte.* I thought you were quite fond of your Uncle Walter?

*GBS.* So I was . . . when he was himself. I remember him as he was when I was a boy. He was a ship's surgeon in those days. He would spend his shore leave in Dublin with us, either at our house in Hatch Street or in our cottage out at Dalkey. He was irreverent, exuberant, skeptical, Rabelaisean. From his filthy limericks alone you could learn the geography of the world. Not really a gentleman, though he knew how to behave like one. He had been sent to Kilkenny College: the Eton of Ireland. If only he had been educated, he might have done something useful in the world.

*Charlotte.* But Kilkenny College . . . two of my own cousins went there. Surely your uncle must have been taught *something* there?

*GBS.* All he learned was how to wriggle out under the College gates at night to make appointments with the Kilkenny whores on behalf of the senior boys. *[A pause.]* I'm glad to see you don't pretend to be shocked. Uncle Walter has always said that boys' schools should be within easy reach of whores. It prevents the boys from becoming homosexuals.

*Charlotte.* It makes us women very happy to know we are of some use to men.

*GBS.* That reminds me. I didn't answer your question.

*Charlotte.* What question?

*GBS.* Why even sensible women set out to annoy their husbands.

*Charlotte.* Oh, let's not go back over that dreary stuff again.

*GBS.* Women annoy men because it's their only way to get even with them. They're not physically strong enough to punch men on the nose.

*Charlotte.* The wife of one of our tenants in Cork used to blacken her husband's eye every week.

*GBS.* There are always exceptions to prove rules. Besides, some men have a taste for being beaten by women. Sidney Webb—

*Charlotte.* I refuse to believe that Sidney Webb requires Beatrice to beat him.

*GBS [Mildly].* I don't imagine he does. Beatrice is now telling everyone that Sidney is the perfect lover by day and by night.

*Charlotte [Shuddering].* How disgusting.

*GBS.* What I was about to say before you cut me short was that Sidney Webb tells me that the poet—oh, what's his name?—Swinburne, that he hires prostitutes to flog him.

*Charlotte.* What an amazing amount of revolting information you seem to have.

*GBS.* Life itself is revolting at many points. The mind has to take the bad with the good.

*Charlotte.* I'd like to hear more about your Uncle Walter.

*GBS.* He's the same breed as yourself.

*Charlotte [Bridling].* I am not in the habit of reciting vulgar limericks.

*GBS.* I'm not thinking of that at all. A repertoire of limericks, filthy or respectable, doesn't make a man interesting. Such things are mere incidentals, mere—

*Charlotte.* Why do you imagine I'm the same breed as your Uncle Walter?

*GBS.* It's not imagining; it's a matter of fact.

*Charlotte.* I asked you a straight question. I want a straight answer—for once.

*GBS.* I cannot understand why people are always accusing me of not giving straight answers. The trouble always is, their questions are so damnably crooked. Nevertheless, my answers are always straight, always direct, always to the point.

*Charlotte.* Are you going to answer my question?

*GBS.* I'm surprised you bothered to ask it when the answer is obvious.

*Charlotte.* You are an aggravating devil . . . George.

*GBS.* Go on, batter a dying man with insults. I'm an aggravating devil, evasive, dishonest, a clown—

*Charlotte.* I said no such things.

*GBS.* I could have sworn I heard the words aggravating devil. No doubt you will now accuse me of having hallucinations.

*Charlotte.* I never said you were dishonest. And I never allow anyone to call you a clown.

*GBS.* You may command, but they're not obeying.

*Charlotte [Earnestly].* You must be more careful not to give them any excuse to call you a clown.

*GBS [Still lightly].* The only people whose opinions I respect *know* that I'm not a clown.

*Charlotte.* If you want to *persuade* the other people, you must show them how serious you really are.

*GBS.* If they thought I was serious, they'd hang me.

*Charlotte [Walking away in despair].* There's no use talking to you.

*GBS.* The reason I said you and Uncle Walter are the same breed—

*Charlotte.* I am no longer interested.

*GBS.* Don't be petulant. The reason is that you are both absentee Irish landlords.

*Charlotte [Hotly].* I am not an—*[Subsiding.]* Well, I suppose in a way . . . if you stretch things . . . *[GBS remains silent. She turns to him anxiously.]* Are you all right?

*GBS.* Perfectly, thank you.

*Charlotte.* You weren't saying anything?

*GBS.* I was enjoying watching you squirm on the hook.

*Charlotte.* Hook?

*GBS.* Trying to deny you're an absentee Irish landlord.

*Charlotte [Angrily].* My home is in Cork.

*GBS [Mockingly].* And you love Dublin.

*Charlotte [Angrier].* Yes, I do.

*GBS.* But you'll do anything except live in Cork or Dublin?

*Charlotte [Gathering her resources for a crushing retort, then finding she hasn't got one].* Pscha.

*GBS.* I'm not blaming you.

*Charlotte.* Oh, thank you very much.

*GBS.* The problem with Ireland and America, is how to make these places fit for civilized people to live in.

*Charlotte.* This is utter nonsense.

*GBS.* In other words, you don't live in Cork for nonsensical reasons. But there are very sensible reasons for not living in Cork, and even more sensible ones for not living in Dublin.

*Charlotte.* I see no point in all this.

*GBS.* On the contrary, there is *every* point. Uncle Walter is drinking himself to death, then *I* shall be the absolute landlord. I'm his heir, you see. *[Mockingly.]* I notice that in spite of your Socialism you're quite impressed.

*Charlotte [Stiffly].* Naturally I'm very happy if you're coming into property.

*GBS.* Actually, it's a case of the property coming into *me*. It's mortgaged up to the hilt. It will be looking to *me* to make it solvent again. *[Dramatically.]* You are battening upon *your* property. *My* property will be battening upon *ME*.

*Charlotte.* You don't have to accept it. Repudiate the legacy.

*GBS.* What? Repudiate my responsibilities?

*Charlotte.* Certainly.

*GBS.* But they are HUMAN responsibilities.

*Charlotte.* Responsibilities generally are.

*GBS.* I mean *literally* human responsibilities. In the shape of my six aunts.

*Charlotte.* All of them demanding furniture polish?

*GBS.* Some settle for brandy.

*Charlotte.* Be thankful for small mercies.

*GBS.* I'm absolutely serious, Charlotte. There are six aunts and God knows how many cousins all depending on that property.

*Charlotte.* Have they any legal claim?

*GBS.* Their claim is much stronger than legal. It's moral. The claim of kinship, of blood, of mercy, compassion, pity, milk of human kindness— God damn them all.

*Charlotte.* I don't see any problem. Simply hand the property over to them.

*GBS.* It's useless to them. It's mortgaged.

*Charlotte.* Sell it.

*GBS.* No one will buy.

*Charlotte.* Nonsense. There's always somebody.

*GBS.* Who would buy an observatory in Carlow?

*Charlotte.* Observatory? Carlow?!! You mean Carlow in Ireland?

*GBS.* I certainly don't mean Monte Carlo. Uncle Walter has no property there. So far as I know.

*Charlotte.* I never heard of any observatory in Carlow.

*GBS.* That's because it's called the Assembly Rooms.

*Charlotte.* Well—which *is* it?

*GBS*. It's both. Uncle Walter says the roof of the Assembly Rooms is so full of holes, it's perfect for observing the stars at night.

*Charlotte*. Am I to understand that your Uncle Walter, your six aunts, and several cousins are all living off the rent of a roofless ruin in Carlow?

*GBS*. We are a very resourceful family.

*Charlotte [After a moment's speechlessness, with a gesture of despair]*. I don't know what to say.

*GBS*. If you weren't a lady, you could say,"Well, I'll be damned." But there *are* other morsels of property besides the roofless ruin. There are a few shops, a few troublesome houses, the best of which are being lived in by my tumbledown aunts. And, of course, there are sixteen acres of land.

*Charlotte*. How many?

*GBS*. Sixteen, not sixty or six thousand. And mostly bog, I should imagine. Or swamp. But you must remember that it isn't necessary to have twenty thousand acres like you in order to qualify as one of the landed gentry. Sixteen acres will do the trick just as well.

*Charlotte [Giving the matter up as hopeless]*. I suppose it will . . . if you are a resourceful family. By the way, I haven't twenty thousand acres. Fourteen hundred would be nearer the mark.

*GBS*. You mean to say that all your millions come from a mere fourteen hundred acres of—

*Charlotte*. My father made some wise investments in railways . . . at the right time.

*GBS*. Oh, worthy sire.

*Charlotte*. He also turned an honest penny or two on the Stock Exchange.

*GBS*. Thrice noble ancestor.

*Charlotte*. Which is why I make retribution by working for Socialism.

*GBS*. Do I detect in this a certain criticism of your father?

*Charlotte [Fiery]*. No such thing. You're only a clever man, Mr. George Bernard Shaw. My father was a good man. There's no shortage of clever men in this world, but you'll wear out more than one pair of boots searching for a good one.

*GBS*. What a father to inspire.

*Charlotte [Combatively]*. Are you sneering at me?

*GBS*. Oh, Charlotte, Charlotte, Charlotte, how little you really know me if you can imagine I'd sneer at anybody.

*Charlotte*. He was a good man, I really mean that. My father was kind. Loving. As straight and honest as the day. And my mother led him a dog's life. He didn't deserve *that*.

*GBS*. Does any man?

*Charlotte*. Yes. I've known men for whom a dog's life would be a thousand times too good. But not my father. My mother made his life one long torment. Even when I was only a child, I could see what he was suffering. I felt he should have beaten her—choked her. But he didn't. He never said a word. He just went away into his room. One day I went in after him. He was sitting there—crying. A man! Crying!! That's what she'd done to him. Broken him.

*[She struggles against tears, then covers her face with her hands and sits on the couch, an old woman once again. GBS comes out of his corner, sits besides her, puts his arm around her, and comforts her. After a while she tries to recover herself.]* I'm sorry, GBS. I seem to have spent a lot of our marriage crying.

*GBS [Cheerfully]*. Oh, most of it, beloved, most of it. For forty years I have been living with a fountain of tears. But that's what husbands are for: to provide a shoulder for their wives to weep on. Oh, by the way, why the present outburst?

*Charlotte [Mournfully]*. I used to think I took after my father. Now I realize it's my mother I'm like, God help me.

*GBS*. I shouldn't worry about that, dearest. All girls take after their mothers. Both of my sisters were my mother all over again. In fact, my younger sister—

*Charlotte [Impatiently, straightening herself]*. Yes, yes, you've told me so a dozen times. She was ginger-haired like all your mother's people.

*GBS*. Not ginger. Red. A fiery Highland red.

*Charlotte*. *You* were ginger when I knew you first.

*GBS*. Red, belovedest. Not so red as my sister Agnes. Red hair, white face. Now I'm red face, white hair. *[Rising moving around restlessly.]* Yet in some ways I haven't changed very much over the years. Neither have you. When I first saw you, you had rosy cheeks, masses of brown hair, and a beautiful skin.

*Charlotte*. That is utter nonsense. When you first saw me, I was already middle-aged and going grey.

*GBS*. I repeat: When I first saw you . . . rosy cheeks, beautiful ivory skin, and not one grey hair on your head.

*Charlotte*. You're imagining things. We were both middle-aged people.

*GBS*. We were the age of Romeo and Juliet.

*Charlotte.* If I didn't know you better, I'd say you'd been drinking.

*GBS.* The trouble is, you don't remember our first meeting.

*Charlotte.* In that house in Surrey which Beatrice rented for the summer.

*GBS.* No.

*Charlotte.* It *was* in Surrey. She rented the house in Middlesex the following year.

*GBS.* Totally wrong.

*Charlotte [Rising, confronting him, and wagging her finger].* Now you listen to me, GBS. My memory is not so good in some ways. But there *are* things which I am certain about.

*GBS.* And there are things I am also certain about.

*Charlotte.* I was staying in that house with Beatrice Webb in Surrey.

*GBS.* Yes, you were.

*Charlotte.* She and I were sharing the expenses.

*GBS.* I didn't know that.

*Charlotte.* Well, you know it now. She wouldn't allow the men to pay anything.

*GBS. I* wanted to pay my share.

*Charlotte [Stopping, confused].* What brought us on to this subject anyway? I thought we were talking about something else.

*GBS.* We were. About when we first met.

*Charlotte.* Yes, in Beatrice's house. And do you know why I was there?

*GBS.* Yes, of course. We all knew that.

*Charlotte.* Beatrice brought me so that I would fall in love with Graham Wallas and marry him.

*GBS.* Wallas was a fine-looking fellow.

*Charlotte.* He was a fool.

*GBS.* Oh now, really—!

*Charlotte.* He had no sense of humor. Absolutely none.

*GBS.* Well, that was why Beatrice brought *me* along. I was to keep you all amused.

*Charlotte.* Especially Sidney.

*GBS.* Especially herself. She was in love with me.

*Charlotte [Flouncing away].* Oh GBS, you can be such a fool sometimes. Beatrice Webb didn't even like you.

*GBS.* I know that. But she loved me. If she had liked me as much as she loved me, I was a goner. She would have swept me off, as she swept off Sidney.

*Charlotte.* I tell you she wasn't in the least interested in you. I know lots of women were interested in you, but not Beatrice Webb.

*GBS.* Why do you use the past tense? They still *are* interested in me. The older I get, the more eager the women are to get their arms around me. Why, I am positively afraid to go out by myself on a moonlit evening.

*Charlotte.* I suppose old ruins do look more romantic by moonlight. *[Remorsefully.]* I shouldn't have said that.

*GBS [Genially]*. Why on earth not? It was fair comment, and quite witty.

*Charlotte.* It was mean and petty. I apologize.

*GBS [Taking her in his arms]*. No need to apologize, dearest. Any apologies between the two of us are owed by me to you. It took me thirty years to become a reasonably good husband to you.

*Charlotte.* I have no complaints.

*GBS.* Then you should have, because I've been teasing you.

*Charlotte.* Oh, you've been doing that since the day we met.

*GBS.* Which is the very thing I've been teasing you about.

*Charlotte [Breaking away and returning to the couch]*. We met in Beatrice's house, and I remember what you said: your exact words.

*GBS.* "How d'you do, Miss Payne-Townshend"?

*Charlotte.* No. You said, "You are exactly as I imagined you would be, Miss Payne-Townshend."

*GBS.* Did I? Yes, I suppose I would have. Because you were.

*Charlotte.* How did you know what I'd look like?

*GBS.* I told you we had met before.

*Charlotte.* No, we hadn't.

*GBS.* You were wearing a blue-green costume.

*Charlotte.* Impossible.

*GBS.* And a little pill box hat on the side of your head like a soldier.

*Charlotte.* I haven't worn a pillbox since I was a girl.

*GBS.* You *were* a girl. You and your mother came into the office.

*Charlotte.* What office?

*GBS.* Your cousin Townshend's office in Dublin where I was an office boy.

*Charlotte.* I don't remember you.

*GBS.* You looked at me hard enough.

*Charlotte.* I did no such thing.

*GBS.* How do you know? You said you didn't remember.

*Charlotte.* I was too shy to look at any boy.

*GBS.* You're still a bit of a shy bird, you know.

*Charlotte.* So are you.

*GBS [Wagging a finger at her]*. But you were staring at me that day.

*Charlotte.* And you were staring back, I suppose?

*GBS.* I was watching you in the mirror.

*Charlotte.* That I would believe.

*GBS [Thoughtfully, after a pause].* It occurs to me that all my life I have been watching people in the mirror, instead of looking straight at them. My father was inclined to do the same. Shy birds, all of us. Not my mother, though. She could always stare you straight in the face. She could make strong men quail.

*Charlotte.* My sister could always look people straight in the face. But *she* was the pretty one.

*GBS.* Not much character, though.

*Charlotte [Contemptuously].* What do men care for *character?*

*GBS. I* do.

*Charlotte.* So long as a pretty face goes with it.

*GBS.* Not essential.

*Charlotte. All* your women had to be good-looking.

*GBS.* You flatter me. How many women do you think I had?

*Charlotte.* That side of your life never interested me.

*GBS.* Is that the truth, the whole truth, and nothing but the truth?

*Charlotte.* So I'm a liar now.

*GBS.* I seem to remember moments of jealousy.

*Charlotte.* I objected to your making a fool of yourself.

*GBS [Sighing].* Doesn't every man make a fool of himself over women?

*Charlotte.* Women do the same over men.

*GBS.* Then the allegations cancel themselves out.

*Charlotte.* I don't see how they do. Men and women makes fools of themselves in different ways.

*GBS.* Is there much to choose between them? Nature is knocking their heads together, even knocking common sense out of their heads, because Nature is merely using men and women to fulfil her own purpose: the replenishment of the Earth.

*Charlotte.* She hardly succeeded with us.

*GBS.* Hang it all, you were past the age of safe childbearing when we married. We couldn't give Nature a chance.

*Charlotte [Harshly].* You know what I think of children.

*GBS.* If you had one, you might think differently.

*Charlotte.* Horrid little creatures.

*GBS.* Some, perhaps.

*Charlotte.* Like rats.

*GBS.* Rats . . . apes . . . elephants . . . birds, fishes, frogs, philosophers, leopards, ladies—we're all distantly related. In some cases the relationship isn't all that distant. I have known some human apes and tigresses.

*Charlotte.* Oh yes, you were very partial to human tigresses.

*GBS.* It was pleasant to stroke their fur, to tickle them behind the ears.

*Charlotte.* Ah pray, GBS, who was tickling whom?

*GBS.* Sometimes I wasn't quite sure. However, I still have *my* ears.

*Charlotte.* Though a little worse for the wear.

*GBS.* Naturally—after more than eighty years.

*Charlotte [Careful not to look at him].* What did you think of me that day you saw me in old Townshend's office?

*GBS* Oh, quite attractive. Very attractive.

*Charlotte.* Liar.

*GBS.* You underestimate yourself.

*Charlotte.* Why didn't you speak to me then?

*GBS.* I had no excuse for speaking to you. I was the office boy.

*Charlotte.* I thought you were the cashier.

*GBS.* That came later. I was cashier until Townshend brought his nephew into the firm and gave *him* the job.

*Charlotte.* I'd have thought you were quite efficient.

*GBS.* I was highly efficient. I always had my books balanced to the last ha'penny.

*Charlotte.* Yet you were pushed out of the job. That hardly seems fair.

*GBS.* Life itself was hardly fair to me in Dublin. I had to go to England before life began to make amends.

*Charlotte.* You're too bitter about Dublin.

*GBS [Very hostile].* That city of derision.

*Charlotte.* And there's no derision in London?

*GBS.* Of course, there is. And in Paris, in Rome, in New York—everywhere. But in Dublin there is nothing *but* derision. In Dublin, more than in any other place on earth, known to me, there is a cheap, vile hatred of everything noble, a base envy of progress, advancement, a distrust of public spirit—

*Charlotte.* People aren't saints.

*GBS [Sweeping on].* —a resentment of energy, contemptible toleration of slovenliness, gracelessness, laziness, dirt, disorder, filth—God in heaven, the River Liffey: the stench, the stink, the dead dogs and cats—and overall the damnable complacency of the jackeens swaggering about in their shabby gentility, sneering and cackling, cackling, forever cackling without a moment's letup, cackling about nothing when the reservoir of dirty stories and lascivious innuendoes has temporarily dried up, anything to avoid thought, anything to avoid responsibility, anything to avoid doing something useful, to achieve something worthwhile; where beauty in women merely feeds lust; where the drunkenness and worthlessness of the husband turn the angel face of eighteen into the worn, weary domestic slave at thirty, exhausted by excessive childbearing, fit only for the scrap heap at forty; where to walk around Merrion Square is to be infuriated by the snobbishness, the pretentiousness, the arrogance, the smug acceptance that We are We and They are They and never the twain shall meet save in the relation of master and servant, Caesar and slave. *[Suddenly subsiding.]* And I know I'm getting ridiculous.

*Charlotte.* I'm always warning you: You could give yourself a stroke when you go on like that.

*GBS.* No fear of that. More likely I'd blow up if I kept it in. The danger is, if I didn't let fly to you, I'd only write it down and publish it. I'd prefer the world not to know how much I am possessed by the devil of Irish oratory. Let it be our secret, beloved, the extent to which I have the fatal Irish urge to get up on my hind legs and blather hot air to the multitude like Parnell and Grattan and Robert Emmet and the whole tribe of patriotic gasbags.

*Charlotte.* You think you've kept *that* a secret?!

*GBS.* Pretty well. The world will never know the worst of me. Most of what I write goes into the wastepaper basket.

*Charlotte.* But most of what you say doesn't. People hear you.

*GBS.* There's enough of the actor in me to make my rubbish sound witty and wise. Besides, my rubbish is still forty times better than the best of other men—if not four hundred times.

*[The lighting changes. Charlotte is again the young woman: GBS is in his corner.]*

*Charlotte.* I have to say something serious to you. Very serious.

*GBS.* It'll only make me frivolous, you know. Natural reaction.

*Charlotte. If* I am to marry you—

*GBS.* If?! IF?!!! The heavens are telling, since the beginning of time, that you and I must be man and wife.

*Charlotte.* Don't be so sure of yourself.

*GBS.* You mean, don't be so sure of *you.*

*Charlotte.* Take it whichever way you like. But if I give up my independence in order to marry you—

*GBS.* If you give up your independence, the whole thing's off. My one and only requirement in a wife is that she shall be independent of me in every way. Besides, I'll be surrendering more of my independence than you.

*Charlotte.* Do you think you could remain quiet for just long enough to let me say five words?

*GBS.* Oh, Miss Payne-Townshend, how you wrong me. My trouble has always been a tendency to silence—morose silence. But now, like Iago, from this moment forth I ne'er shall ope my lips.

*Charlotte.* What I want to say is this. If I marry you, I want my husband to exercise a greater sense of responsibility towards himself than he has perhaps been doing so far. *[A pause.]* I hope I haven't offended you. *[She pauses.]* Why aren't you saying something?

*GBS.* Aren't you being unreasonable? You complain when I talk, you complain when I don't talk.

*Charlotte.* You're so childish.

*GBS.* Yes, ma'am. Anything else?

*Charlotte.* Do you understand what I've been saying?

*GBS.* You mean, about exercising more responsibility for myself?

*Charlotte. To* yourself.

*GBS.* Is there really much room for improvement? Surely I am one of the most conscientiously responsible men who have ever lived. My sense of responsibility is like a woman's.

*Charlotte.* This is just what I'm getting at.

*GBS.* You object to my claiming equality with a woman?

*Charlotte.* Just stop boasting.

*GBS.* Boasting?!!!

*Charlotte.* I'm afraid so.

*GBS [Explosively].* God in Heaven, woman, who has more right to boast than I. Is my brain not one of the wonders of the world? Have I not written five novels of such excruciating brilliance that they were turned down by every publisher in England and pirated by every publisher in America? Have I not been the most penetrating and prophetic London music critic of my time and for a salary of £2 a week begrudgingly paid by that blithering buffoon from Athlone named Tay Pay O'Connor? Have I just not finished four years of the most acutely perceptive London drama criticism of the century, for a salary of £5 a week, intermittently paid by the tenderhearted buccaneer from Galway named Frank Harris—

*Charlotte.* That's another thing. When we are married, that man Harris is never to cross my door.

*GBS [Ignoring the interruption].* Am I not now changing the whole world of the theatre with my half-dozen plays of unsurpassable power? And not only am I toppling the outworn Shakespeare from his throne and replacing him with myself: I am transforming the world with my Fabian Socialism. The twentieth century shall be molded by me in literature and in economics as profoundly as nineteenth century music was by Beethoven and by Richard Wagner. And you, Charlotte Payne-Townshend, reproach me for boasting! Me?! A man who had done so much by forty—by Heaven, my achievement at that early age puts Mozart himself to shame. Think! If only I had lasted until I was fifty, what would I not have done? If only the gods had granted me my three score years and ten, I'd have been one of the marvels of all time. *[Whimsically.]* Which reminds me. If you're going to marry me, hurry out and get the ring. Otherwise you'll miss your chance of immortality as my widow.

*Charlotte [Suspiciously].* I'm beginning to wonder are you really as ill as you look.

*GBS.* Oh far worse, beloved, far, far worse. My hand is on the door of the crematorium furnace. I open it and wearily crawl inside. It slams behind me.

*[The hall door slams shut.]*

*Charlotte [Jumping and clutching her chest].* Jesus!

*GBS.* Not him. Merely my sister Lucy coming in.

*Charlotte [With icy fury].* And does your sister Lucy always close doors like that?

*GBS.* There's no other way of closing our hall door. If you don't bang it hard, the lock doesn't catch and the thing swings open.

*[A hollow bump on the floor overhead.]*

*Charlotte [Looking upwards].* And what was *that?*

*GBS.* My aunt dropping a bottle on the floor to let Lucy know that she wants her upstairs. O course, if we had three hundred servants like you, my aunt would merely ring the bell, and the chambermaid would rush upstairs, and my aunt would tell her to send up a footman with afternoon tea, and up he'd go with a magnum of champagne and a glass on a silver salver. But we haven't got three hundred servants, so my aunt has to notify my sister Lucy in the only way she can that more furniture polish is required.

*Charlotte [Preparing to go].* I don't think I'd be able to face your sister this afternoon—

*GBS.* You'll have to meet her sooner or later.

*Charlotte.* I suppose so.

*GBS.* And you needn't worry. Lucy is just as much afraid of you as you are of her.

*Charlotte.* Afraid of *me?*

*GBS.* Even my mother: You have made her a little nervous too.

*Charlotte.* Your mother's a terror. She'd put the fear of God into Queen Victoria herself.

*GBS.* Of course, it's only your manner. You're really quite soft and sentimental.

*Charlotte [Scornfully].* Sentimental? Me?

*GBS.* Very sentimental about your father.

*Charlotte [Fiery].* If you say one word against my father, I'll leave this house and refuse to see you again.

*GBS [Smiling].* Ridiculously sentimental about your father.

*Charlotte [Glaring at him. He stands firm. She begins to cry.]*

*GBS [As before].* Preposterously sentimental about your father.

*Charlotte [Drying her eyes, looks at him steadily, and speaks in measured tones].* I see you are going to be a very difficult husband.

*GBS.* I see you're the only woman I could ever live with.

[*Lucy comes in. She is in outdoor dress and is just taking off her hat.*]

*Lucy.* Oh, I *am* sorry. I didn't know you had company.

*GBS.* My sister Lucy . . . Miss Payne-Townshend.

*Charlotte [Not stirring].* How d'you do?

*Lucy [Not stirring].* How d'you do?

[*The women stare at each other without speaking. GBS watches them with obvious amusement.*]

*GBS.* Well, you'll certainly recognize each other again.

[*Both women frown at his ill manners.*]

*Lucy [With a rather forced smile].* Will you have some tea?

*Charlotte.* Thank you very much, but no. I fear I must be going.

*Lucy.* I've an idea I've interrupted something.

*Charlotte [Quickly].* Not at all. I was just about—

*GBS.* Oh yes, you have. Miss Payne-Townshend and I are completing arrangements to get married.

*Lucy [Staggered].* I beg your pardon.

*GBS.* You have no objections, I trust?

*Lucy.* Did I hear you say you were . . . you were. . . .

*GBS.* Getting married.

*Lucy.* To each other?

*GBS.* That is the general idea.

*Lucy.* But . . . [*She stops herself.*]

*GBS.* I take it that in the course of the next week or so you'll felicitate Miss Payne-Townshend on the splendid match she is making.

*Lucy.* Oh, I do beg your pardon, Miss Payne-Townshend. Felicitations.

*Charlotte.* Thank you, Miss Shaw.

*GBS.* And although not for the world would I try to prompt you, I'm sure you'd also wish to—

*Lucy.* Congratulations, George. Are there any other votes of thanks for me to propose?

*GBS.* That'll do very nicely for the moment.

*Lucy.* Does Mamma know?

*GBS.* Not yet.

*Lucy.* Where is she?

*GBS.* Gone off to the school.

*Lucy.* Well, in the circumstances Miss Payne-Townshend really must have some tea. *[To her.]* Do, please.

*Charlotte [Uncomfortably].* That would be very nice, Miss Shaw.

*Lucy.* And do please call me Lucy.

   *[A loud bump from overhead. Charlotte starts, clasps her hand to her breast and glances upwards.]*

*GBS [Pointing upwards].* Second call, Lucy.

*Lucy.* Please excuse me. Something seems to have fallen upstairs. *[Going.]*

*GBS.* Miss Payne-Townshend knows it's our aunt.

*Lucy [Stopping dead].* She does?

*GBS.* And I've told her about the furniture polish.

*Lucy [Shrugging].* He seems to have spared you nothing, Miss Payne-Townshend.

*Charlotte [Quietly].* I think your aunt's affliction is very tragic.

*Lucy.* George thinks it's very funny.

*GBS.* All tragedies have their funny side. Just as all comedies—

*Lucy.* Have their tragic side. Oh George, you are *so* predictable.

   *[A louder bump.]*

*Lucy [To Charlotte].* Will you excuse me? *[She goes out.]*

*GBS.* Well . . . now the two of you have met. And you've met my mother. There aren't any more hurdles to be got over.

*Charlotte.* There's my sister.

*GBS.* Is she going to be a problem?

*Charlotte [Stiffly].* Why should she be?

*GBS.* She's a woman.

*Charlotte.* Does it surprise you that my sister is a woman?

*GBS.* Every woman poses a problem to a man. Especially to a man like me.

*Charlotte.* I haven't the faintest idea of what you're talking about.

*GBS.* She's bound to tell you that she hates me.

*Charlotte.* She knows nothing about you. She hasn't even seen you.

*GBS.* The moment she sets eyes on me, she will fall in love with me. Sisterly affection will make her try to hide that fact from you. She will assure you she loathes the sight of me. You will see through that hollow pretence. You will exult because *you* have me, and she doesn't.

*Charlotte [Smiling].* Really, if anyone were to take you seriously—

*GBS.* Aha! That's what everyone says when they realize I have penetrated to their most secret thoughts.

*Charlotte [Complacently].* Listen to me, my dear. When you meet Sissie—

*GBS.* When Sissie meets Me.

*Charlotte.* —you will find that she has eyes for only one man.

*GBS.* I've just told you that. Me.

*Charlotte.* Her husband. *[The snob in her.]* He'll soon be a colonel.

*GBS.* That reminds me. I have a cousin a colonel.

*Charlotte [Surprised].* You have?

*GBS.* He is also a baronet. Col. Sir Robert Shaw. I think he's the fourth baronet or the fifth. They stretch way back.

*Charlotte [Impressed].* Indeed.

*GBS.* Not that we think much of colonels as such. No disrespect to your sister Sissie's colonel. But one of my father's cousins was much more interesting. He was a judge and a member of Parliament. Another of them was hanged as a rebel in 1798. He's the only ancestor I've any real respect for. Incidentally, another cousin of mine is the Chief of the London Fire Brigade.

*Charlotte.* Captain Shaw . . . your cousin?

*GBS.* You've heard the lampoon about him. It's in Gilbert and Sullivan.

> Oh Captain Shaw
> Type of true love kept under
> Could thy brigade
> With cold cascade
> Quench my hot love, I wonder.

Something like that. I may not have got it quite right.

*Charlotte.* What do they mean "type of true love kept under"? Is he impotent?

*GBS.* Not he. He was mixed up in Lady Colin Campbell's divorce case. The butler told the court that he saw them through the drawing room keyhole. They were on the sofa.

*Charlotte.* Just sitting together.

*GBS.* I hardly imagine so. The butler said her legs were up in the air, and the captain was drowning in a sea of petticoats and going down for the third time.

*Charlotte.* Disgusting.

*GBS.* The captain or the butler or Lady Colin Campbell?

*Charlotte.* All three of them.

*[Loud bumps from above.]*

*GBS.* Good Lord, has Lucy not gone up to her yet?

*[Lucy comes in with a tray of tea things.]*

*Lucy.* George, have you any idea where the maid is?

*GBS.* Emigrated to Australia, I hope.

*Charlotte.* I'm putting you to such a great deal of trouble.

*Lucy.* Not in the least.

*GBS.* Our sainted aunt is still summoning spirits from the vasty deep.

*Lucy.* I brought her up a cup of tea when I came in. She'll have to do without her spirits. *[She places the tray on a little table and pours the tea.]*

*GBS.* Talking about Australia: We've hundreds of cousins out there.

*Lucy.* Thousands of them. *[She hands a cup and saucer to GBS.]*

*GBS.* One of them is a chief of police.

*Lucy.* I've never heard what the others are.

*GBS.* Probably bush rangers.

*Lucy.* Or members of Ned Kelly's gang, and no doubt married to Maoris. I've heard that one cousin of ours is—*[Warning.]* Oh George: *That* cup is for our guest.

*GBS [Hurriedly proferring it to Charlotte].* I crave your pardon. My afternoon tea manners are positively atrocious.

*Lucy [Handing him a cup].* That's for you.

*GBS [Examining the cup].* You must be keeping the one with the cracked handle for yourself.

*Lucy [Examining the third cup].* I haven't actually. Poor auntie must have got that.

*[Two bumps from above.]*

*GBS.* Sounds like she did.

*Lucy [Coming around to Charlotte's chair].* Would you prefer to sit beside George?

*GBS [Innocently].* I imagine Charlotte would rather not be on a sofa.

*[Charlotte gulps convulsively over a sip of tea.]*

*GBS.* We were just talking about sofas when you came in.

*Charlotte [Tensely].* I'm quite comfortable here, thank you.

*Lucy.* Then I'll plop down beside George. *[She does so.]* I'm sorry I'm not able to offer you any sweet cake. I looked in the box, but George had scoffed the lot.

*GBS.* I occasionally have a fancy for a finger of cake.

*Lucy.* He eats it by the ton.

*GBS.* If you say so.

*Lucy.* You won't find it much of a problem feeding him. He's a vegetarian, you know.

*Charlotte.* He has told me that.

*Lucy.* Bread and apples.

*Charlotte.* I hope to coax him to extend the menu.

*Lucy.* You'll need to. He makes a terrible noise eating apples. You can hear him in the next street.

*Charlotte.* I hope to turn vegetarian myself, Miss Shaw.

*Lucy.* Oh please . . . Lucy.

*Charlotte.* Forgive me; Lucy, of course.

*Lucy.* And how shall I address my sister-in-law that is to be?

*Charlotte.* My name is Charlotte.

*Lucy.* A lovely name. So soft and cuddly. How do you spell it?

*GBS.* C-H-A-R-L-O-T-T-E.

*Lucy.* Oh . . . just like in the street.

*GBS.* Yes. Charlotte Street.

*Lucy.* I don't mean the street here in London. The one at home in Dublin.

*Charlotte.* Is there a Charlotte Street in Dublin?

*Lucy.* Near where we used to live in Synge Street. But it was pronounced Carlotta Street.

*GBS.* Oh, *that* place.

*Lucy.* George and I were born in Synge Street, and Yuppy.

*GBS.* Our sister Yuppy, officially Agnes.

*Charlotte.* I do look forward to meeting her.

*Lucy [Quietly].* Poor dear Yuppy is dead.

*GBS.* "To be with Christ, which is far better."

*Lucy.* Don't mock, George.

*GBS.* I am not certainly *not* mocking. I quite agree that it is better for Yuppy to be with Christ. She had consumption.

*Lucy.* George didn't approve of Mother having it put on her tomb-stone.

*Charlotte.* That she had consumption?

*Lucy.* The Bible text.

*GBS.* "To be with Christ, which is far better." But I didn't press the point with Mamma. Yuppy was her favorite child.

*Lucy.* Yuppy had the most beautiful hair you ever saw. *[Indicating her waist.]* It came down to here. It was so thick you just wouldn't believe it. On a sunny day it shone. It was like gold.

*GBS.* Burnished gold. But gold.

*Lucy.* I always have this vision of Yuppy. Standing on the hill at Dalkey. A breeze coming in from the sea, blowing her hair around her face.

*GBS.* Do you remember how pale her face was?

*Lucy.* And the sun at Dalkey, shining on her hair.

*GBS.* Manna said that towards the end her face became quite ruddy.

*Charlotte [Sympathetically].* How old was she when she—?
*[She pauses delicately.]*

*Lucy.* She was barely twenty-one when she was taken from us.

*GBS.* With her luxuriant masses of hair and her ruddy complexion, she died the very picture of good health.

*Lucy.* She was skin and bone, George. I was there. You weren't.

*GBS [To Charlotte].* Yuppy died only a couple of days before I packed my bags in Dublin and left the damned place for good and all.

*Lucy.* Manna had sent Yuppy over to the Isle of Wight to get her away from the fogs here in London.

*GBS.* My mother was really very cut up at the time.

*Lucy.* So were you.

*GBS.* Was I?

*Lucy.* Didn't I have to bring you across to the Isle of Wight to the grave? *[To Charlotte.]* He cried like a baby.

*GBS.* Did I?

*Lucy.* Oh yes, you did. But he pretended he wasn't because men aren't supposed to be crybabies.

*GBS.* I see no reason why men shouldn't weep if they want to. If I felt the slightest inclination to cry, then my eyes would drop tears as fast as Arabian trees their medicinal gum.

*Lucy.* But he's quite right about Mamma. Would you care for more tea?

*Charlotte.* Thank you, no.

*Lucy.* Let me relieve you of your cup. *[She rises, takes the cup and places it on the tray.]* Mama has been weeping for poor Yuppy for the past twenty years. Tea, George?

*GBS.* No thanks. *[He gives the cup and saucer to Lucy, and turns to Charlotte.]* Yuppy was her favorite because she was the only one of us to look like her own people, the Gurlys.

*Lucy.* Do you really think so? I know George takes after Mother. That's where he gets all his sentimentality from. George and my mother, they're the two most emotional people I've ever come across.

*Charlotte.* That's not quite how his friends see him.

*Lucy.* Oh, you mean this act he puts on. That he's a real hard chaw.

*Charlotte.* I didn't quite catch what you said.

*Lucy.* A hard chaw. It's an expression we used at home in Dublin. Carlotta Street was full of hard chaws. People who don't care a damn about anybody or anything.

*Charlotte.* I notice George is saying nothing.

*GBS.* What would be the point? My dear sister has allocated highly imaginative roles to everyone she knows, and there's no use protesting that the cap doesn't fit. She ignores the facts and refuses to change her mind.

*Lucy.* And when will the happy day be, Charlotte?

*GBS.* First of June.

*Lucy.* You mean . . . *this* first of June?

*GBS.* What other?

*Lucy.* But that's only a couple of days away.

*GBS.* There is, of course, a very pressing reason for Charlotte to get married.

*Lucy [Staggered].* George!

*GBS [Enjoying the effect].* I am not about to become a father. I'm about to become a corpse.

*Lucy.* Corpse did you say?

*GBS.* I too have decided to be with Christ.

*Lucy.* But in the meantime you're going to be with Charlotte.

*Charlotte [Quietly].* I've asked him not to joke about dying.

*GBS.* Mocking is catching, eh?

*Lucy.* There's no fear of *him* dying. He'll see us all down.

*Charlotte.* Not if he goes on the way he's going.

*Lucy.* Don't judge by appearances. He's been looking that way for as long as I know him.

*GBS.* I have at least seven fatal diseases.

*Lucy.* They seem to be cancelling each other out, George.

*Charlotte.* I've been thinking that he should live in the country for a while.

*Lucy.* George In the country?! He's a city man, my dear. All the Shaws were city men. Put them in the country, and they'd die from fresh air, Carlotta. *[Apologetically.]* Oh, that slipped out in spite of me. You don't mind me calling you Carlotta, do you?

*GBS [Coldly].* The name is Charlotte.

*Charlotte.* Carlotta if you like.

*Lucy.* Thank you, Carlotta. It sounds friendlier, more familiar. Reminds me of Dublin, I suppose.

*Charlotte.* You're fond of Dublin?

*Lucy.* Oh, I love it. Always have. The only place I feel really at home. But then it *is* home, isn't it?

*Charlotte.* Your brother isn't so enthusiastic about Dublin.

*Lucy.* I suppose he has his reasons.

*GBS [Rather harshly].* My reasons are that Dublin is boring. A tedious place. A futile place. A place in which people like me have no business to do, no purpose to serve—

*Lucy.* And in which people like you are humiliated.

*GBS.* If you say so.

*Lucy [Politely ignoring him].* And where will you be married, Carlotta?

*GBS.* Registry office.

*Lucy.* That will be much less fuss.

*Charlotte.* I'd prefer to have as little fuss as possible.

*Lucy.* But how do you think you'll keep George quiet?

*GBS.* Am I such a rowdy?

*Lucy.* You don't exactly melt into the background, George.

*GBS.* In my case that's a virtue, not a fault.

*Lucy [To Charlotte].* Except, of course, when our relatives come over from Dublin to see us. Then he melts into the background pretty quick. Can't get a word out of him.

*GBS.* I couldn't get a word *in* edgewise with our relations. Chatterboxes. Incessant babble. About nothing.

*Lucy.* You'll have a handful in that husband, my dear.

*GBS.* The only interesting kind of husband for a woman to have.

*Charlotte.* Have you never thought of getting married yourself?
*[GBS starts cackling in a high-pitched tone and rubs his hands vigorously. Charlotte looks astonished.]*

*Lucy [Matter-of-factly].* I *am* married.

*Charlotte [Taken aback; to GBS].* But you never told me.

*GBS [Shrugging].* I keep forgetting.

*Lucy.* I wish *I* could forget it too.

*Charlotte [At a loss].* Oh . . . I see.

*Lucy.* Marriage is Dead Sea fruit.

*GBS.* To quote our mother.

*Lucy.* This is hardly the thing to be talking about when Carlotta is just about to be married herself.

*GBS.* I have pointed out to her the drawbacks, the inevitable disappointments—Heaven knows I've not attempted to hide my faults from her, minor though they be.

*Lucy.* She'll find them out soon enough, George.

*GBS.* The voice of experience.

*Lucy.* I'm not saying *I* was completely blameless.

*Charlotte.* I know I'm not perfect myself.

*GBS.* Sweet God, are you pair going to make a General Confession?

*Lucy [Ignoring him].* But my husband did go that little bit too far.

*GBS.* His face looks as if it's carved out of a bladder of lard.

*Lucy.* It's lucky for men we women don't take too much account of their faces. *[To Charlotte, confidentially.]* If a man gets married, his wife has a right to expect that he'll remain faithful.

*GBS.* I deny that she has any *right*. She can always hope so.

*Charlotte [Indignantly].* He expect *her* to remain faithful.

*GBS.* He expects her to make the attempt. To expect any more would be unreasonable.

*Lucy.* Faithfulness is the important thing.

*Charlotte.* Faithfulness is what marriage is all about. My own father was the most faithful of men.

*GBS.* And did that ensure his happiness? *[Quickly.]* You needn't answer. My own father was quite faithful. But that didn't save *his* marriage.

*Lucy [Sharply].* Mother was faithful too.

*GBS.* Well, that appears to dispose of fidelity as a recipe for happy marriage.

*Lucy.* You know perfectly well that the trouble at home was caused by papa's little problem.

*GBS [To Charlotte].* His little problem was that he drank himself silly every day, seven days a week.

*Lucy.* That's one problem you won't have with George.

*Charlotte.* I've no objection to a man drinking in moderation.

*Lucy.* George doesn't know the meaning of moderation. He's a teetotaller, a vegetarian, and a nonsmoker.

*Charlotte [Dryly].* One can't expect everything.

*GBS [Rising abruptly].* Will you excuse me for a moment?

*Lucy [Halting him on his way to the door].* If you're upstairs, perhaps you'll take a look in at auntie.
*[He hobbles out.]*

*Lucy.* Oh, by the way, do you—er—?

*Charlotte.* Thank you, no. I'm quite happy for the moment.

*Lucy.* I'm so glad you're marrying George.

*Charlotte.* Thank you.

*Lucy.* And I know Mother will be very pleased *[Charlotte just smiles.]* He's not a bad stick at all, you know. Very quiet around the house. You wouldn't know he was in the place.

*Charlotte.* I've noticed that.

*Lucy.* He needs somebody to take care of him.

*Charlotte.* Men do.

*Lucy.* I don't fuss about his health, but sometimes I get quite worried.

*Charlotte.* I got a terrible shock when I came back from Italy and saw him.

*Lucy.* You know . . . the oddest thing . . . but I must have it wrong. He said . . . or rather I understood him to say . . . but obviously I got it wrong . . . that you had gone to Italy to get married.

*Charlotte [Obviously uncomfortable].* My goodness.

*Lucy.* To someone else.

*Charlotte.* I wonder how that story got around.

*Lucy.* I somehow got it into my head . . . that it was a doctor. *[Charlotte does not reply.]* Rumors are extraordinary, aren't they?

*Charlotte.* Indeed.

*Lucy.* Oh yes, it all comes back to me now. Somebody met you in Rome . . . or was it Capri?

*Charlotte [In control of herself again].* I *was* in Capri, actually.

*Lucy.* And the doctor . . . a very well-known personality . . . a Norwegian, I think.

*Charlotte.* Swedish.

*Lucy.* And he was called . . . oh, some curious name . . .

*Charlotte.* Dr. Axel Munthe.

*Lucy.* Yes, that's it. But obviously he isn't to be the lucky man. *[Charlotte doesn't reply.]* George *is* very lucky to get you.

*Charlotte.* I regard it as a great privilege to take care of him.

*Lucy.* He thinks he's a genius, you know.

*Charlotte.* I don't think there's any doubt of it.

*[GBS comes back.]*

*GBS.* I was going to hop downstairs to call a cab for you. But the thought of hopping back up all those stairs—!

*Charlotte [Rising].* I prefer to walk. It's such a lovely day.

*Lucy.* George, do you realize you've just *ordered* Carlotta to leave the house?

*GBS.* She has a lot to do.

*Charlotte.* Yes, I really must be going.

*GBS.* She has to see about the license. She has to buy herself a wedding ring.

*Lucy.* You know, Carlotta, he wasn't brought up to behave like that. We reared him as a gentleman.

*GBS.* I am much more important than a gentleman. Charlotte is not interested in mere gentlemen, although many of the breed have pursued her.

*Lucy.* But it was a genius who caught her.

*GBS.* Strangely enough, my dear Lucy, that is the simple fact of the matter.

*Lucy.* Well, may you both be very happy.

*GBS.* Happiness is not our objective.

*Lucy.* Then you will never be disappointed. You may be pleasantly surprised.

*Charlotte [Having put on her hat].* Goodbye, Lucy, and thank you very much for the tea.

*Lucy [Hurrying to the door].* I shall leave you to yourselves.

*GBS.* No need to be tactful. Charlotte and I have no endearments to perform.

[*Lucy stops and turns to Charlotte questioningly. Charlotte remains impassive.*]

*Lucy.* Shall I be seeing you before the big day?

*Charlotte.* I hope so.

*GBS.* She has the strictest orders to report here every day. Now that I'm marrying her, I have to keep an eye on her.

*Lucy.* And are we invited to the wedding? Mother and I, I mean.

*GBS.* There will be no relations, no friends, no enemies. The witnesses shall be the first two persons willing to come in off the street to see us turned off.

*Charlotte.* We have arranged with Mr. Henry Salt and Mr. Graham Wallas to be our witnesses.

*Lucy.* Graham Wallas? Weren't you supposed to be marrying *him?* George, you told me that—

*Charlotte.* Really, Miss Shaw, you seem to be bent on marrying me off to every man in London.

*Lucy.* And Italy. Sorry. No offense.

*Charlotte.* Not even my own sister will be at our wedding.

*GBS.* No relations, no family quarrels. When everybody finds out that nobody was asked, they'll all feel equally insulted, so everyone will be able to stay friendly.

*Lucy.* I'm sure I don't know what Mother's going to say to all this.

*GBS [Snapping his fingers].* Mother doesn't care that much whether I stay single or marry forty wives.

*Lucy [Earnestly].* She's always been very fond of you, George.

*GBS.* I've never given her any reason to be.

*Lucy.* Very well. I shan't argue. And now I insist on leaving you to yourselves for a moment. [*She goes out quickly.*]

*GBS.* Women are incorrigibly romantic. Even Lucy.

*Charlotte.* Really?

*GBS [Jerking a thumb after Lucy].* Well, what d'you think?

*Charlotte.* You're very like each other.

*GBS.* Not a bit of it. *[Opening his arms.]* Come to my arms, my lovely fair.
*[She comes to him but not into his arms. She holds up her cheek. He kisses it lightly. She moves to the door.]*
*Charlotte.* Till tomorrow, then.
*GBS.* Till tomorrow.
*Charlotte [Stopping and turning].* I quite like her, you know.
*GBS.* Oh, everybody loves Lucy. But Lucy loves nobody.
*Charlotte.* Yes, you *are* very like each other. *[She goes.]*
*[GBS leans back on the sofa and whistles. Presently Lucy comes back.]*
*Lucy.* Well, that *is* a surprise. How did *she* manage to nab you when all the others have failed?
*GBS.* Is an explanation absolutely necessary?
*Lucy.* Of course not. Since I'm not asked to your wedding, you've made it quite clear that your marriage is none of my affair.
*GBS.* I can explain *that.*
*Lucy.* You needn't.
*GBS.* She's not inviting her own sister. I can hardly invite mine.
*Lucy.* And Mother?
*GBS.* Her mother won't be there either.
*Lucy.* But I thought her mother was dead.
*GBS.* One of the reasons she won't be there.
*Lucy.* Why isn't her sister coming?
*GBS.* She doesn't know about the marriage.
*Lucy.* But you said they were very close.
*GBS.* They adore one another. That's why Charlotte wants to break the news of me gently.
*Lucy.* Is she ashamed of you?
*GBS.* Quite the contrary. But I gather Sister Sissie from Shropshire doesn't understand about literary genius and the lack of a large income. Her intellectual range is limited to horses. And colonels.
*Lucy.* I still don't see that's any reason for cutting *us* out.
*GBS.* There's one other thing. Her name is Charlotte. I don't wish her to be addressed or referred to as Carlotta.
*Lucy.* She said she rather liked it.
*GBS [Sharply].* Well, I veto it.
*Lucy.* Do you indeed? Then you've made sure that so far as I'm concerned she's Carlotta from now on.
*GBS.* You know Carlotta is just one of your underhand jokes.
*Lucy.* Then you know more than I do.
*GBS.* I remember Carlotta Street very well, and the way the women there earned their living. And I know that Queen Carlotta was

the wife of the mad King George the Third, and you know how I hate the name George, so you are very cleverly killing two birds with the one stone with your Carlotta.

Lucy *[Mildly]*. I didn't even know about Carlotta and King George. As for your name, you were christened George after your father and Bernard after your uncle, just as I was called Lucinda after my mother, and there's nothing either of us can do about it. So there.

GBS *[In a milder tone than before]*. Anyway, drop the Carlotta.

Lucy *[Sharply]*. Certainly not.

GBS. Very well. I am powerless in the face of such petty-minded obstinacy.

Lucy. Really George, you'll make me lose my temper.

GBS. I shan't upset you by saying another word. I am completely in the wrong, as always. You're completely in the right, as always. Shall we leave it at that? I take it at any rate you wish me well in my marriage?

Lucy *[Hurt]*. Oh George, how can you go on like that? You know that both Mother and I want you to have every ounce of happiness you can get. Besides, it's time you settled down.

GBS. I shall continue to look after you both.

Lucy *[Lightly]*. Oh my goodness, George, you don't have to worry about *us*. Mother and I battled on before, and we'll battle on again.

GBS. I shall fix up something with Charlotte so that when I die, neither of you will starve. And you won't have to beg from her.

Lucy. We don't want her money. We don't need it. And what put it into your head that you're going to die?

GBS. I've burned myself out. It often happens to men like me. Look at Mozart. He went at thirty-five. Schubert? He was even younger. I've managed to hold out until forty-two. I may last another year. Two at the outside. Then through the doors of the crematorium to begin a new adventure somewhere else, leaving Charlotte to a comfortable, elegant, prosperous and lengthy— widowhood. She'll be another Queen Victoria.

Lucy. You have it all worked out. George, if you have a fault at all, it's that you're so damned sure of everything. But let me tell you this. You'll live to be a hundred.

*[Three impatient bumps from above.]*

Lucy *[Shaking her fist and glaring aloft]*. And so will that bloody woman up there.

*[The lights fade. Lucy, pale, old, wan, lies on a bed. A chair is beside the bed. From outside, the sound of an amateur pianist*

*playing "After the Ball Was Over." Lucy tosses restlessly. The pianist stops.]*

Lucy. O merciful God, vouchsafe in Thy infinite mercy that the bloody man has stopped playing his damned piano for this day. *[The pianist gives a flourish of arpeggios.]*

Lucy. God, why don't you strike my unmusical neighbor dead, or at least paralyze him so that I can die in peace. *[The light dims slightly on Lucy, and comes up on GBS in his narrating position.]*

GBS. My sister Lucy was like King Charles the Second. She had a lot of lovers, she didn't really give a hoot about anyone else, she was cynical, she was witty, she didn't much care for her brother, and she was an unconscionable time a-dying. *[The light dims on GBS, and comes up on Lucy.]*

Lucy. Oh George, why don't you come and visit me? The strangers keep coming to see me, but I only want my family. And you're the only family I've left.

GBS. She complained to everyone that I neglected her. That I refused to come to her deathbed. But this is always the trouble with people who dither about dying. They lie there, groaning and complaining, you can't satisfy them, they refuse to make any real effort to die, they just linger there, bored with existence, expecting the rest of the world to dance attendance on them.

Lucy. You never came to see your mother, either. I told you, all she wanted when she was lying in this bed as I am lying now, was to see you, her only son.

GBS. Death seems to bring out the theatrical instinct even in those who didn't have it in the days of their health and strength. Let them lead useless, empty, futile lives, doing nothing except converting good food into bad manure; but once they get on a deathbed they feel they have a right to the center of the stage. They put up a performance . . . in life you couldn't trust them to walk on and carry a spear . . . but in death it has to be King Lear, Cleopatra, Ophelia.

Lucy. Surely you could spare me five minutes, George.

GBS. I am one of the most important men of my time. I am the world's oracle. Everyone wants to know my opinion about everything. I am obliged to work a sixteen-hour day, six days a week, sometimes seven. And I am somewhat elderly. I am sixty-four years of age. In the nature of things, I haven't much time left. Another few years and I shall be perambulating the Elysian Fields with Shakespeare, Molière, Ibsen, Handel, Beethoven, and Mozart. Meanwhile, I hope I am a humane man, but I simply *haven't* the time to play leading man to my sisters and my cousins and my aunts in the only big scene they'll ever have.

*[The light suddenly increases. Mrs. Pat Campbell, now entering her ripest phase, sweeps into Lucy's room. She is gorgeously and colorfully dressed. Her hair is raven black. She sparkles with jewels, glows with gold.]*

*Mrs. Pat [With an expansive gesture].* Lucy! My sweetest Lucy! *[She swoops on her and kisses her.]* You look beautiful. You look radiant. How *are* you?

*Lucy.* Dying.

*Mrs. Pat [As if she hadn't heard the remark, settles herself in the chair beside the bed].* Has that *wretch* come to see you yet?

*Lucy.* I'm afraid not.

*Mrs. Pat [Bounding up and sonorously intoning her instructions through the doorway].* Call Mr. Bernard Shaw on the telephone. Inform him that Mrs. Patrick Campbell is with his sister. *[She goes back to the chair.]*

*GBS [Starting, startled].* Is she, by God. Well, *there's* one little conversation piece I'll put a stop to. *[He seizes his hat. He hurries around to the opposite side of Lucy's bed.]*

*Lucy [Sitting up].* Oh George! How nice of you to drop in on your moribund relations.

*GBS [Taking off the hat, elaborately calm and collected].* Hello. *[More lively.]* And Stella. What a pleasant surprise. *[To the audience.]* God God, she must weigh twenty stone.

*Mrs. Pat [Stately].* Good evening, Mr. Bernard Shaw. *[To the audience.]* Poor old boy, he's positively withering away. *[To GBS.]* And have you not brought your sister so much as a grape?

*GBS [Cheerfully].* Not a grape. Not a turnip. Not a head of cabbage. Not even a bag of potatoes.

*Lucy.* George has provided me with everything I want. He is very good to me. He has always been very good to his sister.

*GBS.* You see. I have been barely civil to her. I haven't done a thing for her that I wouldn't do for any stranger who was ill. Yet I am praised to the skies as the most tenderly affectionate of brothers. *[To the audience.]* I see I have to play Laertes to Ophelia.

*Mrs. Pat [Wagging a finger at him].* A bunch of roses to cheer her sickroom—?

*GBS.* In March?

*Mrs. Pat.* Daffodils . . . sweet Heavens, one would think you could have managed a buttercup or a daisy.

*GBS.* She's not a caterpillar.

*Mrs. Pat.* She is a sick woman.

*GBS.* In my presence flowers can safely grow. I have no sadistic urge to wrench their heads off.

*Mrs. Pat.* No, you only wrench women's hearts out.

*GBS.* Oh Stella, don't descend to vulgar melodrama—you, who have been the empress of high comedy—at least, when I wrote the lines for you.

*Mrs. Pat.* I am still available for your lines, even though they are becoming feeble.

*GBS.* Certainly too feeble to be able to carry an actress of your . . . magnitude.

*Mrs. Pat.* Mr. Bernard Shaw, you are what is known among the lower classes as a bloody bastard.

*Lucy [Chuckling].* Oh Stella, forgive me, but when you said that you reminded me of poor Oscar Wilde's mother.

*GBS.* Yes, I'm told she had quite a robust style of conversation when the men weren't around.

*Lucy.* That reminds me. I got another letter from McNulty this morning.

*GBS.* Ah, the ever-faithful Mac.

*Mrs. Pat.* And who, pray, is McNulty?

*GBS [Waving towards Lucy].* Her oldest and fondest admirer.

*Lucy.* A boy I knew in dear old Dublin *[Waving towards GBS.]* They were bosom friends.

*GBS [Carelessly].* We were at school together. He wanted to marry Lucy.

*Lucy.* He was only a boy.

*GBS.* He was merely a couple of years younger than you.

*Lucy [Distinctly].* Three.

*Mrs. Pat.* That's nothing. My present lover is young enough to be my son.

*Lucy.* Three years . . . a lot when you're only twenty. Anyway, he married someone else.

*GBS.* Lucky for him. Poor Mac would ever have been able for *you.*

*Mrs. Pat.* *What* man is really able for any woman?

*GBS.* So long as he can knock her down, that's always something.

*Mrs. Pat [Darkly].* *I* was once knocked down.

*GBS.* How many men did it take?

*Mrs. Pat.* Just one weedy specimen. You.

*GBS [Taken aback].* Me?!

*Lucy.* Oh George! And you pretend you couldn't even pluck a daisy. Do you beat poor Carlotta too?

*Mrs. Pat [Murmuring].* Who could blame him for *that?*

*Lucy.* Stella, you must tell me all about the thrashing he gave you.

*GBS.* None of your lies, Stella.

*Mrs. Pat.* Did you or did you not knock me to the floor?

*Lucy.* I hope the carpet was soft.

*GBS.* It was an accident. I tripped over a footstool. I grabbed hold of her to save myself from falling. We both tumbled down.

*Mrs. Pat.* He was trying to r-r-ravish me.

*Lucy.* And I thought I knew my own brother.

*GBS.* Oh yes, I was trying to ravish you. But you appealed to me to spare your maiden innocence. Maddened with frustrated lust, I broke the furniture, smashed the mirror, tore down the curtains, slashed the pictures, and rushed away to assault the next woman I encountered.

*Mrs. Pat.* There was a witness.

*GBS.* There was no such thing. It's my word against yours, Stella.

*Mrs. Pat.* The parlormaid.

*GBS.* Oh . . . her. She opened the door. She saw her mistress rolling around on the floor, trying to pull a most respectable married gentleman into her embrace, so she went out, knocked loudly, came in again and helped me to my feet. The fact that it was I, not you, who had to be helped up, speaks volumes.

*Mrs. Pat.* *That* I will not deny.

*GBS.* So much, then, for your monstrous allegations of assault and battery.

*Lucy.* Methinks the gentleman doth protest too much. *[She takes Mrs. Pat's hand].* But we don't think any the less of him for his violence, do we?

*Mrs. Pat.* Of course not. So there was really no necessity to bribe the parlormaid to keep quiet about it.

*GBS [Patiently].* I gave the poor girl two pounds because she had to tidy up the room after us. It was extra work for her.

*Lucy.* She must have been very pretty.

*Mrs. Pat.* Quite passable. With men of small discrimination.

*GBS.* She graciously and gracefully helped me to my feet, showing she had more of the instincts of a lady than her mistress—at least on that occasion.

*Lucy.* I'm glad you put that in. She probably had her moments too.

*Mrs. Pat.* She had. I'll tell you later.

*GBS.* Before the conversation becomes totally licentious, may I ask if McNulty had anything to say in his letter?

*Lucy.* He was kind enough to tell me he still regards me as the most beautiful woman he has ever known.

*GBS.* Mac usen't to be quite so soppy.

*Mrs. Pat.* Your sister is a very lovely creature.

*GBS.* She was always the family beauty.

*Lucy.* McNulty was asking after you too.

*GBS.* I must write to him.

*Lucy.* He thinks that now you're the Great Man you no longer have time for old friends.

*GBS.* Everyone who has as much as shaken hands with me regards me as their oldest and dearest friend, and demands a long letter from me twice a week.

*Mrs. Pat.* I know a person to whom you once wrote twice a day.

*Lucy.* You'll get a fortune if you sell those letters, Stella.

*Mrs. Pat.* I cannot bring myself to regard the treasures of a real, a noble, and poetic passion, as mere articles of commerce.

*GBS.* You'd publish every damned word of those letters if I let you.

*Lucy* Have *you* kept Stella's replies to you?

*GBS* I might have kept one or two.

*Lucy.* That means he's kept them all. How d'you manage to hide them from poor Carlotta?

*GBS.* Some respect for my wife, please.

*Lucy.* You had damned little respect for my husband.

*Mrs. Pat.* Or mine.

*Lucy.* He said poor Charlie had a face like a lump of lard.

*GBS.* Worse, he was a lyric tenor.

*Mrs. Pat.* He said that where my poor fellow wasn't brawn, he was beef.

*GBS.* I ask you the old question: Have you ever heard one Irishman speak well of another?

*Lucy.* McNulty speaks very highly of you.

*GBS.* And why wouldn't he?

*Lucy.* Even though you tried to give him pneumonia.

*GBS.* Has poor old Mac gone completely senile? *I* gave him pneumonia!!

*Lucy.* When they were boys, George asked McNulty to take off all his clothes so that he could draw him in the nude.

*Mrs. Pat.* That explains a lot.

*GBS.* It explains nothing except that I was an aspiring artist looking for a model.

*Mrs. Pat.* Boys are expelled from Eton College for doing just that.

*Lucy.* McNulty says he's writing his memoirs of their boyhood days together in Dublin.

*GBS.* Then he has damned little to do. And you can tell him so from me.

*Mrs. Pat [Solicitously].* Lucy dearest, you look quite pale. Shall I get you something?

*GBS.* Hang it all, if you tell her she's quite pale, she'll only feel quite pale. *[To Lucy.]* You're as healthy looking as if you'd just come back from a month in the Isle of Wight. *[Too late he realizes he was maladroit.]*

*Lucy [Smiling at him, turns to Mrs. Pat].* That's where our sister died.

*Mrs. Pat [Rising and glaring].* Well really, Mr. Bernard Shaw, that joke was definitely tasteless and singularly unamusing.

*Lucy.* It's all right, Stella; he didn't mean it that way at all.

*Mrs. Pat.* Lucy, you are a perfect saint that you can forgive him for such a brutish remark.

*GBS.* Oh, chuck it, Stella. Lucy is perfectly able to defend herself if I had an intended an innocent remark to have any such monstrous meaning.

*Mrs. Pat.* Do keep quiet, Joey.

*GBS. Now* who's being gratuitously offensive! Joey! Is that all a great man means to *you?* Joey!

*Mrs. Pat.* Your sister is *ill.* Can you not get that into your great man's brilliant clever brain?

*GBS [Bending towards Lucy].* Are you feeling particularly ill just now?

*Lucy [A little weary].* Not more than usual, George.

*GBS.* Shall I tell the nurse to come in?

*Lucy [Rousing herself].* Oh no no, don't do that. She'll only ask you both to go, and I'd much rather you stayed.

*GBS [Straightening, triumphant].* There you are, Stella, Are you satisfied *now?*

*Mrs. Pat.* Shall I get you a little brandy?

*Lucy [After a quick, nervous glance at GBS].* Oh, no thanks.

*GBS [Casually, as if the thought had just occurred to him].* Lucy, do please excuse us for a moment. I've an idea for a play. I'd like to get Stella's opinion.

*Mrs. Pat [Angrily].* This is neither the time nor the place to discuss plays.

*GBS [Smiling ingratiatingly].* It won't take a moment. *[He signals to her with his eyes, then takes her arm and leads her away from the bed. While his expression remains smiling, his voice is angry.]* Do you want to kill her with your brandy?

*Mrs. Pat [Taken aback].* What on earth are you going on about?

*GBS.* Her heart isn't strong. A glass of your brandy will simply stop it altogether.

*Mrs. Pat.* What do *you* know about it? *[She turns to smile at Lucy.]* You won't even come to visit her.

*GBS*. Don't try to change to subject. *[To Lucy, smiling.]* Are you all right?

*[Lucy smiles and nods.]*

*Mrs. Pat*. She's not getting enough to eat and drink.

*GBS [Almost exploding]*. Are you accusing me of letting her starve?

*Mrs. Pat [To Lucy]*. So sorry, darling, but he insists on talking business. *[Facing GBS belligerently, but still smiling glassily.]* I am merely saying she isn't eating enough, and you're neglecting her.

*GBS [Belligerently]*. I have provided her with everything she needs, everything she asks for.

*Mrs. Pat [Hissing]*. Damn your money: It's *you* she wants.

*Lucy*. Will you two stop fighting and come and talk to me.

*Mrs. Pat [Going back, beaming]*. Fighting? We weren't fighting, my darling.

*GBS [Going back to his side of the bed]*. We were fighting like two devils. And over *you*.

*Lucy*. I know you were. And you needn't worry, George. I'm not going to take brandy. *[She leans back and closes her eyes.]*

*Mrs. Pat [To GBS, defiantly]*. A little brandy when you're feeling peaky is the best thing in the world for you.

*GBS*. Ha!

*Mrs. Pat*. Any doctor will tell you that.

*GBS*. Especially when he has shares in the drink trade.

*Mrs. Pat [Suddenly bending over Lucy]*. Lucy! Are you . . .?

*[Lucy opens her eyes and smiles weakly.]*

*GBS*. My God, you've talked her into a weakness.

*Mrs. Pat [Putting her arm around Lucy's shoulders and glaring at GBS]*. Go home, Joey. Go home.

*GBS*. Let us both go home and let her get some rest. I'll call the nurse in.

*Mrs. Pat [Softly]*. Perhaps you *should* try and rest.

*GBS [Taking up his hat]*. Come, Stella.

*Mrs. Pat [Not moving]*. Are you sure you'll be all right?

*[Lucy whispers to her.]*

*Mrs. Pat [To GBS]*. She wants you to leave us alone for a moment.

*GBS*. Are you sure she doesn't want *you* to leave *us* alone for a moment?

*[Mrs. Pat motions him away.]*

*GBS [Coming forward, to the audience]*. I'm damned if I'll allow that wretched Thespian play Me off the stage at my own sister's sickbed. Lucy is now *her* oldest and dearest friend. And, of course, Lucy has an audience. An audience that wants to know *all* about me, *all* about my childhood in Dublin, all about my father, all about my mother, and Vandeleur Lee. And now even McNulty wants to start blabbing. *[He pauses, draws a deep breath and makes a declaration.]* I myself have told all that need be told. I have told it coherently and more important, artistically. There is nothing else of the slightest interest to anybody. The rest should be . . . silence.

*Mrs. Pat [Rising].* You may come back.

*[GBS strides back jauntily.]*

*Mrs. Pat [Kissing Lucy].* Goodbye, my darling Trilby.

*GBS [Startled].* Your darling who?

*Mrs. Pat.* My darling Trilby. *[Sweetly.]* Didn't you know that Lucy is Trilby—or Trilby is Lucy, whichever you like.

*GBS.* Lucy, you haven't been raking up that silly idle gossip-mongering—

*Lucy.* I haven't. I've no ambition to be the heroine of a sentimental novel.

*GBS.* Thank God for that.

*Mrs. Pat.* Everyone in London knows about Lucy and Trilby.

*GBS.* Everyone in London knows no such thing.

*Mrs. Pat.* You are appallingly rude. Lucy is Trilby and that peculiar singing teacher who lived with you—

*Lucy.* Poor dear old Vandeleur Lee.

*Mrs. Pat.* He is Svengali. We know all about it, Joey.

*GBS [To the heavens].* Why in God's name am I forever being singled out as the victim of preposterous legends, insane romances, fantastic imaginings—

*Mrs. Pat [Calmly, but delighted to get him on the raw].* Nobody has mentioned you at all, darling. *You're* not in it. It's Lucy . . . and Mr. Vandeleur Lee . . . and your mother.

*GBS.* Not even my poor mother is to be spared.

*Lucy.* She was my mother too, George.

*GBS [Suddenly changing tactics, he goes over to Mrs. Pat, folds his arms and grins down at her].* Stella, you are turning into a mischievous old gossip. Get these facts into your poor addled head. Vandeleur Lee was a Dublin singing teacher and orchestral conductor.

*Mrs. Pat [Gesturing dramatically at him].* A hypnotist. A mesmerist.

*GBS.* He was no such thing. But I would not object to the description, mesmeric. He taught Lucy to sing. And taught her very well. Before that he had taught my mother—*[Smiling, to Lucy.]*—*our* mother.

*Mrs. Pat.* And your mother ran away with him.

*GBS [Patiently].* He came over to London. Mother followed him later on.

*Lucy.* George, it was a matter of days.

*Mrs. Pat.* Thank you, darling Trilby. We get the truth from *you,* just the pure and simple.

*GSB.* Poor Oscar Wilde used to say the truth was seldom pure and never simple.

*Mrs. Pat.* Don't try to change the subject.

*Lucy.* She's well able for you, George.

*GBS.* Let's not lose sight of the facts of the matter.

*Lucy.* Since when did *you* know the facts of the matter?

*GBS.* Mother left Dublin because Father couldn't afford to keep her and you and Yuppy, not to mention myself.

*Mrs. Pat.* So she packed her bag and followed Mr. Vandeleur Lee the next day!

*GBS.* It wasn't like that at all. She didn't come to London to *live* with him. They lived in separate houses, miles apart from each other.

*Mrs. Pat.* You and I lived miles apart from each other, but that didn't stop us from—

*GBS.* Woman, have you no shame?!

*Mrs. Pat.* What on earth is there to be ashamed of?

*Lucy.* You're perfectly right. There's nothing to be ashamed of in the love of a man for a woman or a woman for a man.

*GBS.* Did I say there was?

*Mrs. Pat.* You did, you did, you ludicrous flesh-and-bloodless old maid.

*GBS.* I merely object to the detail of sexual encounters being described for the amusement of third parties.

*Lucy.* I've known cases where the third party was herself romping around with the other two.

*Mrs. Pat.* I had a lover who always said it takes three to make it interesting.

*GBS [Outraged].* This is monstrous.

*Mrs. Pat.* But it was interesting for *us.* He overestimated his powers.

*Lucy.* Poor old Vandeleur Lee. He was in love with *me,* you know.

*Mrs. Pat.* Everyone knew that, darling Trilby. And with your mother as well.

*Lucy.* I think it was more a case of her fancying him. Wouldn't you say so, George?

*GBS.* I would say all this is women's magazine twaddle. I know he took a fancy to *you,* and I know that poor Yuppy had an innocent kind of young-girl crush on him.

*Mrs. Pat.* What a *fascinating* man he must have been.

*Lucy.* He had wandering hands.

*Mrs. Pat.* Haven't they all?

*GBS.* God in heaven, can't you utter three words without lapsing into lewdness? *[Abruptly.]* Lucy: You must rest. We're tiring you.

*Lucy.* Indeed you're not. I've enjoyed talking about the old times.

*Mrs. Pat [Kissing Lucy].* Goodbye, dearest Trilby. I shall come again on Thursday, and you can tell me more.

*GBS [Nodding to Lucy].* I might be able to manage Thursday myself, too.

*Mrs. Pat.* How lovely. Three *will* make it very interesting.

*GBS.* Fiend. *[To Lucy.]* If there's anything you want, just let me know. *[He offers Mrs. Pat his arm and turns to go.]*

*Lucy.* Kiss Carlotta for me.

*GBS [Dropping Mrs. Pat's arm and turning abruptly].* I nearly forgot. Charlotte told me to give you her kindest regards, and best wishes.

*Lucy.* Kiss Carlotta *twice* for me.

*GBS [Taking Mrs. Pat's arm again, and waving].* Goodbye, goodbye.

*Mrs. Pat.* Come along, you poor old would-be Svengali.

*[They go out. The light dims over Lucy. GBS and Mrs. Pat reappear at the front.]*

*Mrs. Pat.* Why are you always playacting?

*GBS.* A devastating question, coming from *you.* And what monumental statement did Lucy make to you when you were whispering together?

*Mrs. Pat [With a mocking smile].* *That* I shall never tell you.

*GBS.* Then it cannot have been of the slightest importance. Otherwise you'd be bursting to tell me.

*Mrs. Pat.* Would I?

*GBS.* The only secrets worth knowing are the secrets everyone knows. And those secrets keep themselves.

*Mrs. Pat [Grinning].* But you'd still love to know?

*GBS.* Would I?

*Mrs. Pat [Slowly].* Oh yes, you would. *[Holding out her hand.].* Goodbye, Professor Higgins—

*[Instead of shaking it, he kisses it ceremoniously.]*

*Mrs. Pat [Sighing wearily].* Oh dear . . . I suppose, Professor, for the sake of auld lang syne I must let you kiss me. *[She holds up her cheek.]*

*GBS.* In the public street? Not bloody likely, Eliza. It might frighten those famous horses of yours. *[Waving his hat and moving off.]* Goodbye, goodby . . .

*[Mrs. Pat goes on her way. GBS flops on the sofa, puts his hat beside him, leans back and stretches his legs.]*

*GBS.* According to that blackguard, Frank Harris, the only way to treat a women is put her on her back. What Frank doesn't tell us is, how to get her off *your* back afterwards. *[Pointing after Mrs. Pat.]* It's hard to believe that eight years ago that woman was an enchantress. I do not exaggerate. She enchanted *me*. She had me at her feet. Poor Charlotte nearly went out of her head. And I don't think I cared whether she did or not, as much as a reasonably decent husband should. *[Gazing after her reflectively.]* I risked the most sacred obligations for that woman. *[He jumps up restlessly.]* That's the damnable thing about Nature. Nature doesn't care a hoot for our most sacred obligations. She wants *[Pointing]* you or you or me to father a child on her or her, and it doesn't matter a fig whether we marry or not. *[Wagging his finger at the audience.]* That is why the Book of Common Prayer is talking through its hat—or rather talking through the collective mitres of the Bench of Bishops—when it purports to lay down the law about marriage. *[He takes a prayer book from his pocket and reads.]* First, marriage "was ordained for the procreation of children." Utter nonsense. Children are not the object of marriage: They are its incidentals. Sometimes its accidents. Marriage is primarily a scaffolding to build a relationship between a man and a woman, and all the rest is gas and gaiters. *[He reads.]* Secondly, it was ordained for a remedy against sin." Sin? *What* sin? *[He reads.]* "To avoid fornication." To. Avoid. Fornication. What is fornication? A sexual act performed outside marriage. What is marriage? Ordained to avoid fornication. Well, you could run around in that circle all night, if you were fool enough. *[He reads.]* And ordained "That such persons as have not the gift of continency might marry, and keep themselves undefiled. . . ." *Have* you ever come across such impertinence? I got married in a registry office. I wouldn't have objected in the least to getting married in a cathedral—in fact, I should have been only too happy to plight my troth to Charlotte in some charming old village church—if only I hadn't to expose her, and myself, to being informed by a person in a black gown and a white vest that he was marrying us because we hadn't the gift of continency. What self-respecting man or woman could submit to such a monstrous accusation? What is wrong with brides that they don't slap the clergyman's face? Why don't the bridegrooms knock him down? *[He pauses. Then with a spacious gesture.]* Procreation there must be. Of course. But the considerations that guide us in choosing a domestic partner are not necessarily the proper ones for you, my friend, to choose a mother for your children, or you, madam, to choose a father for yours. When it comes to procreate, listen to the voice of nature. As you go about your daily business, thinking of anything but sex, Nature will suddenly take hold of you and say: Look—that person there—*that* is the person I want you to have a child with. And if the person feels the same about you, just arrange to meet in the dark, couple . . . and part. And let the children be brought up by the State in orphanages. We would not know where we were born, why we were born, who our parents were. We would not have to hate any woman because she was our mother, despise any man because he was our father. Life, and love, would be far less complicated. *[He pauses, then resumes less vehemently.]* You may ask: Is there not then a danger that a man might marry his own sister? *[Sweetly reasonable.]* Well, what harm if he did? Even under the present dispensation, many a man might be marrying his own sister if only he knew it. In the Garden of Eden, men had to marry their sisters. There were no other women for them. Well, it was either marry their sister or marry their mother. *[More seriously.]* But I think the danger is greatly exaggerated. In my own experience, and from what I've noticed in other men, we are *not* attracted in that way by our sisters or our mothers. On the contrary, we feel an instinctive repulsion from them. Take my sister Lucy. I always found it a severe trial to live under the same roof as her, let alone anything else.

*[Lucy suddenly raises herself in the bed, as if waking from a nightmare, and cries, "George!"]*

GBS *[Rubbing his hands uneasily]*. There's really no need for her to die. But she has lost the will to live. That, and tuberculosis. I suppose I have tuberculosis myself. The three of us have it. Poor Yuppy gave up the struggle at twenty-one. But Lucy and I battled on . . . although I was sure I was taking my departure at forty-two. Lucy is . . . now, let me see. I'm just sixty-four, that makes her sixty-seven. Mother was over eighty. Father was . . . was it seventy-six? Astonishing, for a man who drank so much. *His* father died at fifty-something. My mother's father . . . bloody

old scoundrel . . . he was over eighty. I may make the seventy
mark myself. Charlotte will go on forever. Takes damned good
care of herself. She'll end up ninety and a nuisance to everybody.

*Lucy [Weakly].* George.

*GBS.* I suppose I'd better go and give Lucy a call.

*[He takes his hat and goes off jauntily. The pianist starts playing
"After the Ball." GBS comes to Lucy's bedside. She is lying still,
her eyes closed. He stoops over her, alarmed.]*

*GBS [Whispering].* Lucy . . . *[A little lower.]* Lucy.

*Lucy [Stirring, opens her eyes].* The maiden is not dead, George;
she only sleepeth.

*GBS [Immensely relieved, he sits on the chair beside her].* And
how are you?

*Lucy.* Very tired.

*GBS.* Has our theatrical friend been in bothering you?

*Lucy.* Mrs. Pat? Haven't seen her for ages. How are *you?*

*GBS.* I've been in bed with a dreadful dose of flu. *[He rises restlessly and walks in the direction of the music.]* Does the damned
fellow never stop at that piano?

*Lucy.* It's a lady.

*GBS.* I might have known. Very insensitive player. That song—
what d'you call it?

*Lucy.* "After the Ball."

*GBS.* Ah yes, of course. After the ball is over, after the something
is done, many a heart is breaking . . . after the ball. It may not
be a world masterpiece. But there's a certain amount of feeling
in it. It shouldn't be rattled off so heartlessly as that. But then,
women have no heart.

*Lucy.* You used to have such lovely hair.

*GBS [Passing his hand over his head].* I'm not bald yet.

*Lucy.* Oh, I nearly forgot. Put your hand in here under my pillow.
I have it her to remind me.

*GBS [Slipping his hand under her pillow and draws out a baby's
cap].* Glory be to God, what is it?

*Lucy [Slightly irritably].* What d'you think?

*GBS.* It could be a baby's bonnet.

*Lucy.* It was yours.

*GBS [Derisively].* How on earth d'you know?

*Lucy.* After mother died, I found it in her secret box.

*GBS.* It was probably yours. Or more likely Yuppy's. Yuppy was
the only one of us she cared tuppence about. You know she had
no particular feeling for *me.*

*Lucy.* She had a note pinned to it. Yours was the only one she kept.

*GBS [Lightly].* I wouldn't have believed it. What d'you want me to do with it?

*Lucy.* Put it in the fire, if you like. Give it to one of your maids to polish the brasses with.

*GBS [Stuffing it into his pocket].* I shall keep it. An heirloom for the family neither of us ever had.

*Lucy. I* have no regrets about that.

*GBS.* Neither have I. *[He jingles the money in his pocket.]*

*Lucy [After a pause].* I am leaving McNulty the piano.

*GBS.* It'll cost him a packet to get it over to Ireland.

*Lucy.* Carriage paid . . . I've put *that* in my will.

*GBS.* Then there'll be no problem. Except for the neighbors. Pianos shouldn't be allowed except in soundproof rooms. *[Irritably.]* Confound it, doesn't that woman know any other tune?

*Lucy.* She never plays anything else. *[A pause.]* Carlotta.

*GBS.* What about Charlotte?

*Lucy.* Is she well?

*GBS.* Thriving as usual. Threatening to take me over on yet another visit to our dear native land.

*Lucy.* I'd love to have seen Dublin just once more.

*GBS [Cheerfully].* And so you shall. Come with us if you like.

*Lucy.* March is always . . . so very windy . . . in Dublin. Always a bad month.

*GBS.* As far as I'm concerned, every month in that place is a bad month.

*Lucy [After a pause].* George.

*GBS [Without turning around].* Yes, Lucy. *[A pause. He turns.]*

*Lucy.* I am dying.

*GBS [Coming over and sitting beside her].* Nonsense. You'll be all right in a moment. *[He takes her hand.]* Just rest yourself. *[He keeps staring towards the music, not at Lucy. The piano stops.]*

*GBS.* I wonder if that wretched woman has stopped at last? *[A pause.]* You might even be able to get a little rest then. *[A pause.]* There was a hopeful air of finality about the way she thumped that last chord, wouldn't you say? *[A long silence. He steals a look at Lucy. He bends down to her.]* Lucy. *[More urgently.]* Lucy. *[He gently takes away his hand and rises. He moves a step or two away, undecided. Then he goes back to her.]* Lucy . . . are you asleep? *[He can hardly articulate the name.]* Lucy. *[He straightens, breathing heavily. He puts his hand to the top of his breast as if something was catching him. He is in shock. He touches her hand.]*. Lucy . . . it's me.

*[He suddenly breaks. Terrible sobs rock him. He covers his face.*

*At length he recovers himself, takes a handkerchief from his pocket, wipes his eyes. Then one more step towards the bed.]*
GBS. Lucy. *[A long silence. He sighs and takes up his hat.]* Well, here I am, the last of the line. Nobody left to contradict me. *[Slightly louder.]* Friend McNulty, burn all my letters to you; I shall burn all yours to me. Let us draw the curtains. *[He calls off.]* Nurse. *[Gravely.]* Miss Shaw has died. You had better send for the doctor. *[He comes forward.]* You know, this may sound heartless and cruel, but if we were to be absolutely honest with ourselves, to face unpleasant truths, then we would admit that when a relation dies, even one that we have been very fond of—*[He taps his breast]*—then in here we have a certain feeling of relief at being rid of them at last. Yet—*[Pointing back towards the bed, without looking around]*—she had many friends. They had a genuine regard for her. *[He drops his hand again.]* I am myself a much-hated man. *[He points again.]* But she was extraordinarily popular. Not only with men, but with women too. She cared for nobody, certainly not for me. Oh yes, she was kindly; she wouldn't harm people; I don't think she was vindictive. *[With a little smile.]* I suspect she had many love affairs. If she thought a man really ached for her, and she didn't find him too repulsive, well. . . . *[He shrugs.]* And now the comedy is finished. *[He goes back to the bed and gazes down at Lucy.]* Well . . . goodbye, and safe journey. *[He stoops in the act of turning away, takes his spectacles from his waistcoat pocket, puts them on, and stares hard at her. He takes off the spectacles and puts them away reflectively.]* Hmm. When you were young, you were the image of mother. And now . . . you're the image of her again. *[He sighs, pulls himself together, and waves his hat to Lucy.]* Safe journey. *[Over his shoulder as he goes.]* And give Mother my regards. *[He goes off. Blackness. When the light returns, Lucy and the bed have disappeared. Charlotte is looking out into the garden.]*
Charlotte. Playacting, playacting, always playacting. *[She sighs, continues to stare out for a moment, and then calls.]* It's time to come in. You'll catch cold.
GBS *[Off]*. Coming, belovedest, coming.
Charlotte *[Coming to the sofa and sitting]*. Playacting . . . always playacting.
*[GBS comes in jauntily. He wears a miner's helmet and a sage-green tweed cape.]*
Charlotte *[Acidly]*. Are you going to wear that thing even in the house?

GBS *[Drawing the cape closer around him]*. But it *is* rather chilly.

*Charlotte*. What do you expect . . . in late September . . . in the depths of the country?

GBS. Never mind. We shall go up to London in a day or two, to the nice, warm, thick, dirty air.

*Charlotte*. I'm not talking about your cape. I'm talking about that thing on your head.

GBS *[Putting up his hands to the helmet, but not taking it off]*. Good Lord, I didn't realize I still had it on. *[Folding his arms and meandering around.]* Extraordinarily comfortable, these things. They mighn't look it, but they are.

*Charlotte*. You look quite ridiculous, you know.

GBS. Striking is the word, belovedest. I put it on while they were taking photographs of me chopping wood.

*Charlotte*. But it's a *miner's* helmet.

GBS. Merely to save my precious head in case any logs flew up in the air and came down to top of it. However, if it irritates you. . . . *[He takes it off, goes out to the hall to leave it there, and comes back without his cape.]*

*Charlotte*. Now you really *will* catch cold.

GBS. It's quite warm in the house.

*Charlotte*. I thought you said it was quite chilly.

GBS. Outside, yes. Inside, no. *[A pause.]* Are you feeling out of sorts?

*Charlotte*. If you had all the pains and aches that I have—

GBS. Why not stay in bed?

*Charlotte*. My bones seem to be grinding off each other. It's worse when I lie down.

GBS *[Sitting beside her and putting an arm around her]*. Old age, my dearest. *[Almost exuberant]*. But don't worry. It'll soon be time for us to shuffle off the mortal coil, to discard these greasy, ill-designed commonplace bodies. Then . . . no more aches and pains. No more desires, regrets, ambitions, appetites, disappointments, fears, maneuverings, worries, frustrations. *[Gesturing spaciously with his free hand.]* All will be peace. Serenity. We shall just go on floating through space through all eternity.

*Charlotte [Shrugging off his arm, rising and moving around the room]*. *I* don't want to go on floating around space. I just want to be *nothing*.

GBS. What you want beloved, is a good smart trot around the garden. You've been frowsting too much indoors. Go and fetch your coat.

*Charlotte [Stopping and glaring at him]*. I'm not going out there to be frozen to death. And my goodness, look at *you*. Your nose has gone blue with the cold. *[She marches out purposefully.]*

*GBS [Feeling his nose].* My nose feels quite warm. And why wouldn't it be? An hour every afternoon chopping wood, sawing logs. That's the way to get the circulation going. *[He leaps up.]* By heaven, *I* don't feel my age. *[He folds his arms, dances around in a burlesque sailor's hornpipe, trolling the music.]*

*[Charlotte comes in, carrying a woolen rug. She stops, appalled. He executes a few high kicks for her.]*

*Charlotte.* Will you sit down before you give yourself a heart attack.

*GBS [Desisting, and patting his chest].* Sound as a bell, my heart.

*Charlotte.* You're all out of breath. Sit down at once.

*GBS [Shrugs and sits].* Anything to oblige.

*Charlotte [Tucking the rug in around his legs].* You're worse than twenty children.

*GBS.* *Only* twenty. I must be failing.

*Charlotte [Straightening and surveying her handiwork].* Tomorrow you're to stay all day in bed and rest yourself. And the day after.

*GBS.* No, I shan't. The red flag of revolution I raise aloft.

*[He raises a clenched fist.]*

*Charlotte [Sitting in a chair].* Well, I can't force you if you don't want to. But you must give yourself a rest. Not one word are you to write for the remainder of this week. I'm not going to have you like your friend Mr. Joyce.

*GBS [Puzzled].* Who's my friend Mr. Joyce?

*Charlotte.* The man who wrote that book about Dublin.

*GBS.* Oh, *him*. What has he done now?

*Charlotte.* He has died.

*GBS.* Really?

*Charlotte.* Didn't you read it in the paper?

*GBS.* The headlines must have been either too big for me to see or too small for me to notice.

*Charlotte.* It was just a couple of lines.

*GBS.* What happened him? Walked under a bus?

*Charlotte.* He died in hospital. In Switzerland. He wasn't very old.

*GBS.* Sounds like drink.

*Charlotte.* The paper didn't say *that*.

*GBS.* The papers never get anything right.

*Charlotte.* Don't they? They get *you* right.

*GBS [Settling himself more comfortably]* You *will* be, you know. Whether you like it or not.

*Charlotte [Sharply].* Will be *what?*

*GBS.* Floating. Floating through space forever.

*Charlotte.* I'll be doing no such thing.

*GBS.* Oh yes, you will. Dust we are, and unto dust shall we return. When the crematorium has done its job on us, particles of Charlotte and her preposterous old husband will be . . . *[He flutters his fingers through the air.]* . . . for ever and ever. Hallelujah!

*Charlotte.* Don't say things like that.

*GBS.* Let me draw your attention to one of poor old Shakespeare's blinding glimpses of the obvious. Death, a very necessary end, will come when it will come.

*Charlotte.* I wasn't talking about that. I meant calling yourself preposterous.

*GBS.* Oh, but in many ways I am. So is everyone. Man is a preposterous creation. He will have to be improved upon.

*Charlotte [With something like a sniff].* Man has already been improved on.

*GBS.* Ah . . . you mean Woman. Well, I wouldn't altogether disagree. I have always maintained that the feminine element in a man is more valuable than the mere masculine.

*Charlotte [Dryly].* And I suppose *I* have a man in me somewhere?

*GBS.* Of course. Men and women contain elements of each other, and are the better of it. I even have rudimentary breasts.

*Charlotte [Frowning].* And what have *I* got?

*GBS [Uneasily getting away from the point].* Oh, these physical odds and ends of no real significance. What's important are the mental attributes, the intellectual standpoints. By the way, I meant to ask you. Did James Joyce get the Nobel thing?

*Charlotte.* I don't think so. The paper didn't say so. *Should* they have given it to him?

*GBS.* Of course. Good God, look at the people they do give it to.

*Charlotte [Dryly].* They gave it to Yeats and you.

*GBS [As if this were the explanation].* Yeats was a poet, and he had the name of running the Abbey Theatre, although Lady Gregory— *she* was the real genius there. It was *she* who should have got the Nobel Prize. I suppose they thought Yeats needed the money.

*Charlotte.* Did you ever find out which of your plays they gave it to you for?

*GBS.* The damned fools wouldn't have known.The Nobel Prize is supposed to be awarded to whoever has rendered the most notable services to literature during the previous year. Well, I wrote nothing the previous year. *That* was my notable service to literature.

*Charlotte.* How do they pick the winners then?

*GBS.* The same way as other tomfools try to pick winners. Stick

pins in a list. *[He rises and throws the rug aside.]* They should
have given it to Joyce. He could have done with the money.

*Charlotte [Rather dryly].* I'm surprised you think so highly of Mr.
Joyce.

*GBS.* Oh, a literary genius. No doubt of it.

*Charlotte.* But you didn't finish his book.

*GBS. Ulysses* was too unbearably vivid a picture of Dublin for me.
Thank God, I'm finished with the place. I shall never set eyes on
it again.

*Charlotte.* Yes, you shall. You must scatter my ashes there.

*GBS [Frowning].* In Dublin?!

*Charlotte.* On the Three Rock Mountain, on the side that looks
down over the city.

*GBS.* Why not in our garden?

*Charlotte.* I'm Irish. Why should I leave myself to England?

*GBS.* Your mother was English.

*Charlotte.* I hated her. She made me like herself: a selfish bully.

*GBS.* I cannot comment. I never knew the old lady.

*Charlotte.* I knew *your* mother.

*GBS.* And did *she* make me like herself?

*Charlotte.* She was vindictive. So are you.

*GBS.* Vindictive? Me?!! Surely my Christian forgiveness shames
the saints.

*Charlotte.* The most vindictive man I've ever known. You never
forget, you never forgive.

*GBS [Beckoning her over to him].* With *you* there has never been
anything that needed forgiveness. *[He kisses her hand.]*

*Charlotte [Moving away].* I wonder. *[Looking hard at him.]* You
took your revenge with laughter.

*GBS.* The kindest way.

*Charlotte.* Again, I wonder.

*GBS [Trying to disentangle himself from the rug].* My dear Charlotte, I have never wasted time on taking vengeance—

*Charlotte [Sharply].* Stay where you are. Keep that rug around
your legs. You'll catch your death.

*GBS.* Never! Death will have to catch me. *[He puts the rug up
around his shoulders.]* All the same, Death isn't doing too badly
with the others. They're dropping like flies. Yeats has gone.
Joyce. AE. Augusta Gregory.

*Charlotte.* Beatrice Webb.

*GBS.* It was very remiss of her to die. She had no right to go like
that and leave poor Sidney to try to struggle along on his own.
Look at the poor devil. A sheep without a shepherd.

*Charlotte.* I want to leave him some money in my will.

*GBS*. What makes you so sure he'll live to get it? He won't last long without Beatrice.

*Charlotte*. How long would you last without me?

*GBS*. Not a day. I'd follow within the hour.

*Charlotte*. I wouldn't be too sure about that.

*GBS [Marching around, swirling the rug]*. I *daren't* stay alive after you. I should be the world's most eligible bachelor. The women would be queuing up out there, ravenous to become the Second Mrs. Bernard Shaw. Life wouldn't be worth living. No. Charlotte. *[He comforts her.]* I order you to stay alive. It is you who must escort me to Golders Green, not I you.

*Charlotte*. You must help me to make my will.

*GBS*. What? Again?!

*Charlotte*. Now that my poor sister's gone, things have changed.

*GBS*. She never liked me, that woman.

*Charlotte*. I don't know what put that notion into your head. She was quite fond of you.

*GBS*. It never showed.

*Charlotte*. Sissie wasn't one of those dreadful women who keep throwing their arms around every man they meet.

*GBS*. Oho, *I* saw her draping herself around the colonel often enough.

*Charlotte*. That's exactly what I am saying. She kept her endearments for her husband.

*GBS*. I must say I rather liked the fellow.

*Charlotte*. May I remind you that "the fellow" became a brigadier.

*GBS*. Technically yes. But he remained a colonel spiritually and morally. He hadn't an idea in his head. But it was pleasant to go out rambling with him. Like taking an amiable and woolly dog for a walk.

*Charlotte*. If you're quite finished slandering my late brother-in-law, I'd like to discuss my will.

*GBS*. You're going to cut me off with a shilling?

*Charlotte*. Everything will go to you for your life.

*GBS*. Don't worry. I'll die before you. Women live longer than men.

*Charlotte [Ignoring the remark]*. And after that, it's to go to educating the Irish.

*GBS [Stopping in his tracks, then flopping on the sofa]*. Now let me get this right. You're proposing to leave all your money to educate the Irish?

*Charlotte*. Irishmen are uncouth.

*GBS*. Well, since you've been married to one for forty years, you should know. And Irish women?

*Charlotte*. Even more uncouth.

*GBS*. Oh, I wouldn't say that.

*Charlotte*. Well, *I* would.

*GBS*. Your entitlement. And how, pray, are the Irish to be educated? You realize that they do have schools.

*Charlotte*. I don't mean that kind of education. I mean art. Irishmen don't know how to talk.

*GBS*. They don't know how to *stop* talking.

*Charlotte*. They don't know how to do that either. I mean elocution. They need to know how to speak properly.

*GBS*. Undoubtedly. But his vowels are excessively broad, he minces his consonants, he says "dis" and "dat," "dese" and "dose," and he has no chest voice. *[Rising enthusiastically.]* By heaven, Charlotte, you're doing the right thing. The Charlotte Shaw National Institute for Voice Production. There isn't an Irish man, woman or child who can sing a note properly.

*Charlotte*. John McCormack.

*GBS*. Pah. I heard a record of him singing "Blayss Thees Howss." He sounded like a confidence trickster.

*Charlotte*. If you will allow me to continue.

*GBS*. I understand perfectly what you're aiming at. You are absolutely right. You have my wholehearted support. Educate the Irish. They have the brains. Educate them, and they'll become the true Master Race.

*Charlotte [Quietly]*. I have no intention of educating them to be the Master Race.

*GBS [Soothingly]*. You use educate in the sense of "civilize," "cultivate."

*Charlotte*. That is the word I'm looking for. Give them some *culture*. A little polish.

*GBS [To the audience]*. The IRA burned down her old family home. It broke her heart. But she never said a word. *[To Charlotte, fingering his beard thoughtfully.]* There will be difficulties, practical difficulties about polishing the Irish.

*Charlotte*. All I want is for them to have the chance to hear fine music, see beautiful paintings—

*GBS*. Witness fine plays, hmm.

*Charlotte*. That goes without saying.

*GBS*. Thank you.

*Charlotte*. Above all, to learn something of the social graces. Nice manners and the social graces.

*GBS [With a hint of irony]*. A nation of ladies and gentlemen.

*Charlotte [Quietly]*. Real ladies, dearest GBS, real gentlemen.

*GBS [To the audience]*. Who don't burn down each other's houses and murder each other.

*[Charlotte falls into a profound silence. GBS approaches her, lays his hand affectionately on her shoulder, then comes forward.]*

GBS. Charlotte disobeyed my wishes . . . for the first and only time in all our married life. She died before me . . . and made me the world's most eligible bachelor. *[He pulls the rug closer around him. He seems very old, very frail, but the eyes twinkle with mischief.]* All I had to do was lift my little finger . . . beauty . . . youth . . . maturity . . . wealth . . . wit . . . charm . . . blonde . . . brunette. . . . *[He chuckles, then sings.]*

> La ci darem la mano,
> La mi dirai di si.

CURTAIN